OUR MAN IN ORLANDO

HUGH HUNTER

MONDAY BOOKS

A CIP catalogue record for this title is available from the British Library

ISBN: 978-1-906308-15-5

Typeset by Andrew Searle
Printed and bound by CPI Cox and Wyman

www.mondaybooks.com
http://mondaybooks.blogspot.com/
info@mondaybooks.com

For mum and dad, with love.

Acknowledgements

IT'S never possible to mention everyone who helps in a project like this, so I'll start by apologising to those I've left out here, and to thank those who helped me anonymously – you know who you are!

Secondly, I would like to thank Mike Creasey, Mark Hunter, Margaret Luongo and Billy Simms who all read my first draft and offered useful criticism and encouragement.

Particular thanks also to Craig Taylor, who read my extremely long, painful second draft and gave me helpful advice over a long coffee in Oxford one beautiful summer's afternoon.

A special mention to Chris Bonner, Nora Maxwell, Alex Sloane and Maria Woodcock, who were the first to hear these stories and laughed in all the right places.

Thanks to Fiona Hunter, whose help towards the end was much appreciated.

My deepest appreciation to Farisse, and the staff at Costa Coffee in Upminster – my second office! – various Starbucks baristas around the world, the guy at the little café off of Place de la République, and everyone at Einstein's on Sand Lake Road, all of whom on many occasions allowed me to sit working for hours with only a small latte on my table.

A very special thanks to Catherine, mon amour, mon refuge, ma vie.

Finally, my deepest thanks go to my parents, without whose love and support this book could never have happened. This one's for you!

Foreword

Hundreds of Britons are arrested in Florida each year. During the decade I spent as Our Man in Orlando, it was my job to deal with them.

It was busy work: the British consulate in Marseilles, which covers all of the south of France, might only see a dozen arrests per year; we often got that many in 24 hours.

Some were detained for relatively minor crimes – driving drunk, petty theft or assault – but plenty of others were taken in for murder, rape or large-scale drug dealing. Some of them ended up doing serious jail time, too – from 30 or 40 years (with no hope of parole) to, in one case, more than a thousand years. A few faced Old Smokey, the electric chair.

Many of these cases never made the UK press – in fact, because of the sheer scale of crime in the USA, many made only two or three paragraphs in the local newspapers.

As British consul in Florida, I got to know these prisoners – those inside for a few days, and those inside for the rest of their lives (often I was the only visitor they got).

I also dealt with people whose American business dreams had turned into nightmares, mothers and fathers whose children had been snatched away and families for whom a sunshine holiday had gone tragically wrong.

It was exciting, fascinating and occasionally distressing work; I loved almost every second of it, and this is my story of that time.

For reasons of consular confidentiality, and to protect innocents, the names of some of the people I dealt with have been changed. Additionally, some locations and times have been changed for the same reason. But everything I describe is true, and actually happened.

Hugh Hunter, London 2010

1

THE HUGE METAL DOOR slammed shut behind me.

Once again I was locked inside a Florida jail, as I had been hundreds of times during the previous nine years.

I glanced up at the CCTV on the ceiling. Unseen eyes would scan my every move until the moment I left. I winked at the camera. They hate that.

I walked alone down several corridors. Each time I came to a secure door, it opened remotely and I passed through. Eventually I arrived at a waiting area where inmates congregated to meet with their lawyers in the adjacent interview rooms.

I reported to the sergeant in charge of the section. Three stripes stood proudly on the sleeve of his crisply-ironed shirt below a Palm Beach County Correctional Department badge.

'Name?' he enquired.

'Hugh Hunter. I'm the British vice-consul.'

'Take a seat,' he said. Custodial officers in Florida are rarely conversational.

I sat down. I knew I could be here a while. Regrettably, I was not permitted to bring any books or other reading material into the secure zone, lest I conceal within them a map or an escape plan. All I had was a small folder containing some case notes.

My eyes fell on a television set mounted on the wall, which was tuned to a news channel. After a short story about a man trampled to death by an ostrich, the British journalist Trevor McDonald appeared on the screen, reporting from some godforsaken corner of the world.

The only other people in the holding area were two inmates, both African-Americans, who were waiting to meet their attorneys. When they heard McDonald speak, their mouths fell open in shock.

'Listen to the brother speak!' shouted one of them.

'I never done heard a nigger talk like that!' exclaimed the other, in awe.

The one closest to me turned to me. 'You ever hear a brother speak like that?' he said.

'Yes,' I said. 'He's a well-known broadcaster – he has a great reputation in England.'

The other man turned to his friend. 'What he say?'

'He said the nigger's got a reputation over in England.'

The second man leaned forward now. 'Is that for real?'

'Yes,' I said. 'He's held in high esteem.'

'Damn!' he said. 'That sounds like some serious shit.'

They returned to their own private conversation, but I overheard one whispering, 'High esteem! Nigger'll get ten years for that shit.'

After a short while, a guard entered and beckoned me to follow. He showed me to a small interview room where my prisoner was waiting. He was 22 years old, and his name was Paul Carr. He was from Burnley in Lancashire, and he had been arrested a few days before. I love freaky-looking people, and I couldn't help but smile. He looked like someone had unscrewed the bottom off a toilet brush and glued it to a Toby jug; to make matters worse his ginger hair clashed horribly with the bright orange of his prison boiler suit.

He did not return my smile. We shook hands, and I sat down across the table from him. I started to introduce myself, but he did not wait to hear my name.

'I didn't do this,' he snarled, 'I've been framed! What are you going to do about it?'

Officially, as a British consular officer I was concerned primarily with the young man's health and welfare, not his innocence or guilt. Most British consular officers around the world simply refuse to discuss the details of a given crime; in fact, the policy of the Foreign and Commonwealth Office (FCO) is to keep conversation strictly to mundane matters such as the prisoner's diet and family contact.

Unofficially, I had realised a long time ago that to be of any real assistance to my compatriots I would have to tread a fine line between following FCO policy and telling the prisoners what they needed to know.

British inmates in foreign prisons are in an extremely vulnerable position.

It's often difficult, if not impossible, for them to find out what's happening and what *might* happen from anyone else, including – if they're lucky enough to have one – their lawyer. A consular officer probably has a good idea of what lies ahead; in my experience the average prisoner needs some straight talking, quickly.

Unfortunately, they don't usually like the straight part of the talking.

I looked at the young man across the table from me. He was legally an adult, but he still had much to learn about life. He'd managed to land himself in an American jail when he should have been back at Boots in Burnley buying some acne cream. It would be hard for him to be in this place. He was vulnerable and would certainly be a target for other, bigger men. I would help him as much as I could, but to do that I would need to know more about the situation.

I looked at my file, to check his name again.

'All right Paul,' I said, 'what's the story?'

'I was a passenger in a car that had drugs, but they say they were my drugs as well as his drugs even though it was his car. It wasn't my car and I don't even really know the bloke. I only went with him because I wanted to buy some cigarettes.'

'Well, that was a stroke of bad luck,' I said.

'Yeah, it was,' he replied, with no obvious sense of irony: a bad sign.

'What evidence have they got against you?'

'Just the drugs they found in the car.'

'Where were you when you were arrested?'

'Martin Luther King Boulevard.'

In tribute to the great civil rights leader, almost every American city has an MLK Boulevard, but they tend to be in the poorest parts of town, where crime is more prevalent.

'There's a lot of drug dealing and prostitution going on down there,' I said.

'Is there?'

I looked down at his arrest sheet, which I had in front of me. 'It says here you were arrested at 2.30am. Is that correct?'

'Er… yeah, that would be about right.'

'At the time of your arrest, it says you had cocaine in your system.'

'Did I?'

'You know you did.'

'That doesn't have anything to do with anything. It isn't illegal to have cocaine in your blood.'

'Whether it's illegal or not, and I think it probably is, being coked out of your head isn't going to go down well in court, trust me. You're in Florida, here – not Sweden. This doesn't look good. You should probably prepare yourself to be here for a while.'

Possession of cocaine and, more specifically, conspiracy to distribute it was likely to earn him three to five years in a state correctional institution – and that was if he pleaded guilty. If he was convicted at trial he was facing five to ten years.

'You can fuck right off!' he snarled, 'I didn't do it.'

'Hang on,' I said. 'Don't take it out on me. I'm only telling you what to expect.'

I didn't mind him venting his anger a little – it was only to be expected – but I didn't want to get embroiled in a pointless argument.

We sat in silence for a few moments. Although he didn't yet know it, Paul had been arrested during a police sting operation. He and his co-defendant had purchased a significant amount of coke from an undercover officer in a major drug-dealing neighbourhood. They had not bought cigarettes. There was no doubt in the minds of the arresting officers that he had gone there for drugs, and I knew from experience that a Florida jury would have no doubt either.

After a while, he calmed down and looked at the table in front of me, where I had placed a packet of mints.

'Whose mints are they?' he asked.

'Mine,' I said.

He reached over, took two of the mints and put them into his mouth.

'Whose are they now?' he said.

'Still mine,' I said. 'But you're in possession of them. You were from the moment you took them and ate them.'

'What if the mints got into my mouth by accident?'

'By accident?'

'They could have fallen in whilst I was asleep.'

He was being perfectly serious.

'What's that got to do with your charge?' I asked.

'It proves the drugs weren't necessarily mine, even if I had coke in my blood,' he said, slipping the packet of mints into his pocket.

'It proves nothing of the kind,' I said. 'And please don't test that argument in court. Now, can I have my mints back?'

'Oh, yeah, sorry. I forgot they were yours.'

He knew he was guilty, but thought he'd be able to talk his way out of this. He did not understand that in the United States evidence and due process were not for the likes of him. He was in the country illegally – having overstayed a tourist visa – he had taken drugs and he had no money to pay for a lawyer. He was unemployed, uneducated and dripping with attitude. None of this augured well.

I knew he would spend the next six to nine months in that Palm Beach County Jail, during which he would receive little information about the development of his case.

Eventually, when his spirit was sufficiently depleted, the prosecution would approach him and offer him a deal: he could plead guilty to a reduced charge, have the whole thing resolved with just a brief court appearance for sentencing and be on his way in a matter of months. Alternatively, he could plead 'not guilty', wait perhaps a year for a trial date and take his chances on the more serious charges. If he were to be convicted of them, he could face many years in prison.

In Florida, less than three per cent of prosecutions end up in front of a jury: the rest are resolved by plea bargains. The Floridian judicial system has more to do with economics than justice. Depending on your viewpoint, it is either ruthlessly perverse or extremely effective.

From out in the corridor I heard a buzzer sound, followed by a loud click. A metal door then slammed shut, and there was the sound of a big key being turned in a lock. There was a shout in the distance, which echoed down the hallway. Somebody banged something metal against the pipes. These are the sounds of confinement.

A sorry-looking son-of-a-gun with a broom shuffled up to the window of our room. He was wearing the distinctive blue tunic of the jail 'trusty', one whose good conduct permitted him to work and earn credits within the jail system. He made no effort to sweep anything. When he saw us, he came right up to the glass and smiled. He only had one tooth, which was gold, and his gums were bleeding. He was a black man who had dyed his hair blond, but his dark roots were showing: evidence of his months in pre-trial detention. He grasped the broom handle like a microphone and in a fine tenor voice he began to sing us a Frank Sinatra song. He had, apparently, done it his way. That was probably a mistake.

'We haven't got any cigarettes so fuck off!' shouted my client, before he'd got past the first verse. Frank grinned and hobbled away.

'What's he in for?' I asked.

'Arson,' he said.

'What did he set fire to?'

'His granny.'

'Bloody hell! Did she survive?'

'She was already dead. He was trying to melt the gold fillings out of her head before the undertakers got there.'

We both contemplated this in silence for a moment. I was getting hungry and I wanted to return to the relative sanity of the outside world. I started to put my papers away.

'What happens now?' Paul asked me, his tone more conciliatory.

'Probably nothing much for a while – my guess is not for several months, maybe even the best part of a year. You can't make bail because you're in the United States illegally; if you paid the bond you'd only go straight to an immigration detention centre. Let me ask you, how well do you know the bloke who was driving?'

'Hardly at all.'

'Can you be sure he won't give the police a statement incriminating you?'

'No, he won't do that, he's a mate.'

'Well, is he your mate, or a bloke you don't know?'

'Bit of both, I suppose.' Even he was embarrassed by his lie.

'Be prepared for the fact that the prosecutor will almost certainly approach this guy in about six months and offer him a sweet deal in exchange for a statement implicating you. They may even come and offer you the deal first. You need to think about what you're going to do when that time comes.'

'I can't grass him up.'

'Well, that's your prerogative. I'm only telling you what I think will happen. Besides, you might feel different about that after you've been in this hellhole for six months.'

'No, I won't.'

I sensed a slight anger in his tone again.

'Listen, I'm here to help,' I told him. 'I'll do whatever I can, and if you need anything you can either write to me at the consulate, or you can call us reverse-charge. They call it a "collect call" here. Ask for me or my assistant, pro-consul John Corfield.'

I stood to indicate that the meeting was over, and he rose to shake my hand. He muttered a few words of thanks. I rarely got even that much from most prisoners.

On the way out, I stopped at the jail's reception area to retrieve my leather jacket and bag from a locker. I had two missed calls on my cell phone. One from my girlfriend, who'd left the four-word message that no man ever wants to hear: 'We have to talk.' The other was from my colleague, Linda, at the British Consulate General in Atlanta. There was no message, but I returned the call anyway.

'Hey there, it's me,' I said. 'I think I missed your call earlier?'

'Hey Hugh,' she said. 'Listen, I have to go into a meeting right now, but I just wanted to let you know something before it gets out.'

She was whispering, which usually meant something interesting was happening.

'Is everything okay?' I asked.

'Well, they offered me early retirement this morning, and I'm just going back in to tell them I accept it.'

I wasn't too surprised at this news, but it was sad. I wondered if she was the first one to desert a sinking ship. I didn't say anything.

'I'm sorry I won't be able to watch out for you any more, but you'll be fine without me,' she said.

'Yeah, I'll be fine,' I said. 'Listen, I have to go, but I'll call you in the morning. Good luck.'

'Thanks, drive safe.'

In the car park, I prepared my Triumph motorcycle for the ride back to Orlando. Most British diplomats don't conduct their business trips on motorbikes, but most British diplomats weren't paid as badly as I was.

Thick, black clouds gathered to the north, which was exactly where I was going. I knew it was going to rain, and rain hard, but tried to persuade myself that maybe it would blow over. Driving a bike through a Florida storm is wet and dangerous and exhausting.

Half an hour later, as I headed up the Florida Turnpike, it burst right in front of me. Two hundred metres up the highway was a curtain of heavy rain, literally a dark grey wall of water, and at that point there's nothing to be done other than grit your teeth. Within seconds every part of me was soaked; I could smell the rain in my clothes and the roar of it drumming on my helmet filled my ears.

Within seconds, the water on the road surface was an inch or two deep and the bike began to aquaplane slightly; I slowed as much as was safe – the visibility was extremely bad and cars can come up behind you fast – and a speeding dump truck passed me on the outside and threw up a torrent of water, temporarily reducing my visibility to zero. My heart rate accelerated, and I could feel the adrenalin pumping through my body. The bike wobbled a fraction. In anticipation of a grim death, I braced myself and gripped the bars tightly.

2

MY STORY ACTUALLY begins at Toronto's Pearson airport in the spring of 1996. I had just spent the weekend visiting my brother, and was attempting to go back to my apartment in New York. At Pearson you clear US immigration at the airport before you fly to the States, and I was in the middle of an uncomfortable discussion with the US immigration officer about my domicile arrangements.

'Are you living in the United States?'

'What do you mean exactly by "living in the United States"?'

'Is your main residence in the United States?'

'No, as I've told you, my main residence is in London, England.'

'I think you're living in the United States.'

'Well, you're wrong. I've already shown you my air ticket to London in two days' time.'

My flight back to New York City was due to leave in less than an hour. The immigration officer looked at me for a few moments. She sensed I was lying, but I'd chosen my words carefully and I was not about to change my story, no matter how many times she asked me. It was a stalemate.

'Take a seat over there and wait,' she said.

She took my passport and my air tickets to New York and London and went off to speak to someone else. I'd already been in the secondary-interview room for half-an-hour answering the same questions over and over. This wasn't looking good, and I figured the game was up. I had moved to New York in 1990 to study at the American Academy of Dramatic Arts. After graduating I worked for a year – acting in obscure, *off*-off-Broadway theatres – on a practical training visa, which expired in 1994. By that time I was living on the Upper West Side of Manhattan. For the next two years there was a kind of grey period, where I was in and out of the United States on my B1/B2 tourist visa. I never overstayed the time restrictions of any given entry, but on the whole I was probably spending more of my time in America than I was supposed to.

I went and lay down on the seats, and I must have fallen asleep because I awoke with a start over an hour later, when the immigration officer shouted at me to get up and come back to the desk. From the look on her face, I guessed I was going to be refused entry to the US.

I wandered over, trying not to look too despondent.

'I've spoken to my supervisor,' she said, 'and I am under instruction to admit you to the United States. But only for a period of 48 hours.'

'Okay,' I replied casually, furiously trying to calculate where that left me.

'If it was down to me, you wouldn't be getting in at all,' she said, as she stamped my passport with unusual vigour and stapled inside it a white I-94 departure card before tossing it back across the counter at me, along with my flight ticket.

'Please thank your supervisor for me, he is eminently wise.'

I don't think she appreciated that last remark because, as I turned to leave, she offered a parting shot.

'You'd better be on the plane to England in two days,' she said. 'And the next time you come back to the US, you can expect some problems at immigration.'

That was all I needed, some black mark against me on the computer. I waved goodbye over my shoulder as I left the interview room and headed through to the departures lounge.

I'd missed my flight, and had a three-hour wait for the next one – though fortunately the check-in staff understood the situation, and stuck me on the next flight without penalty.

On the way back, I considered my options.

I didn't want to go home to England: that was for sure.

Flying to London on Wednesday would keep me within the strict letter of the law, but I doubted I'd get back in to the States any time soon.

Failing to leave the country by Wednesday would leave me in the States unlawfully.

After landing at La Guardia, I disembarked and found myself mingling with a large crowd of people in the lounge waiting to take the next flight out. The atmosphere seemed unusually tense, so I asked one of the passengers what was going on.

'The earlier flight to Toronto was cancelled,' he said, 'so we're all waiting for the last plane back tonight. They've oversold it, so most of these people don't have seats yet and they're trying to get on the flight.'

There was a scrum of desperate passengers around the desk, gesticulating and shouting at the airline staff. At that moment I had an inspirational idea. I approached the desk and stood at the very end. Just under the counter was a pile of I-94 immigration departure forms, which had been collected from the passengers who had already checked onto the flight. I removed the I-94 card from my passport and placed it inside the sleeve of my jacket. At a certain moment a man at the other end of the desk demanded loudly to be given a boarding pass, or to be checked on to a flight with another airline. As the staff members turned to deal with him, I gently tucked my I-94 to the middle of the pile on the desk, turned and walked away.

The records would now show that I had entered and left the United States on the same day. That solved the first part of my problem, but I was still unsure what to do about the long-term situation.

* * * * *

The next day I called a mate of mine, Lance, who worked at the British consulate-general in New York. He'd once told me that if I could get a job at the consulate, I would get a diplomatic visa, as he had done a couple of years before. We went for a beer and I explained my problem.

'Well, I've got some great contacts,' he said. 'I'll see what I can do.' (Months later, I discovered that he'd been sleeping with a woman in the personnel department. He lost his job a few years afterwards when he tried to put his hands down the knickers of a young secretary working in the political section: she subsequently turned out to be with MI6.)

With Lance pulling a few strings and maybe some bra straps, a week or two later I found myself interviewing for a position as a visa officer at the consulate. There was only one other applicant. I was offered the job the next day, and I started the following Monday.

Two weeks after I began, I was given a few days off work to go to London and get my visa from the American embassy. My visit to the embassy went without problem, and the next day I boarded a flight back to New York. My arrival at JFK didn't go so smoothly.

The immigration officer took one look at my passport and told me I'd have to go for a secondary interview. I went into a large separate room adjacent to the admissions desks and waited. After about an hour the senior immigration officer called me forward.

'Are you Mr Hugh Hunter?'

'Yes, I am.'

'Have you ever had any problems with US immigration?'

'No, I have not.'

'Well, I don't like this,' he said. 'I don't like it at all.'

'What's the problem? Is there something about me in the computer?' I asked.

'No, not exactly, but if you didn't have this diplomatic visa in your passport, I would refuse you entry and send you back to London. As it is, there's not much I can do about it.'

He didn't explain further. I was mystified, but he gave me my passport back and wished me a good day.

I went back into the consulate the next day. My job involved processing visa applications from people in the United States who wanted to travel to the UK. For obvious reasons, I never mentioned the incidents at Toronto or JFK to anyone in the office, but I wondered what had actually happened. I found out about two months later when I was sent to JFK airport for a day's training on fraudulent and counterfeit travel documents. The two instructors were US immigration officers. Towards the end of the day, one of the officers mentioned, almost in passing, that they had an unofficial system to identify people who they were suspicious about, but could not record on the computer.

'As you've learned,' he droned in a flat, nasal monotone, 'the ink we use to stamp passports is red in normal lighting conditions, but it glows blue under an ultraviolet light. If we have a suspicion about someone, but maybe for legal reasons we can't log it on the computer, we simply take several pages from the middle of the document and scuff the corners in the ink. When you look at that passport under an ultraviolet light, the whole corner of the passport glows bright blue. If you ever see that, you'll know that there's been a problem of some kind but, probably because we couldn't prove it, it hasn't been logged. Treat such visa applicants with caution.'

The next day I took my passport to work. That evening, after everyone else had left, I looked at it under an ultraviolet light. The corner was bright blue. I removed the edges of the affected pages surgically with a scalpel, shaving off a little more each time until all the ink was gone. I never had a problem with US immigration again.

I worked in the consular and visa section at the British Consulate in New York for around 18 months. It was a zoo. In those days consular and visa work was of marginal importance to the FCO, so we were inadequately funded and understaffed. Money was spent, instead, on the commercial work done at consulates – most of that money was, in my opinion, completely wasted, a good proportion of it on pointless lunches for diplomats. For most of the commercial officers, their only qualification to do the job was a brief FCO training course and almost none of them had had any hard experience in commerce, but within the closeted confines of the FCO, where there were few commercial realities, they were pretending to be businessmen. The truth was easy to see: by lunchtime on the Friday before a long weekend, the trade and investment offices were empty. In the visa section, by contrast, a dozen of us would be working into the evening to process hundreds of last-minute applications from people needing to travel to or through the UK that weekend. We never got so much as a word of thanks for it from the management.

It was actually an embarrassment. Every day, the visa queues would stretch out of the waiting room and past the elevators. Having stood in such lines many times myself, I knew how that felt and I often wondered how many people contemplating investing or working in the UK had taken one look at that line and gone elsewhere with their money and skills. Yet dozens of diplomats, whose remit was trade and investment, sat idle just a few metres away. It was a joke.

One morning we had a security briefing from a London-based officer. He told us how important our safety was to the FCO, and reminded us to be vigilant for unattended bags and suspicious behaviour. When I returned from lunch that afternoon, I stopped by our security guard, a young Puerto Rican employed via a local agency to save money. He spoke a kind of restructured English and he had a metal detection wand he waved all over the visa applicants before he allowed them into the waiting area.

'Hey there, Juan, how are you?' I said.

'Hangin' good, amigo, takin' it easy on the tenth floor.' He then attempted one of those complicated urban handshakes, but I failed miserably so he just punched me in the hand.

'Tell me, what do you have to do when the metal detector goes off? Do you have to pat people down?' I asked.

'I don't know. I've been working here two years, and this thing didn't never gone off. Not even one time.'

'Really? Can I see it please?'

'Sure thing.'

I took the end off of it and gave it a brief examination.

'You need batteries in here, my friend.' I told him.

'Nobody said nuthin' to me about no batteries when I got this job,' he replied, snatching back his wand indignantly.

That was how important our safety and security *really* was.

* * * * *

As the months passed, I began to find myself at odds with the management. It all culminated in the autumn of 1997, when we were told to expect a visit from a London-based FCO inspection team. We got the news on a Thursday afternoon, and the team was going to be in the office on the Monday morning. The inspectors were going to audit our visa operation to see whether we had sufficient resources and whether we were doing our jobs properly. We didn't, and we weren't. Naively, I was happy: I thought the inspection would reveal this and that the parlous situation might be rectified. Instead, our bosses panicked and asked for volunteers to come in and work over the weekend to clear the enormous backlog of applications. I spoke up to refuse, and encouraged the others to do the same. The request was fundamentally dishonest, and would prevent the audit team from ascertaining the real situation.

I ended up in an argument with my line manager. In front of the whole office, she screamed at me that I wasn't a team player and criticised me for my attitude. *My* attitude?

In the event, they got their volunteers, the auditors came in, spent the entire day in the consul's office and left on the Tuesday afternoon without even stepping foot into the processing office where the work was done. The hours spent over that weekend clearing the backlog had been wasted. The pile of folders could have been plonked in the centre of the office and strewn with fairy lights and the auditors would not have seen them. That was an interesting lesson for me on how the FCO conducts its oversight.

After this incident I was certain that my card was marked, and that I needed to think about an exit strategy. Then, just before Thanksgiving in November, I arrived at work one morning to see a notice on the message board.

Vacancy: British Vice-Consul, Orlando

This was a significant position. The successful applicant would have responsibility for all consular protection matters pertaining to British nationals in Florida, which meant anything from dealing with holidaymakers who'd lost their passports to visiting murderers in prison. But I was mostly interested because the successful candidate would be in charge of the office, reporting to the British Consulate General in Atlanta 400 miles away. Whoever got this job would be largely free of micromanagement and interference. From my experience thus far in the FCO, that was no small consideration.

Owing to my relative lack of consular experience I didn't think I had much chance of getting the job but I flew down to Atlanta for an interview anyway.

I've done many things in my life, and for several years I had been a London firefighter. During my interview, the consul general asked me what skills from that job I might be able to bring to this one. I didn't actually think there was much crossover, but I didn't want to say that. So I said the only thing I could think of. 'I'm pretty good at putting out fires.'

'Ah, yes,' he said, as he noted my answer down, 'that would come in useful.'

I was momentarily confused by this comment, until it dawned on me that he was speaking metaphorically. He obviously hadn't heard that all firemen are secret arsonists; I thought everyone knew that?

The next morning I was offered the job. It was time to escape from New York.

* * * * *

The British vice-consulate in Orlando had opened a few years earlier after the explosive growth of charter airline travel to Florida from the UK and a large increase in the resident British population.

My first day in the vice-consulate was in February 1998, a month before my 36th birthday. I was replacing vice-consul Linda Nassar, an American from Georgia – not all British consuls are British. A glamorous southern belle, she was blonde, in her early 50s and spoke with a laconic confederate drawl. But her easy, laid back nature disguised a keen intelligence and a wealth of knowledge about consular work, which she'd been doing for 30 years. She'd seen it all, and I would draw on her experience repeatedly.

After Linda and I had breakfast together, she introduced me to my two staff. Viv McCulloch was a gregarious, open, smiling woman; Sarah Bishop was not.

I spent the rest of the day drinking coffee and talking to Linda whilst she smoked.

'I didn't think you were allowed to smoke in office buildings in Florida,' I said.

'Well, I've sealed it off,' she said, pointing to the ceiling. There were yards of nicotine-stained tape covering every vent and fire alarm. 'Besides, this is, technically, British territory so British laws apply here. You can still smoke indoors in England, right?'

'Er… yes,' I said. You could back then. 'So anyway, I assume most of my work here will be lost passports and expired air tickets?'

'Well,' – almost all of her sentences started with 'well' – 'there's a bit of that, but you'll spend most of your time dealing with British prisoners.'

'Are there a lot of them?'

'Hundreds.'

'*Hundreds*? Are you kidding?'

'Well, we probably deal with more arrests and more long-term prisoners than any other British consulate in the world. Serious criminals, too, some of 'em.'

'Murderers?'

'Yeah, we have a couple dozen of those, and new ones every year.'

'Anyone I would have heard of?'

'Well, maybe one or two, but mostly they never made the news in the UK.'

'How come?'

'Well, the newspapers here rarely report on the nationality of defendants in trials. And if the press here doesn't mention it, the press in the UK doesn't usually get to hear about it.'

The job was beginning to sound even more interesting than I had originally anticipated.

I subsequently found that Linda had been right. The consulate in Orlando did deal with more arrests and prisoners than any other British consulate in the world. In fact, for several years, we dealt with more British prisoners than all of the British consulates in France put together.

I had a few days with Linda, during which we reviewed case files, talked about resources and ran through staffing issues. Then she left for the British Consulate General in Atlanta, from whence she had come four years before, to take up a promotion. She would also be my main point of contact in Atlanta.

I didn't feel remotely qualified for the job I'd taken on.

Florida is the size of England and Wales combined – the distance from Pensacola at one end to Key West at the other is over 500 miles. I was there to deal with pretty much any problem you can think of involving British nationals, as well as taking on a few statutory functions, such as signing certain official documents and undertaking 'maritime investigations' – mostly inquiries into deaths on board British-flagged vessels. There would also be occasional representational duties, such as public speaking and media relations.

But mostly I would deal with criminals.

If the job was big, the pay wasn't. There are two types of people who work in an embassy or consulate – 'diplomatic service personnel' and 'locally-employed staff'.

'DS' personnel are your traditional, career diplomats – known within the Foreign and Commonwealth Office as 'UK-based'. They generally work a rolling pattern of three years in a developing country, followed by three years in a developed country, followed by two or three years in the UK, until retirement, and they are extremely expensive. They're paid good salaries in UK pounds, but the many allowances and expenses they receive whilst abroad usually dwarf their salaries, and their children are normally entitled to a Government-paid private education. They also usually have lavish accommodation – the consul at an adjacent post to mine was UK-based and the rent on his apartment, paid by the FCO (i.e. the British taxpayer), was almost $10,000 per month. This was a huge and entirely unnecessary extravagance: it was almost never used for official government business, such as entertainment of local dignitaries, or accommodation of senior British officials who might be visiting the area, which were the only reasons that I could see might be used to remotely justify such expenditure.

Sadly, that wasn't something I personally had to worry about. I was locally-employed (LE), and LE staff were contracted to a particular position at a specific post and paid a salary in the local currency. Rest assured that 'LE' personnel don't get the big money or the flashy perks; when I started I was paid less than $2,100 per month, and from that I had to fund my own accommodation, transportation and airfares back to the UK.

I had found an apartment within walking distance of the office, which meant I didn't need to rush out and get a car, but I couldn't afford much furniture. Fortunately, the second day I was there I found a perfectly good old armchair in the car park outside my front door where somebody had abandoned it. A cheap bed from a company by the railway station and a small table and chairs from a second-hand store made it habitable. It was Spartan, but it would do.

A few weeks later I solved my transport dilemma with a 1996 Triumph Trident motorcycle. It was black with red trim, a gorgeous bike and cheaper than a car, if not so convenient. For long distance travelling, I'd fly and rent a car at the other end.

The day after I bought the Triumph, I rode it over to a small airfield in Orlando and booked my first flying lesson. I had always wanted to be a pilot and instruction in Florida was relatively inexpensive: now was the time to make it happen.

Back in the office, the workload was heavy from day one.

Consular relations between the United Kingdom and the USA are governed by the terms of the Anglo-American Agreement on Consular relations (AACR) of 1951. The terms of the treaty are far reaching, but one of the most important aspects of it concerns the arrest of British nationals in the States (and, conversely, the arrest of American citizens in the UK, as the treaty is reciprocal). Whenever a British citizen is arrested in the US it is mandatory for the police (or other arresting agency) to notify the British consulate, even if the arrested person does not want this.

In fact, the police frequently fail to notify the consulate of arrests, which was an ongoing problem, but the number of notifications was still high and the phones rang constantly. We received faxes informing us of arrests several times each day. It was hard to stay on top of it all, but I worked long hours to do so – invariably more than 60 hours a week during the first few years. Normally, I would need to travel a couple of days each week, usually to visit prisoners, but also others who were in trouble of some kind, which meant working weekends to catch up.

Notwithstanding the low pay and the long hours, I was excited and enthusiastic about the new job: it looked as if it would be fascinating. I was immensely proud to be in charge of a Foreign Office post, and, above all, it offered a real opportunity to help people in difficulty.

3

WHEN I STARTED in Orlando I must admit that I had a morbid curiosity about going to visit people in prison. I'd never been into a jail, and I was keen to found out what it was like. More than anything, I was interested to know what kind of mishaps and poor decisions could land you there. Over time I began to consider each case and try to determine whether it was a single, isolated error of judgment in an otherwise blameless life, or a series of angry, self-destructive events leading inevitably, inexorably to prison. I saw plenty of both kinds, and most shades in between, but one thing that struck me quite early on was the incredible stupidity of some of our crooks. Occasionally, the American cops have their work cut out in bringing British offenders to justice. Mostly, though, the criminals more or less throw themselves in jail through their own ineptitude in ways that reflect badly on our educational system, if nothing else.

Andy Cunningham was one such.

He was a fat, 44-year-old skinhead from London, who was, coincidentally, arrested the day I arrived in Orlando. He was booked into Dade County Jail in Miami on charges of stealing a car – or 'grand theft auto', as the Americans call it – and, for good measure, the jet-ski it was towing.

I went to visit him as soon as I could. He was pleased to see me, and, as fellow Londoners, we struck up something of a rapport. After some initial pleasantries, he started to give me some of his background, which included a large number of previous UK convictions. This seemed to be a matter of great pride to him.

He had not long since been released from prison in England, having served a sentence of 12 months for car theft. I knew that was a long sentence for car theft (in the UK, anyway), so there must be an interesting story behind it.

'We nicked luxury cars to order,' he said. 'Found the motors and sent them abroad. There's lots of places where they're not too bothered where the vehicle came from.'

His role had been to steal an almost new Range Rover in London, and deliver it to a lock-up garage in Liverpool. He'd been given a key to the car, copied or stolen by a mechanic who had previously serviced it. The plan called for an accomplice to visit the owner's house after midnight, an hour or two before Cunningham, to switch the number plates with fakes assigned to another, identical Range Rover which was legitimately being driven around in Cornwall; if the police stopped Cunningham and ran a check on the car, he would be able to supply the name and address of the real owner and, hopefully, he'd be on his way.

So far, foolproof.

'Problem was, the guy got there and found he'd lost the fake for the back,' said Cunningham. 'He couldn't be arsed to go and look for it – he just decided to go with one plate. He reckoned it was better to have a back number plate than a front one, even if it was the wrong colour, so he stuck the fake front plate on the back.'

He was shaking his head as he told me the sorry tale, and I had to smile. He held up a hand. 'Wait... it gets better. In the dark, and in his rush to get out of there, he put the bloody plate on upside-down. Course, he never told me any of this.'

Early next morning, Cunningham arrived at the target vehicle. His job was just to drive the Range Rover 200 miles without drawing police attention to himself.

'Trouble with *that* was,' he said, 'I was pissed when I got there. Plus I brought three of my mates along for a laugh and they were pissed as well. And still drinking. Well, I'm anxious to get going, it never occurred to me to have a look at the plates. Didn't even give it a second thought. We got in, it was a nice motor, cranked up the sound system and got going. We hit the rush hour, and somewhere on the North Circular, just before the M1, one of my mates says he feels sick. I wasn't going to stop, so he put the window down and threw up outside. The puke went all over a motorcyclist, who stopped and rang the Old Bill.'

By now, four drunk skinheads are roaring up the M1 at 100mph in a stolen, £70,000 vehicle which is covered in vomit and has a white number plate upside-down on its rear. Chumbawamba is playing at around 120db. Do things like this happen anywhere other than in the United Kingdom?

Ten miles out of London, the police caught up with him. They put on their lights and sirens to indicate to Cunningham to pull over, but he was having none of that, and immediately put his foot down: the chase was on.

'It lasted for about half an hour, and in the end there was about a dozen cop cars, a couple of motorbikes and a helicopter after me. What happened was, I flipped it over the central barrier. We hit some cars coming the other way, spun over a few times and landed upside down. Me and the front passenger was alright because of the airbags and that, but the lads in the back were proper fucked up.'

Immediately after his release from prison, he'd come to the USA for a holiday with his girlfriend, Tracy. They'd been having a difficult time, he told me; he felt this was because of their enforced separation, but I suspect it was because he was an idiot. In the States, they only fought more, and Tracy had gone back home early. Cunningham decided to stay on for an extra week, or two.

During that time he chanced upon a man in a bar in South Beach, Miami, and they fell into conversation. By the end of that evening he was falling-down drunk and had been recruited into a new criminal enterprise, which involved stealing a pick-up truck and the jet-ski on its trailer from an underground car park in downtown Miami. The plan was stunning in its simplicity: the American would keep watch whilst Cunningham, a skilled mechanic and experienced car thief, stole the truck and trailer. They would then head straight to a waiting cash buyer and off-load the jet-ski; the truck could be quickly stripped for parts, and then dumped. What could possibly go wrong?

The next afternoon they arrived at the parking garage, and the American took up his position. Cunningham was soon inside the truck and had the engine started. Unfortunately for him, he had failed to notice two important things. The first was that the trailer was secured (by means of a metal cable passing around its axle) to a metal ring concreted into the ground. The second thing was that there was an alternative entrance/exit from the car park.

As he pulled smartly forward, he heard a terrific crash as the axle was torn from under the trailer. The trailer swung around behind the truck and collided with a concrete column, destroying itself and the jet-ski; at that moment, a security guard on a routine patrol arrived through the second entrance and discovered the unfolding carnage.

Cunningham panicked and attempted to drive off; but the trailer had become entangled around the column. As he accelerated, the wheels simply span around on the spot, creating noise and smoke. He bailed out and tried to run for it, but being clinically obese he was quickly taken down by the guard and arrested at gunpoint.

His American accomplice fled, but was caught a few days later.

Cunningham went on to spend 18 months in jail before he finally accepted a plea of guilty, was sentenced to time-served and deported. During that time he persisted in calling us several times each day – reversing the charges, and therefore at the British taxpayer's expense – to demand that we pass on his ridiculous messages of love to the estranged Tracy. It is part of the role of a consular office to act as a conduit between British nationals imprisoned abroad and their family and loved ones in the UK, and often the consulate is the only such link. But consulates tend to be busy, and the amount of time available for such activities is limited. Cunningham was of that breed which is not much given to consideration of the needs and problems of others; in the end we had to limit his phone calls to once per week. It was a blessing to everyone, with the possible exception of Tracy, when he was finally deported home.

James Black was another unbelievably foolish Brit I came across. After completing his studies at Strathclyde University in Scotland, James decided, like many of his contemporaries, to take a gap year. His first stop was Florida, where he had a friend at the University of Florida in Gainesville. He quickly fell in love with the place and its sub-tropical climate. The university is large – it dominates the city – so his life there was full of young students, wild parties and day trips to the beach. Unfortunately, before long his money started to run out. His parents helped him out for a while, but eventually they told him to get a job, or cancel his world trip, come home to Scotland and *then* get a job.

One evening, as he took a walk around the city to think about his problem, he happened on an unlocked car. This was a young man who, by all accounts, had never had so much as a criminal thought in his life, so what happened next was almost surreal. He opened the vehicle and then its glove compartment. Inside was a loaded pistol, which he stole. He considered selling the gun, but didn't know how or where he could do so, or how much money to ask for. He thought about pawning it, but he would have had to supply personal information to the pawnshop.

So in the end he did what any British gap year tourist would surely do, and decided to use it to rob a bank.

The next morning he ran into the Mid-Florida Credit Union bank with his shirt pulled up over his face, brandishing the pistol. In his broad Scottish accent he demanded all the money in the cash till, and fled from the bank with about $4,000. Not having really considered his getaway plans, he stole a child's pushbike and pedalled off down the street.

So the police had a pretty good description to go on when they arrived at the scene moments later: a white male, with a strange accent and a shock of red hair, several thousand pounds stuffed down his underpants, riding a red bicycle with a wicker basket.

Unsurprisingly, he was caught within a few minutes when a patrol car cut off his escape, causing Black to go spectacularly over the handlebars.

He was taken to the county jail and booked for armed robbery.

He immediately made a full confession. All of the stolen money was recovered, and, apart from Black grazing his knee when he fell off his bike, not a single person had been harmed in this bizarre enterprise.

The Alachua County Sheriff's Department failed to contact the consulate, but I found out about it the next day when Black's father called from Scotland to find out more about his son's arrest, having heard garbled details in a phone call from James' friend in Florida.

Before we finished our conversation, Mr Black asked me a question. 'What kind of sentence could he get for this?'

I hesitated to answer; there was no good news here. 'It's difficult to say, at this point,' I said. 'We don't know whether he threatened anyone, or even fired the gun, which could make all the difference. Another thing we don't know yet is whether he'll be charged by the US federal authorities or by the state of Florida.'

In the United States, you are subject to both federal laws and state laws. Some offences – bank robbery is one of them – are both federal and state crimes. If a federal authority, such as the Federal Bureau of Investigation (FBI), the Drugs Enforcement Agency (DEA) or the Secret Service, prosecutes you, you appear in a federal court, and, if convicted, serve your time in a federal prison (which could be anywhere in the US). If a state authority, like a city police department or a county sheriff, prosecutes you, you appear in a state court and you serve your time in a state institution. For any given crime, the federal and state sentencing guidelines can be quite different.

'Which of those authorities would probably pass the longest sentence?'

'The State of Florida,' I answered.

'What if he fired the gun, and he's prosecuted by the State?'

There was no point in being evasive. 'If he fired the gun, even if he didn't hit anyone, it is a minimum of 20 years without chance of parole,' I said.

Florida's Governor Jeb Bush – brother of George W. – had won the recent gubernatorial election race with the slogan '10/20/Life'. If you carried a gun in the commission of a felony, you would automatically get a 10-year minimum mandatory sentence; if you fired it, 20 years; if the bullet hit someone, life without parole.

I heard his unspoken, but audible reaction. From the conversation I could tell that, whatever his son's actions may have been, Mr Black was clearly a decent man. I tried to say something positive. 'He would still be a relatively young man when he got out.'

Another difficult, but short, silence followed. 'Yes,' he said. 'But I won't be.'

In that moment, I saw his possible future: no weddings, no grandchildren, no family Christmases. Maybe dying before his son was free. Often the people most harshly punished as a result of criminal behaviour are not the criminals themselves.

'I'm really very sorry,' I said. 'I can't imagine what you're feeling.'

He was gracious in reply. 'Well, thank you for being so direct with your answers, it does make it a little easier to know where we stand.'

The next morning I headed north up the Florida Turnpike to Gainesville.

James Black could not have been a more unlikely bank robber. He was shy, softly-spoken and slightly built. We discussed his case and he was keen to know the lay of the land.

'A great deal depends on who prosecutes you,' I said. 'If it's the State, as opposed to the federal authorities, you're in a heap of trouble. Fortunately for everyone concerned, you didn't fire the gun, but it's still a minimum of 10 years.'

He blanched on hearing that. Then he gave a sardonic laugh. 'At least my dad won't be able to get his hands on me for a while,' he joked, shaking his head, 'because then I'm dead for sure.'

Back home in Scotland, the story had for once hit the papers and a couple of dozen newspaper reporters and photographers were camped outside the family house, with mobile television vans blocking the street. One paper ran the story with a picture of James in his graduation gown, with the caption, adapted from an advert, 'Your degree from Strathclyde University can take you to new places.' A bit tasteless, if you ask me.

Several weeks after his arrest, Black got his first break. The federal government elected to pursue the prosecution, as was its prerogative. Any bank robbery in the USA is considered, in principle, to be an offence against the Federal Reserve, and the federal authorities get the first choice on whether to prosecute. If they decline, the State can then prosecute for armed robbery. As I've said, somewhat counter-intuitively, the federal sentencing guidelines for armed robbery are less onerous than the State of Florida's.

Around that time, Mr and Mrs Black came to visit me at the office, on their way to Gainesville. They were good, honest and hardworking people, and I don't suppose they ever expected to find themselves in a position like this.

As soon as the proper court papers were in place, Black admitted the offence and entered a plea of guilty. He wrote a lengthy letter of apology to all the parties concerned – not least to the people he had waved the gun at during the robbery. Most of them, in turn, wrote letters of mitigation to the judge on his behalf, saying, essentially, that he was a nice, friendly and polite bank robber, and that he should be treated with whatever leniency was available to the court. His parents also secured many dozens of letters from friends, employees and college professors to support his good character. If ever a man had robbed a bank by accident, James Black was he.

A few months later, on a rainy Thursday, the sentencing hearing was held at the federal courthouse in Gainesville. I attended as an observer (the FCO does not normally permit consular officers to give evidence in a foreign court). The prosecution presented the undisputed facts; the defence offered Black's total admission of guilt as charged, along with his apologies and some character witnesses. Finally, the judge addressed the defendant.

'I've read all the letters of support,' he said. 'And having reviewed the case notes and listened to the evidence, I just cannot comprehend how this robbery happened. It was clearly an aberration. Nevertheless, it was a serious offence, and I am bound by law to order a sentence of incarceration of not less than five years.'

He then did something quite extraordinary: he ordered James into the custody of his parents for the three remaining days of their stay, and he ordered that he present himself into the custody of the US Marshals at Alachua County Jail by 8pm on the Sunday. This act was a significant honour to the integrity of the Black family, and they left the court for what would be their last few days together for some time.

After the sentencing, as the crowds were melting away from the courtroom, the clerk of the court approached me and said that the judge would be honoured to host me in his chambers for tea. The honour, of course, was all mine, and we spent a pleasant half hour in his room discussing various subjects. During this, he mentioned that he'd never been to England. I told him that he absolutely should go, and sooner rather than later.

'Why?' he asked me, 'is it particularly beautiful at this time of year?'

'No,' I said, 'we desperately need the money you'll spend while you're there.'

He laughed.

Black duly reported at the jail by the appointed time a few days later and began his sentence. He was soon transferred to a federal prison in Wisconsin, where his consular care fell to my colleague at our consulate in Chicago. His parents stayed in touch with me, though, for the duration of his sentence and kept me informed of his progress. Within two years, he was allowed to transfer to a prison in Scotland to finish his jail term. International prison transfer requests from British nationals in the USA rarely succeed, and when they do they usually take many years to come through. In Black's case, I have no doubt that his success was largely due to the temerity and dedication of his mother, who became something of an expert in the legal and political intricacies of international prison transfers. Once back in Scotland, he moved through the prison system quite quickly and was in an open prison within a relatively short time, before his eventual release on parole. It had undoubtedly been a tough time for him, but it could have been much, much worse. The relative leniency of his sentence was due to his own essentially good character, and the diligence of his parents.

Consular work is rarely much appreciated by the people who receive the services – it's more usually seen as a right that is funded by taxpayers (there's some truth in that, but not much) – but the Black family were extremely gracious to us and they sent a Christmas card to the consulate each year, along with a personal note of thanks and goodwill.

* * * * *

One day, the police in Clearwater called to tell me about the arrest of a British man called Mike Sigston.

It turned out he'd committed one of the most gruesome murders the state had seen in recent times.

I went to visit Sigston in Pinellas County Jail the next day. He was brought into the interview room in shackles, chains rattling as if he were a ghost in a Jacobean drama. He was around 50, but looked much older, with pale skin, sunken red eyes and a face that needed ironing. His hands were stained with tobacco, and they shook. He sat down heavily – it is hard to sit elegantly when you're manacled, hands and feet – and looked at me as if struggling to get me in focus.

'Hello, I'm Hugh Hunter, the British vice-consul,' I said.

He started to try to and introduce himself, but instead gave out an almighty, involuntary cough, and half-a-litre of phlegm sprayed across the desk at me. This is one of the occupational hazards of being a consul. He made no attempt to apologise or excuse himself, but simply snorted up some more mucus from his throat, swallowed it and then bent forward to wipe his face with his manacled hands.

'How are you doing?' he said, and then wiggled his chains to show that he was unable to shake hands with me. *Thank God for that*, I thought.

'I'm fine, thanks. How did you get yourself into this mess?'

'I drink,' he said.

'Do you?' I replied. I tried to sound surprised.

'Yeah, I drink a lot. It's kind of a problem.'

'Are you an alcoholic?'

'Yeah, I guess so.'

'Have you ever been treated for it?'

'Nope, I never really thought of it as a problem until now.'

'Do you take drugs?'

'When I can get them.'

'Which drugs? Cocaine? Marijuana? Heroin?'

'Yeah, those and anything else I can get my hands on.'

'Have you ever been treated for drug addiction?'

'No, I haven't.'

While I was making notes on this he said, 'Do you have any painkillers on you? I could really do with some painkillers.'

'Sorry,' I said, 'I can't help you there.'

'Fuck me,' he said, looking out the window of the interview room and across the prison courtyard, 'this place is ugly when you're sober.'

'Well, you'd better get used to it,' I said. 'I suspect you'll be here a while.'

'You definitely don't have any painkillers, then?

'I'm afraid not.'

He went on to tell me that he had been living in America illegally for a few years, and he had moved in with his girlfriend, an American woman from Florida who was also an alcoholic. A few days before his arrest, they had been drinking at home one night. They had consumed so much vodka that he could remember almost nothing of the evening, except that they might have had an argument and a fight about something. As far as he could remember he thinks that they made up, and maybe had sex before going to sleep. He said that when he woke up the next morning he had a tremendous hangover. He looked over and saw his girlfriend on the other side of the bed and spoke to her, but she didn't reply. He pulled the sheets off her to wake her up, and suddenly realised that there was a huge pool of clotting, sticky blood in the bed. He shook her, but immediately knew from her cold skin that she was long dead.

'Oh, my giddy aunt!' I said. 'What did you do then?'

'I was pretty freaked out,' he said. 'I didn't know what to do. I thought about it for a while, you know, tried to sober up and think straight. That was when I made my mistake, though.'

I grinned inside. He'd murdered his girlfriend with a hunting knife whilst in a drunken rage, probably had sex with her corpse and then spent the night sleeping in a pool of her blood – and *then* he made a mistake? I couldn't wait to hear this.

'What was that?' I said.

'Well, you know, I didn't think the cops would believe that I didn't mean to do it, so I rolled her body up in an old carpet, put her in the trunk of my car and drove out to the woods over by Tarpon Springs and buried her. Came home, had a beer, watched a rerun of the *Texas Chainsaw Massacre* on the box and tried to forget about the whole thing.'

As you do.

Nothing happened for a couple of days, but then his girlfriend's father grew concerned because she hadn't called him, and rang the police. A sheriff's deputy from Pinellas County turned up at the prisoner's apartment to ask a few questions. Probably unsatisfied with the answers he was getting, he asked for a quick look around the place.

'Did he find anything?' I asked.

'Well, when he looked in the bedroom he saw all the blood on the bedclothes and called for back-up.'

I was incredulous. 'You hadn't cleaned or changed the bedclothes?' I said.

'No, I... I just forgot, I suppose. I just slept on the couch. I was trying to put it out of my mind. It was freaking me out.'

'I'm not surprised. It's freaking me out, and I wasn't even there.'

Some homicide detectives soon arrived and questioned him further. He tried denying any knowledge of what had happened, but eventually told them the whole story, or at least as much of it as he could remember. He even took them to the burial site, where they were able to recover his girlfriend's decomposing body.

Unusually, in my experience, the police officers and the prosecutor did, in fact, believe his claim that he didn't mean to kill her, and that he had panicked when he buried her body the next day. It didn't help him that much, though. He pleaded guilty to manslaughter and got 40 years in prison.

The story didn't even make the front page of the local newspaper. Well, Florida's a dangerous place.

It's also a weird place, as the story of Barbara Batt confirms.

Batt had been married to a British prison officer for almost 30 years when he left her for another woman.

To help overcome the pain of her husband's sudden and unexpected departure, and the subsequent divorce, she travelled to New Jersey to spend a couple of months with an old school friend who'd emigrated there. During this sojourn, she met a Spanish woman, Rosa Lopez, with whom she became friendly. Rosa had a boyfriend who was on Death Row in Florida and for some reason this fascinated Barbara.

When Rosa mentioned that men on Death Row were looking for people to correspond with, Barbara got busy with a biro.

In no time at all, she was writing to one Gary Bond, a man 25 years her junior who was facing the ultimate judicial punishment for having killed his ex-girlfriend and her new lover.

Whether it was because of the photograph of herself she sent him or her electric prose, we will probably never know. Anyway, he fell in love with her – at least, that's what he said.

He wanted her to come and visit him, but there was a small problem: the only people ordinarily allowed to visit death row prisoners are family members or officials, such as lawyers or consular staff; anyone else would need a special permission, which, frankly, Batt was unlikely to get.

This little obstacle, however, was soon overcome when Bonds wrote and proposed marriage and Barbara accepted.

A few months later a ceremony took place at the Death Row facility in Union Correctional Institution.

Consummation was not permitted.

In order to be closer to her new husband, Batt moved to a small caravan in a trailer park near the prison. From this vantage, the relationship grew. They wrote to each other daily, and she visited him every Saturday, which was the maximum permitted frequency. There was no touching permitted during the visits, and his hands were manacled behind his back; at least that would protect her from the same fate as his previous girlfriend.

This arrangement continued for some months before Rosa Lopez showed up from New Jersey. She had been making frequent visits herself to her boyfriend, but this time she had something different to discuss with Batt. She explained that her boyfriend and Bonds had conjured up an escape plan, and she wanted to know whether Batt was up for it.

Batt was up for it, and that was where it all started to go downhill.

A few weeks later, two women – one middle-aged and British, and the other young and Spanish – arrived at a heliport near Starke, Florida, in a rented car. They had booked a helicopter flight to get an aerial view of some property they were thinking of buying a few miles out of town. The large bag they were carrying, they explained to the pilot, was full of photographic equipment.

Two or three minutes after take-off, the pilot felt a poke on the back of his head. When he looked round, he saw at close range the wrong end of a gun barrel. The other passenger was also armed.

'Keep flying north west!' shouted the Englishwoman.

'Okay, take it easy,' he replied. 'Where are we going?'

'You'll see,' she hollered.

After a few more minutes the prison was in sight. Batt then explained to the pilot how it was going to work.

'I want you to fly over the exercise yard of that prison over there,' she said (I'm paraphrasing). 'We're going to drop this bag down to a couple of prisoners who'll be waiting for us. They're going to give us some covering fire and chuck some grenades about the place. We'll be shooting at the guards from up here. Once you get low enough, the two prisoners will be jumping into the helicopter and we'll return to the base at full speed. Do you understand me?'

It's loud in a helicopter, and difficult to communicate without headphones. You have to shout a lot, and wave your arms about. Economy of language is best, which might explain the pilot's response: 'You are fucking joking, right?'

'Not in the slightest,' said Barbara Batt.

The pilot was a local man with knowledge of the area, and he was able to explain to his two passengers several fatal flaws in their plan.

'First of all, there are observation towers all around the prison, and in those towers are some bored, trigger-happy guards with big guns. Before we even get close to the place they are going to shoot us down and we will all die. Secondly, there are wires across the exercise yard that will prevent us from getting anywhere near the ground – if the blades of this aircraft hit those wires, we will all die. Thirdly, the weight of two grown men climbing onto this aircraft will put us over our maximum payload – we simply won't be able to fly with them on board. We will crash and we will all die. Besides, what if even more prisoners decide to take their chances and jump on board? We'll be pulled to the ground and we will all die.'

His words of aeronautical good sense had some effect on the women: they relented and told him to fly back to base. As soon as they landed, they jumped into their car and drove off at speed without even paying for the flight.

The pilot called the police and the women were arrested a few miles away. Soon after her arrest, Batt made a full statement to the authorities.

I went to visit her a few days later. I've met a few unlikely criminals in my time, but she takes the biscuit. She was nearly 60, quite short and unprepossessing, and I listened in astonishment as she told me her story. By the end she was in tears, feeling extremely sorry for herself. She had grown up children, and was anxious that she might not see them again – at least, not as a free woman. I thought she was probably right, but this didn't seem the best time to say so.

As Batt was beginning to learn, American jails are hell. They tend to be full of young, loud, aggressive morons. They are so dangerous that everyone is trying to be crazier than everyone else in the hope that they'll be left alone. Many of the inmates have nothing to lose. Most of the facilities are either sealed shut, with the air conditioning set so cold you are constantly shivering, or open to the elements, in which case they are, for most of the year, insufferably hot and humid. For someone slow and frail, like Batt, it would be hard to survive.

She was eventually arraigned and charged by the federal authorities for the crime of air piracy. She was assigned a federal public defender based in Jacksonville, and soon after the arraignment I went there to talk with him about the case. He told me that it didn't look good for her. She had been caught red-handed in the execution of a serious crime, and the absolute minimum she would receive would be a sentence of 20 years; it would probably be longer.

There was also another problem, he told me. After the women were arrested, the police went to Union Correctional Institution to arrest the two inmates concerned for attempting to escape. (I know it sounds absurd to arrest someone on Death Row – after all, how much more can you do to actually punish them? – but that's how it works.) They both admitted the plan, but they said they had been induced to commit the offence by Barbara, and that she had threatened to kill Rosa if they did not acquiesce. Rosa had also made a statement to the same effect.

My immediate reaction was to laugh: I couldn't see how these idiots thought that anyone would actually believe this nonsense. The lawyer also permitted himself a smile.

'I'm sure they're lying, too,' he said. 'And I doubt that any judge or jury will believe them. Nevertheless, if that allegation sticks, her sentence could be significantly increased.'

'Poor woman,' I said. 'She thinks she's marrying a decent bloke – just an average hardworking double-killer – and he turns out to be no good. Men, eh?'

Despite the seriousness of the charges, I had some measure of sympathy with Batt. I suspected she was fundamentally decent, though deeply confused. She had done something really stupid, but it had been quite out of character. She was certainly going to pay a heavy penalty for it.

It was several more months before I went to see her again. She was living through a nightmare. We talked for a long time about her life in England, her family and how much she would miss them. She was full of regret, but it was too late to change anything now.

She was eventually sentenced to a minimum of 20 years in a federal prison, and soon after she was sent to the women's federal correctional institution in Danbury, Connecticut.

She is still in that prison today, and, I understand, looking for a pen friend.

Very few people are fundamentally evil, but I have come to believe that some people have inherent character weaknesses that almost compel them to their fate. Sigston had struggled most of his adult life with addictions and dependency, and in the end this flaw led directly to his downfall. Cunningham was a profoundly lazy, stupid and inconsiderate man who was determined he would rather steal than work, but he had run out of ideas years ago: I have little doubt he will spend most of his life behind bars. In the classic sense, they were both tragic: their fundamental character will always lead them to failure. But Black and Batt were, it seemed to me, basically good people who had, under strange and trying circumstances, made a flawed judgement, and compounded mistake upon mistake. In the classic sense, this is comedy or even farce, and it fascinated me, and would occupy my thoughts for hours. Mostly I wondered whether this sort of thing could happen to anyone – whether it could happen to me. Would my life be a tragedy or a farce?

From a practical point of view, whatever these people had done, they needed all the help they could get. I was proud to serve in this role, and I quickly felt that this was work I was born to do.

* * * * *

As a consulate team, we quickly gained experience and settled into our work well. I spent almost half my time travelling on business, and worked in the office most weekends to compensate for the time away. As I'd hoped, I had almost no contact with Atlanta other than my frequent, friendly calls with Linda. They were content to let me get on with it. My consul general in Atlanta gave me only one instruction when I started: 'I don't want any surprises, so make sure I hear it from you first.'

Most of my contact with the wider FCO was through the consular desk officers in London – simply known to us as 'London', or 'The Desk'. We reported our important work to them, they let us know what was happening back at the 'centre' and gave us news, requests or instructions as appropriate.

The consul based at our Embassy in Washington was nominally responsible for overseeing the consular network throughout the United States, and was another point of contact and advice. When I first started in Orlando, the lovely Carol Priestley held that post. After a couple of years, she was posted to Moscow and replaced by Graeme Wise. Both of them were dedicated public servants and a source of wisdom and encouragement when needed.

Late one Saturday afternoon, not many months after I first arrived, I was alone in my favourite coffee shop. On a nearby table was a copy of *Orlando Weekly*, the city's listings magazine. I had a quick look through to see what was going on, and came across the personal ads section. One ad in particular caught my eye. An African-American woman was looking to meet someone, and her description sounded interesting. I rang and left my details on the message machine saying simply that I hoped she'd call me sometime.

That evening I stayed home, watched television for a bit, and then went to bed. At around 12.30am my phone rang, waking me from a deep sleep.

'Hi, this is Cheryl,' came the voice on the other end of the phone, in the most sultry, sexy southern accent I'd ever heard. 'May I please speak to Hugh?'

'Hello, this is Hugh Hunter here,' I said. 'I'm sorry, but do I know you?' I'd forgotten about my earlier phone call.

'You called and left me a message from the personal ads.'

'Oh, right. So this is you, then?'

'This is me.'

'Fantastic. Fantastic. Er… what time is it?'

'I have no clue. What are you doing? Were you asleep?'

'No, not at all, I just got back from dinner with friends.' I didn't want her to pigeonhole me as a boring English curmudgeon just yet – there was plenty of time for her to discover that later.

'Why don't you come over and meet me? I'm with a friend at a club over on East Colonial.'

'OK, I'll be there in half an hour.'

I had a quick shower, jumped on the Triumph, and was there in double-quick time. She had told me she would be wearing a red dress and standing by the bar over to the left as you go in. I saw her immediately, and, to be honest, you couldn't have missed her. She wasn't far short of six feet tall, and she had an extremely athletic build. She was looking the other way when I arrived, and I quickly noticed that most of the men around her couldn't take their eyes off her. How could they not – she was stunning. The first question that crossed my mind was 'Why does a girl like that need to place a personal ad?' There must be an answer to that, but I still have no idea what it is.

I approached her and introduced myself. She smiled, turned to her friend and shrugged. Her friend nodded vaguely back at her.

'Have I passed the audition? I asked her.

The music was loud and it was difficult to hear people talking, so she leaned in close and said, 'Not yet.'

I bought drinks for her and her friend.

'What's that you're drinking?' Cheryl asked me.

'Soda water. I'm driving.'

'I respect that.'

'I can assure you it's the only respectable thing about me.'

The briefest of American comprehension-pauses and then she laughed. I was off to a good start.

'Where are you from?'

'I'm British.'

'Are you here on vacation?' she inquired.

'No, I'm on Crown service.'

'What's Crown service?'

'I'm working here on a commission from Her Majesty Queen Elizabeth the Second,' I replied.

'I work for commission. It sucks!'

'It certainly does.'

After this brief exchange she turned her back on me and began to look over towards the dance floor again. I looked at her dress more closely; it was long, flaming red and at the back there was nothing: the shoulder straps kind of came down to meet just about at the base of her spine, leaving her entire back visible. I wondered how her substantial breasts were supported, and whether I'd get a chance to find out for myself. Her shoulders were powerful but feminine, and I was entranced by the enticing curve of her spine.

At this point I was half-sitting on a high barstool. In front, with her back still turned to me, Cheryl started to sway gently from side-to-side with the music. Then she began to move slowly backwards until she was essentially grinding her backside against me. I put my hands softly on her hips and felt her move. It was intensely erotic. She put her hands gently on mine, still without looking at me. I thought, *This is going to be amazing*.

When the club closed she invited me back for coffee at her place, and I accepted.

'Where's your car?' she asked.

'I don't have one, I'm on a motorcycle.'

'Really? So how do you go on dates?'

'I don't.'

'Follow me then, it's not too far.'

Back at her apartment, which was miles away, we had coffee and talked for a while. She was an engaging conversationalist, and although I teased her gently, in a typically English way, she took it all in her stride. I have mostly found mainstream white-American culture to be quite direct, and lacking a sense of irony; I wondered whether Cheryl's ability to play with words and meaning was a black thing.

Whatever the reason, she seemed to 'get' me, and her laughter was compelling. I felt powerfully attracted to her. Soon I was standing in front of her in the lounge, and we were kissing gently. After a respectable period of time, I took the shoulder straps of her dress, pulled them to the side and let go. She dropped her arms down as I did so and the dress fell to the floor, and there she was in just a thong and a pair of Manolo Blahniks – this tall, powerful woman rising from a lake of red silk. The only thing supporting her breasts were her genes. It's good to be the British consul.

The next morning I awoke early, as I had a flying lesson. I pulled the covers over Cheryl and gave her a tender kiss on the shoulder before trying to leave quietly and avoid waking her.

Just as I was about close the front door behind me I heard her shout out 'You better call me, you freak!'

I smiled all the way home.

4

I HAVE ALWAYS TRIED to see the best in people.

Unfortunately, try as I might, I could find absolutely nothing redeeming whatsoever in the man who was sitting in front of me in the Broward County Jail in Fort Lauderdale.

The day before flying down for my first visit to Geralt Owen I had reviewed his substantial case file. One of the documents was a copy of Owen's criminal record from the UK. It made interesting reading. He had committed his first offences, for theft and public disorder, at 13. By 15 he was still stealing, but had added assault to his repertoire. His later offences also included a conviction for forcing a 13-year-old girl to fellate him.

A Welshman, he had spent much of his 20s and early 30s in-and-out of prison, but in his mid-30s he married a presumably unsuspecting woman. I could not imagine what she might have seen in this artless, lying thug, but the marriage was not very old before his violent and controlling behaviour became a problem. The situation became so bad that she moved back to her parents' house, some distance away, but he followed her there and attacked her. Eventually she divorced him and fled to Florida to stay with an old school friend who had settled in Fort Lauderdale, hoping that that was far enough away.

Unfortunately, Owen managed to discover where she had gone, and followed her. He turned up at her new home one day, taking her by surprise, and, after failing to persuade her to return to the UK with him, beat her up. He was arrested and spent a couple of months in Broward County Jail before being deported and excluded from the USA.

You might think that would be that, and I'm sure his ex-wife did. But, once back in Wales, Owen simply changed his surname to Evans, his mother's maiden name. He successfully applied for a fresh passport in this new name, and was back in Florida within weeks, passing easily through US immigration despite his recent deportation.

On the evening of his arrival back in Florida, he went straight to his ex-wife's new residence, stopping only to purchase a hunting knife. He lay in wait for her there, and sprang upon her as she got out of her car. Shouting abuse at her and screaming at her that she must go back to Wales with him, he held her by the hair as he punched and kicked her. She tried desperately to get back in to the vehicle, and found herself half-in and half-out of it, all tangled up in the seat belt. At that, Owen pulled the blade from his jacket and launched a frenzied attack on the woman he claims to this day was the love of his life. He stabbed her 37 times, and then ran off down the road, leaving her to die in a pool of blood on the driveway. The neighbours, alerted by the screams, called the police and an ambulance; but, terrified of a return by the hysterical knifeman, no one went to the assistance of the fatally wounded Englishwoman. As her life ebbed from her, she spent her last horrifying minutes alone, presumably in tremendous pain, and unable to say goodbye to her children and her sisters, thousands of miles away.

Owen made a run for it up the east coast, heading for the Canadian border, but his escape attempt was always doomed to failure; at 5ft 8in, he weighed almost 20 stones, he sported a full beard and moustache and was wearing a Welsh rugby shirt with his own name on the back. Despite this, he did make it almost 1,000 miles to Maryland before he was spotted by an alert police officer who was aware of the nationwide alert. He was taken into custody at gunpoint, the arresting officers treating him with considerably more mercy and respect than he had shown his ex-wife a few days before.

He was soon extradited back to Broward County to face a charge of first-degree murder, which can carry the death penalty in Florida.

I first met him well over a year later as he waited for a trial date, which, at best, was still likely to be a further year away. I saw him in a small visiting room in the county jail. He looked like what he was, a modern Neanderthal, and his greeting was confined to a grunt. As I took the relevant papers from my folder, he stared at me for a long time. An annotation in the case file informed me that he intended to plead not guilty to murder on the grounds that he had not meant to attack his wife, much less kill her, when he travelled to her house that day. He later told me that he had purchased the knife because Fort Lauderdale was such a dangerous place.

We talked for quite a long time during that first meeting, and he was at pains to convince me that he had murdered his wife in a fit of loving passion. He cared about her so much, he said, that he could not face the prospect of life without her. I think he had convinced himself that this was actually true. 'I'm Welsh,' he told me, 'and I have a Gallic temperament.'

I told him that that was an insult to all decent Welsh people: he didn't like that. In truth, of course, he knew nothing of the qualities of selflessness and tenderness evident in real love. He knew only of his own needs, desires and frustrations in life. He was a selfish, manipulative, violent individual.

He said that his attorney, appointed by the court and paid for by Florida taxpayers – for Owen was, of course, indigent – was trying to secure a plea bargain on a charge of second-degree murder, but that the prosecutor was under pressure from his ex-wife's family in the UK to prosecute and convict him of first-degree murder. One essential difference between first-degree and second-degree murder – premeditated killing against a spur-of-the-moment act – is that, in Florida, the former can carry the death penalty while the latter does not.

We talked about a number of other issues, including his health and the conditions in the jail. He complained about everything; the whole world was against him, and he was a victim of injustice. As soon as I felt I reasonably could, I made my excuses and left. It is truly exhausting to spend time with someone like that, and when I departed my shoulders were tight with tension.

By the time I went to see him again, almost a year later, he had secured his plea bargain to second-degree murder. The victim's family had reluctantly accepted that a conviction for first-degree murder was uncertain, and that it would be in their best interests to accept a plea of guilt on the lesser charge.

The judge had accepted this plea, and Owen was now scheduled to appear in court again in several weeks time to be sentenced.

Before I went to the jail, I had dropped by to see Owen's attorney, at the attorney's request. He gave me an update on exactly what had happened during the plea process. Owen had accepted the plea to avoid any chance of the electric chair, but he would be incarcerated in the Florida Department of Corrections for the rest of his natural life. He went on to explain that he, the lawyer, was now done with the case: he would appear at the sentencing hearing, which was a formality, and he would then have no further involvement in the matter. I asked what would happen if Owen wanted to appeal. He told me that as Owen had accepted his guilt, and agreed to the sentence, there could be no realistic grounds for an appeal. If one *did* take place, it would require a specialist appellate lawyer which would be an expensive undertaking and Owen would have no recourse to public funds. I thanked him for all his efforts on behalf of this British citizen. Just before I left, he passed me some legal papers and a box.

'What's in this?' I asked him

'It's a collection of photographs of the victim taken in the mortuary, before the autopsy started. They had been scheduled as evidence in the trial, but, in the event, they were superfluous.'

I quickly perused them. They were horrific: Owen's ex-wife looked as if she had been butchered in a meat market. I couldn't really imagine what I would do with them, nor did I really want to take responsibility for them, but it seemed churlish to refuse them. I asked him to whom they actually belonged. He told me that they had belonged to the state of Florida, but that they had been relinquished to him, and he was giving them to me to take on behalf of the British Government.

When I went to see Owen that afternoon he was upbeat and pleased to see me, which I found surprising; but I soon found out why. He felt that the court, in accepting his plea to second-degree murder, had exonerated him of malice and aforethought in the killing, and that everyone now accepted that it was all just a terrible accident and that nobody was really to blame.

'I'll get 20 years,' he said, 'but if I behave myself I'll only have to do about 14. I done more than a couple already, so I'll be back in the UK in 10 years or so. It's bad, but it ain't that bad.'

'I'm not sure you have that right,' I said. 'Your lawyer says you're in for life.'

'Oh, no, no, no,' he said. 'You've misunderstood him there, see. I'll be home before long, don't you worry.'

We talked for a while longer, and then he mentioned the photographs: 'I asked my lawyer if I could have them, but he said they had to be handed over to you for safekeeping. So can you let me have them?'

I realised I'd been set up. Clearly, and with good reason, the lawyer hadn't wanted to send the pictures to Owen, but nor did he wish to put up with all the correspondence and arguing that would likely ensue from a refusal so he had sidestepped the problem.

'I do have them,' I said, 'but I don't think I can send them to you. For starters, the prison wouldn't allow it.'

His attitude changed in an instant, and he became aggressive with me. This belligerence went on for a short while, but when he realised that I was unfazed by his antics he started to wallow in self-pity.

'I really want those photographs,' he said, almost in tears.

'Why?' I asked.

'Because they are the only pictures of my ex-wife I have left,' he said, with a straight face and, as far as I could tell, no irony.

And then, right on cue, his tears began to fall.

A few weeks later, he was in court for sentencing. He was given a life sentence, with no chance of parole, precisely as his attorney had told me he would. I wasn't there, but I was told that when the sentence was passed he erupted in fury and started to threaten the judge and the prosecutor, as well as his own attorney. He refused to sign the form acknowledging he had been sentenced, and lashed out at the courtroom officials. I'm told that the guards put him in a headlock, tied his arms and legs together and dragged him out of the place feet first. As he was pulled down the steps of the dock, his head bounced on each one like a football. I wish I'd seen that.

The next time I saw Owen was about six months later at the Florida Department of Correction's South Florida Reception Center. A 'reception center' (RC) is like a 'prison school', and there are three in Florida: South Florida RC in Fort Lauderdale, Central Florida RC in Orlando, and North Florida RC, in Lake City. All inmates spend the first few months of their sentence at one of these facilities, and are given medical and psychiatric assessments before being allocated to a permanent prison.

When Owen came into the interview room, I hardly recognised him. He had lost several stones in weight, and had shaved off his moustache and beard. I had expected that he would be terse and difficult, and that he would complain about his sentence and, once again, the photographs. I was wrong. He liked it at SFRC. It was a vast improvement on his conditions at Broward County Jail. He had a nice cell, which he shared with a pleasant murderer from Mexico who, coincidentally, was as innocent as Owen himself. He had a job in the laundry that wasn't too taxing and gave him the chance to get some perks. He was confident that the application he had just filed on his own behalf to appeal his sentence (he had no access to a lawyer now) would be heard by the appellate court and granted. It was all laughter and smiles, as if we were old mates. After we had finished the interview, I watched him leave the interview area; he was joking with the guards and the other inmates, shaking hands and slapping backs. I remarked in my notes that, bizarre as it might seem, he appeared about as happy as I could imagine him ever being. In some way this prison life seemed to suit him.

It wasn't to last.

I next saw him about a year later at Union Correctional Institution in Lake City in Northern Florida. The correctional officer led me to a large room – probably a mess hall or muster area of some kind – and showed me to a small desk. On the other side of the room were the two inmates I was scheduled to see – Owen, whom of course I knew, and a young black guy that I'd not met before. I saw Owen first. He was clearly depressed, and he was uncommunicative. He hardly looked at me for the short duration of the interview. Although he gave no reason, he said he was unhappy at this prison, and he wanted me to try and get him transferred elsewhere. He said he had yet to hear anything about his appeal. I tried a few times to get him to talk, but he didn't really respond. There was a long silence, before I suggested that I needed to see someone else. He just nodded. Then as he got up to leave he looked at me and, like an orphan left in a brutal care home, simply said: 'Please get me out of this place.'

He was, by this point, quietly weeping.

After he left the room, my next prisoner came over. He was in his early 20s, had been born in London and had come to live in the USA with his family when he was a child. He sounded American. As he sat down at the desk, he looked over at the departing Owen.

'That guy English?' he asked me.

'Welsh,' I said.

We both watched as Owen underwent a compulsory body search before he was admitted back into the prison's general population. After patting him down, the guard inspected inside Owen's mouth and then put on elastic gloves before searching around his testicles and then up the crack of his backside. He was like a pig being inspected at a market: this is just one of the ritual humiliations that constitute daily life in Florida prisons. Finally, the door closed as he left the room.

'I don't think he's very happy here,' I said.

'I ain't surprised,' he said. Then he leaned in close to me and spoke in conspiratorial tones. 'He's in my dorm. There're 90 men in that dorm, and only two of them are white. He's got 44 boyfriends, if you know what I'm saying. I'm not even going to tell you some of the stuff your man there has to go through to survive, but whatever you think it is, it's worse. I'm surprised he can still walk.' He paused before saying to nobody in particular, 'You do not want to be a white boy in a Florida prison. No, sir, you do not.' He looked at me. 'My friend,' he said, 'if you are ever convicted of a crime in Florida, and they are going to send you to one of these places' – he paused for dramatic, but authentic, effect – 'take a gun, put it in your mouth and pull the trigger.' As he said this, he mimed it with his hand to drive home his point. He meant it.

'Thanks,' I said. 'I'll be sure to remember that.'

Driving home on the Triumph that evening I thought of Owen. Prisons in the United States are extremely predatory – the strong exploit the weak, to horrible effect. A correctional officer once told me that the staff managed the security of the prisons, in that they made sure that none of the inmates escaped or harmed the officers. But the prisoners managed most of their interpersonal affairs themselves. Violent gangs constituted along racial lines – blacks, Latinos and whites (invariably meaning white supremacists) – dominate the inmate culture. The rules of the gangs are strict and oppressive. There is no interracial contact permitted, which ensures that the culture of violence is self-perpetuating. If you decline to join a gang, you are victimised as a 'race traitor'. If you *do* join a gang, you will make enemies of everyone else. Either way, if you're weak, you lose. The only possible respite for the vulnerable is to seek protective custody within the prison system, which brings its own problems.

Despite his violent background, Owen, like all bullies, was a coward. He had a stocky build, he was ugly and he could appear intimidating, but he was physically and mentally feeble. All his victims in life had been women or children. His life in the prison must have been insufferable, but I could not help but reflect on the irony of his being subjected to the kind of treatment he had so often inflicted on others.

When I returned to my office the next day, I wrote to the prison warden (the equivalent of a prison governor in the UK) and requested that Owen be transferred to another prison owing to his 'personally difficult circumstances' at Union CI. Writing a letter like that was tricky, as the governor would have been perfectly entitled to ask what specific 'difficult circumstances' I was referring to. As Owen had not given me any information about why he wanted to move, I would not have been at liberty to divulge it to the governor. I cannot say whether this letter achieved its objective or not, but within a few months Owen was moved to Avon Park CI, which is in the middle of a US Air Force bombing range and has a reputation for being probably the best-run correctional facility in Florida.

Shortly after moving to Avon Park, Owen was transferred, temporarily, back to Broward County Jail to hear that the appellate court would not consider his request for a new sentencing hearing. So, it would be life without parole after all. He wrote to me a few months after the court hearing to say that, although he was disappointed at the result, he was happy to be at Avon Park. I continued to visit him once a year for the duration of my time at the consulate. He never warmed to me, nor I to him, but I was the only visitor he ever had, so despite his ambivalence towards me, he always seemed to appreciate the visits.

About a year before I left the consulate, his mother died in Wales. I went to Avon Park CI to break the news to him. He was clearly saddened by his mother's passing, but it caused him to become strangely philosophical about his life sentence in Florida. He said that he now had no real reason to ever go back to the country of his birth.

'I actually feel liberated,' he said. 'Like she's off my hands now, I got no duty towards her.'

I felt that if such a duty had existed he had failed to meet it at every turn, but now was not the time to say so.

I try to be philosophical about his lifetime of incarceration, and on the whole I think it is a good thing. He will be relatively safe, warm and comfortable in Avon Park. For the rest of his life he will get three square meals a day, and any medical attention he requires. When he was on the outside, he demonstrated virtually no appreciation of his own freedom. He never worked, he had no interests beyond his own gratification, and he did nothing of value for anyone. More importantly, he was a constant and habitual menace to others – he ruined many lives as well as his own – and there is no question in my mind that he would have continued to have been so if he had escaped capture.

The Florida Department of Corrections maintains a comprehensive web site. It is a source of much useful information concerning how the state prison system is operated: the operating expenditure of the department, the rules for visiting prisoners, the various types of educational courses available for the inmates and so on. Most interestingly, they maintain a database of all the prisoners incarcerated within the system, as well as those under supervision (i.e. on parole or probation), those who have escaped, and those released from prison. The database is accessible by the public, and if you locate a specific inmate, you can see not only his or her photograph, but you can read all about their date and place of conviction, as well as the offence(s) for which they have been found guilty and their sentence. It is a remarkable public facility, and I have long wondered why we have no such thing in the United Kingdom. Lawyers in the UK I have spoken to about it tell me that it would contravene human rights legislation; but they have human rights legislation in America too – they even have constitutional guarantees to protect their citizens from the government, which is more than we have – and it doesn't prevent the information being in the public domain there.

Behind this there is a simple truth. There is a different social contract between the community and criminals in the USA. In the United States, those that break the law can expect to face significant consequences for their actions – actions arising from their own personal choices. In the United Kingdom criminals rarely expect to face meaningful consequences for what they've done.

From time to time, I have a look at Owen's photo on the web site, just to remind myself of all the hours I spent with him over the years. (Owen is not his real name – I have changed it to avoid causing distress to his children, and to avoid indentifying his 13-year-old victim.) Notwithstanding that I loathed him as a person, as a consul I am proud to have served him according to the best principles and traditions of the British consular service. But it comforts me that he will be incarcerated for the rest of his natural life. The world will manage perfectly well without him on the streets and in a strange way he will manage perfectly well without us. Of course, had he killed his ex-wife in the UK, he would almost certainly be at large by now.

* * * * *

During the previous months I had started seeing Cheryl regularly. She was ten years younger than me, and a great antidote to the pressures and problems of work. We sometimes went out on the bike, but she liked to dress up so we mostly went in her car. Notwithstanding her humble beginnings – she came from a large, poor family in Arkansas – she'd done well for herself in the real estate business and she drove a metallic-blue convertible Jaguar. Next to her I felt a bit of a fraud. She looked decidedly glamorous, and I did not. She was stunningly attractive and always immaculate, whereas I am plain and dress like Worzel Gummidge. She made people's heads turn; with me, it was more their stomachs. But she didn't care about that at all and we delighted in each other's company.

Sometimes we talked about race. I had dated black women before, in London and New York, but it was different in the American south. Black/white mixed-race relationships are still relatively rare in the United States, particularly in the south, and when you do see them it's more often a black man with a white woman. We attracted interest when we went out together, and while we never had an unpleasant remark made to us I quickly became aware that, to some southerners, the American Civil War was not something that had happened all that long ago.

'You never really forget that, for almost all blacks in the United States, your ancestors were slaves,' she told me.

'I can't imagine what that feels like,' I said. 'I guess we think of our ancestors as conquerors of the world.'

'I think of mine as men and women packed into crates so small that they couldn't even roll over,' she said. 'People put on ships and sent to sea for weeks and weeks and then, if they survived, being sold into slavery for the rest of their lives. If they ever had children, their families would usually be broken apart and sent away. I find it humiliating, even now, and it breaks my heart to think of it.'

Even 150 years after abolition, the issue was clearly still affecting her life. I asked her how.

'All sorts of ways. Like, I almost never date black guys.'

'Why not?'

'It's complicated.'

'Tell me, I'm interested,' I said.

'It's hard to find one, for a start. There are more black guys in prison than in college in this country. A lot of black guys just have different values than me.'

'In what way?'

'In how they feel about being involved with a family, for one,' she said.

'So, by dating a white guy do you have a higher expectation of marriage and children?'

'I don't know. Should I?'

This was the first time that marriage and children had come into our conversation, and I immediately felt uncomfortable about it – more uncomfortable than talking about race, strangely enough. I didn't know why. Maybe it just seemed to bit too soon to be talking about that. So I did what I often do in such situations and said nothing.

Cheryl was the first to break the awkward silence. 'You know, the problem with a lot of black guys is that they can't or they won't take responsibility for themselves.'

'Is that because they're black, or because they're guys?' I said.

Cheryl fixed a steely stare on me.

'You better not fuck with me,' she said.

'I won't,' I answered, with a nervous laugh. I wasn't quite sure what she meant, exactly, but it sounded ominous.

* * * * *

Cheryl's sense of the need for people to take personal responsibility for themselves was reflected in wider American culture. You have a choice, and you alone are responsible for that choice and its consequences: that's the American way. That mindset permeates many areas of American life: education, work, relationships and particularly the criminal justice system.

Take burglary, for example, which is a relatively safe occupation in the UK – not least because any householder who uses force against an intruder is quite likely to find himself arrested along with the housebreaker. If the burglar is badly hurt, the homeowner can easily wind up doing several years in prison, while the burglar – assuming he's charged and convicted – can expect community service or a short jail term if he's unlucky.

As with so many other things, it's not like that in the States – as a scalliwag over from the UK on a cheap package tour will occasionally discover to his cost.

So if you're of the light-fingered persuasion, and are planning a trip across the Atlantic, here are a few things to bear in mind before you set out.

First, there is at least one gun in a quarter of homes in Florida.

Second, the homeowner is pretty much allowed to shoot you as soon as you break in, under a thing called 'Castle Doctrine' – a legal principle based on the unfortunately outdated principle of an Englishman's home being his castle. This doctrine lays down that it is a person's right to defend his property against intruders, even if it means using life-threatening force.

Thirdly, if someone is injured or killed during the course of your committing a felony – and burglary is a felony – then you will be held responsible for that death or injury, whether or not you actually did anything specific to cause it.

All this was rammed home pretty hard to a 15-year-old British boy called Christopher Gould on one pleasant spring evening not long after I'd arrived in Orlando.

Christopher had been born in the UK and, like many others, his parents had followed their dream of the good life to Florida recently.

He and another kid decided to burgle a house that they thought was empty, having been told by another boy that the owner was on holiday. They broke in through a downstairs window, and were moving through the darkness at the bottom of the stairs when two shots rang out.

Gould tried to flee, but as he scrambled around in the dark the lights went up and he saw a man at the top of the stairs with a pistol levelled at him. The man shouted to him to get on the floor and freeze and he did as he was told immediately; he later told me how, as he lay there, he could see blood and brain matter sprayed all over the expensive hardwood floor. One of the rounds fired by the householder had hit the other teenager in the head and killed him stone dead.

Unfortunately for the boys, the man had not been on vacation – instead, he'd been at home sleeping, and had been woken by the sound of breaking glass. He was prepared to defend his house and family by whatever means necessary, and had taken a loaded pistol from the drawer next to his bed, moved quietly to the staircase and opened fire.

In the UK, he would have been charged with manslaughter, and possibly murder. In Florida, he was lauded as a hero by the police on television and it was Christopher Gould who carried the can because he had been acting in concert with the fatally-shot youth.

Originally charged with murder – which sounds ludicrous to British ears – he eventually pleaded guilty to manslaughter, and was sentenced in a juvenile court to eight years in a juvenile correctional facility. Essentially, these are the same as adult prisons but without adults, the idea being to keep vulnerable youngsters away from highly predatory males. Of course, some young males are every bit as violent and manipulative as older ones; the tough kids quickly identify the weaker and all sorts of horrors can follow. Gould was not strong.

I had called his parents and offered to meet with them to discuss the situation, but they had abruptly declined my invitation, declaring rudely that they didn't want my 'fucking interference'. Sometimes, when you talk to the parents of young prisoners, you can easily see why they end up where they do. Still, I went to visit him, as I was duty bound to do. He was a tall, thin boy, maybe 6ft 3ins, with a poor complexion, greasy, unkempt hair and bad body odour. He collapsed himself onto a chair in the visitation room like a marionette whose strings had been cut, and stared at the floor. Despite my efforts, the best I could get out of him was the occasional monosyllable; he was a profoundly shy and insecure kid and I could imagine how he could have been talked into the burglary. He was lucky to be alive, and he knew it, but he had done an unthinkably stupid thing, and would now have to suffer the consequences.

His biggest worry was that, as a British citizen, he would be deported after completing his sentence. 'I don't have any family back in England,' he would say. 'My mom and dad won't move back so I'll have no-one.'

In that respect, he had a lucky break. When he finished his prison sentence a few years later, he was simply released and no immigration official ever came to speak to him. This can only have been the result of an oversight, and I'm pretty sure it was the only case during my time in Orlando where that happened. On a couple of occasions, people were able to beat a deportation order, but I cannot remember any other case where someone simply slipped through the net on a mistake. As far as I know, they never caught up with him and he is still living with his family in Florida today.

Cases like that were rare, but not *that* rare. I dealt with another young Briton, a 16-year-old called Adrian Parker, who had also recently moved to live in Florida. He went out one night with two friends, and they decided to steal a car and go for a drive – as you do. They chose a two-door sports car and, after somehow getting inside and getting it started, they sped off, with one of the other kids driving. Parker had hopped into the passenger seat and the third guy, a tall, gangly American youth, was sat in the back.

They prowled around the streets of Sarasota for an hour or so before heading out into the countryside for a fast, wild drive. Unfortunately, somewhere out in the middle of nowhere the driver lost control of the car on a bend and careered into a telegraph pole, coming to rest in a field. The impact had split the petrol tank and the vehicle burst into flames. Parker and the driver got out and, instinctively, they both ran off down the road. But Parker stopped suddenly when he heard the screams of his friend trapped in the back of the car, which was now well alight. The boy was in a desperate struggle for his life, but in his panic he had become uncoordinated and was unable to push the front seat forward. Parker ran back to the blazing car and tried to free his friend from the car, but it was futile. The young man in the back was burned alive: a truly horrible death.

When the police arrived they arrested the two survivors on a charge of grand theft auto. They were both subsequently charged with manslaughter, to which Parker pleaded guilty. He did four years for it.

After I'd been in Orlando for about a year, the caseload had increased so significantly that I was awarded extra staff to cope with it – a rare occurrence in the FCO! Viv McCulloch was still with us, but Sarah Bishop had moved to Texas with her family, and I replaced her with pro-consul John Corfield (pro-consul is the consular rank immediately below vice-consul). I also recruited Sheila Scott as a consular assistant, and a few years later Rebecca Budgen joined the team.

The American judicial system is far from perfect but I could see a purposeful system of punishment in action. The Americans never call it punishment, mind you: they call it 'correction', a strangely euphemistic term for the straight talking Americans to use, especially when there was little correcting going on in those places. Nevertheless, in Florida and the wider federal system, a prisoner must serve at least 85% of a sentence – the maximum relief you can earn for good behaviour (known as 'gain time' by the prisoners) is 15% of the sentence.

The subject of whether prison actually 'works' came up sometimes during conversations I had with lawmakers and law enforcers. One politician put it to me very simply: 'Ninety-five per cent of all crime in Florida is committed by less than three per cent of the population. If we can find those people, catch them and convict them, we can put them in prison for a long time, during which they will be unable to commit crime against the public. My job is to facilitate that, and the public in Florida supports it overwhelmingly.'

The message I was getting from friends and family in the UK was quite different. The levels of anti-social behaviour on British streets were rising as quickly as the levels of violent crime – the statistics to the contrary being issued by the British government and the police chiefs were widely mistrusted by everyone I knew – and, most significantly, the people responsible for it appeared to be beyond fear of any consequence. It seemed that every British authority traditionally responsible for shoring up order and civility – the police, the schools, the prisons, social services, and so on – had succumbed to the extremes of political correctness and statistical manipulation, with dire consequences on the streets. With the exceptions of a few poor, urban areas, antisocial behaviour is virtually unknown on American streets.

Unfortunately, as a British consul, I was not entirely protected from the effects of outrageously offensive behaviour by British people.

5

I WAS SITTING IN a large bar-cum-restaurant on International Drive in Orlando one afternoon, waiting for Cheryl to arrive. I was drinking coffee and reading a book. My concentration was broken by a terrific crash at the table just next to mine. A young man – clearly mentally and physically disabled – had attempted to stand but had stumbled and fallen in the process, knocking over the table and breaking most of the cups and glasses that were on it. The next sound that I heard was a roar of childish glee and the eruption of a spontaneous chant. It went: 'You're a fucking idiot... you're a fucking idiot.'

I looked over to the bar: a group of six or seven young Englishmen were standing at the bar of the restaurant. They were wearing football shirts, and they were sunburned, fat and drunk and they were laughing and shouting at the poor guy with no concern for the others in the diner.

Fortunately, the young man who had fallen did not appear to have hurt himself, but he was clearly embarrassed and was having trouble getting back to his feet. The elderly couple who were with him were struggling to help him up, and I jumped forward to assist. As he got to his feet, I wiped his hands of the food and drink that had been on the floor. The chanting from the Englishmen continued until they realised that their victim was suffering from a disability, at which point it changed to the horrific, 'Eng-er-land, Eng-er-land, Eng-er-land.'

I helped a waitress clean the broken items from the floor, and began talking with the couple. They were dismayed at the behaviour of the men. The young man now seemed to think that he'd done something wrong and became distressed. The couple told me they were from Oklahoma and were in Orlando to take their grandson to Disneyworld. The grandfather assisted his grandson from the restaurant with love and dignity, and the grandmother told me that when their daughter had died a few years before, they had taken her son in as their own. They had been planning this trip for over a year. She wanted to help the waitress clear up, but the waitress insisted that it was not necessary and urged her to join her family.

I sat back down and pretended to read my book, but my eyes filled with tears.

I knew from a circular that the British Ambassador was due to speak that evening to a group of politicians and businessmen in Houston, Texas. I knew he would speak well, and would made an impressive mark on his $200-a-ticket audience. But I couldn't help thinking that the real British ambassadors were there in that bar with me this afternoon. They, too, made their mark on all those present, and it was visceral, immediate and shocking. I felt diminished beyond explanation that afternoon, both as an Englishman and as a human being.

Unfortunately, as a British public servant, it is your duty to serve people such as this professionally and without judgment, and it can exact a heavy emotional toil on you. It has been said that our interests plus our values give us the foundation for our foreign policy, and I spent many hours in contemplation of what British values had now truly come to represent. Anti-social behaviour and low-level criminal activity was commonplace amongst sections of the British community visiting Florida, and it often fell to me to deal with the consequences. I wanted to be promoting the best of British ideals, but most often I was mitigating national embarrassment – putting out fires.

One of the two most common offences for which British people are arrested in Florida is 'petit theft' – essentially, shoplifting. This is due to a cultural phenomenon: a significant minority of the British people who go there on holiday are thieving bastards.

In Florida law, petit theft is defined as the taking of an article, or articles, with a value of less than $300.

Often when British people are arrested for this offence it concerns items stolen from the theme parks. The theme parks in Florida are generally welcoming, orderly and clean places. They are also inclined to be expensive, though I recognise that 'expensive' is a relative term; 30 years ago, Florida was still a slightly exotic location for the British traveller, and the United States was a destination for the sophisticated and adventurous. Now it's our most visited long-haul destination, served by cheap package holiday firms, charter airlines and inexpensive scheduled flights. (It was almost always cheaper for me to fly to London from Orlando than it was to fly to Tallahassee, the state capital of Florida, less than 300 miles away.)

Along with the package holiday, comes the welfare tourist. I have nothing against being on the dole – I've often thought I'd quite like to be on it myself – and there are as many types of people on welfare as there are grains of sand on a beach. But stereotypes are stereotypes for a reason, and the fact is that there is a certain model of behaviour associated with the underprivileged families, or fractions thereof, from our nation's council estates, and it doesn't translate well abroad.

The theme park gift stores are large and welcoming, and instead of doors there are just wide openings to draw you in. They don't seem well-protected against theft, but that is deceptive: hidden cameras observe your every move, and the staff are trained to be vigilant. If you steal, there is a high chance of getting caught. Lots of Britons fail to understand that, or, perhaps more accurately, are indifferent to the consequences; in fact, stealing novelty items seems to be something of a field sport for some of them. The consequences of getting caught are a trip to the Orange County Jail, and, if you're lucky, affordable bail.

Whilst most people who end up in this situation get bailed within hours, and therefore don't require immediate consular assistance, there are often repercussions months or years later. The perpetrators of these offences are expected to appear in court in Orlando several weeks after their arrest, but most of them head straight back to the UK, forfeiting the bail money but not otherwise giving the matter another thought. But some always chance it and return to America for another holiday a few years later. That's when they find themselves collared by the US immigration service on arrival at the airport owing to an outstanding arrest warrant, and back in Orange County Jail – facing the original charge of theft *and* a new charge of failing to appear in court. Guess what happens when they try to get bail this time?

Additionally, they find that when they entered the USA under the terms of the visa-waiver scheme, they answered incorrectly a question on the immigration form about whether they have ever been arrested before. If you have previously been arrested (not *convicted*, I must point out, merely arrested) for a crime involving 'moral turpitude', which could mean anything, you are not permitted to enter the USA without a visa. If you have been arrested and you answer that question incorrectly on the visa-waiver form, you are considered to have made a false representation to US immigration officials. This is a federal offence.

Not infrequently, people in that situation set out for a week's holiday in the sun and find themselves in jail for a month or more, sorting the whole thing out.

So, although petit theft in itself is not an especially serious crime, it can have serious repercussions and it can most certainly cause problems for us: consular officers can easily spend hours working on a case like that.

Here's just one of example, chosen from among literally hundreds.

A mother from Liverpool had come on holiday to Orlando with her seven children. They chose an inexpensive hotel on Orange Blossom Trail, where the rooms are usually rented by the hour, and they had pre-purchased passes to Disneyworld for the duration of their stay. On the third day of their trip, the mother had been arrested and taken into custody, and her children had been sequestered into foster care overnight. The next morning an official from the Florida Department of Children and Families (DCF) called me from Orange County Jail and asked if he could talk to me about the situation as he was having some difficulties with the family. He explained the background to me on the phone.

'The kids are all aged between six and 15,' he said. 'The key kid is nine. They were out for the day in Disneyworld, and the nine-year-old goes into a Disney store, picks up a toy, it was quite expensive, and carries it out to his mother. She then places it in her backpack. A security officer sees this on a camera, and the undercover security team in the store are alerted and decide to follow them and watch what they're doing before making their move. So the family moves on to another Disney store, and here the mother is seen speaking to the nine-year-old, in the manner of giving instructions. The boy goes into this store and he steals another item. And it goes on like this for a little while.'

Eventually, he told me, the security staff had moved in with a sheriff's deputy and arrested the mother.

'She tells the deputy she knows nothing about where the toys have come from,' said the DCF official. 'She'd just assumed the boy had paid for them, or won them in competitions or something. Yadda, yadda, yadda. The sheriff's deputy says he's taking her off to the jailhouse, and that the kids are being taken into protective custody. So she starts screaming, "He's not even ten yet... that's too young to be criminally liable".'

I couldn't help grinning – I knew what was coming next.

'So the deputy says, "Maybe not where you live, lady, but it's different here. And you're going to jail."'

She'd made the fatal mistake of assuming the police, and the system, were as soft in Florida as they were back home on Merseyside.

She started protesting her innocence loudly – in my experience, it was always the least-deserving Brits who are keenest on demanding their rights – but the deputy sheriff didn't want to hear it.

'So what's the problem?' I said.

'She appeared in court for arraignment this morning and to request bail.' (In fact, she had appeared via a video link from the county jail five miles away. This convenient facility reduces the cost and security implications involved in moving the prisoners around unnecessarily. It is frequently used for preliminary hearings in less serious cases.) 'The judge set bail at $800, which, amazingly, she had. Trouble is, that's *all* she had.'

The woman was able to pay the bail immediately, but when she began processing out of the jail her problems snowballed. The DCF officer who called me had met her at the prison to discuss what was going to happen upon her release.

'I told her, "You don't have the money to continue this vacation. You don't have any money for your hotel, or food, or transport, or anything else. This is a serious situation, and I recommend you make arrangements to fly home as soon as possible."'

'Right,' I said.

'But she takes a different view. She wants the kids back, she wants to continue with the vacation, she's paid for the damn Disney World passes and she wants to use them. At this point, I tell her she and the kids are barred from Disney premises and the passes have been forfeited. So she becomes argumentative and abusive, demands I refund her for the passes – like it was my problem.'

It sounded depressingly familiar to anyone who has witnessed the behaviour abroad of aggressive Britons with a misplaced sense of entitlement and no shame.

The DCF guy then reached the real point of his call. 'Anyways, we had a meeting about the children earlier this morning and there were some real concerns raised about their welfare. These kids are abusive – they've been threatening their supervisors during the night, the oldest boy stated that if they were not reunited with their mother soon, he would make an allegation of sexual abuse against a staff member – and all of them have significant hygiene issues. I mean, they are dirty, their clothing is soiled, they smell terrible. So the senior officer in the department has decided that the mother is an irresponsible and incapable guardian, and that there is no question of them being permitted to return to her custody whilst they're in Florida. If they don't leave the United States within 24 hours, the DCF will seek to take the children into care.'

In trying to persuade the mother of the need to return to England, the DCF officer, unfamiliar with the mores of the British welfare classes, had become exasperated with her responses. It was about then that he had called me for assistance.

'Okay,' I said. 'Maybe the best thing is to bring the whole family over to the consulate so we can see if we can sort it out here.'

What the hell was I thinking?

Later that morning, we all congregated in the waiting area of the consulate – the mother on a chair, the children parked around her on the sofa, the tables and the floor. The DCF official and I remained standing. I suggested to the mother that I speak with her privately, but she wasn't embarrassed to discuss the situation in front of the kids: in fact, she seemed positively keen to do so, perhaps thinking this would affect my attitude. In retrospect, I should have insisted on the private discussion, but I didn't. We live and learn.

With all the children present – some of the younger ones hanging off their mother, pawing at her hair and her arms – we tried to resolve things.

'How do you think we can move forward?' I said.

'I wanna go back to the hotel with the kids and carry on with the holiday.'

'But that's impossible,' I said. 'You don't have any money left. How would you feed yourselves?'

'Well, yeah. But it would be too horrible for the children to go back so soon. They've been looking forward to this for years, know what I mean?'

'But the situation has changed. It's impossible for you to stay. Maybe you could come back again next year, but for now you have to go home.'

'No, we'd rather stay now. I can find the money somehow, I can ask someone at home to send it over.'

'That's simply not an option,' I said. 'You must understand that there really isn't any choice to make. You have to be sensible about this.'

At this point the oldest child, 15-year-old boy, turned to me, his face a picture of rage. 'Don't fucking tell us what to do, you fucking cunt!' he yelled. 'We'll do what the fuck we like and there's nothing you can fucking do about it. Don't listen to him ma, we'll stay if we want and he can fuck off. Who the fuck do you think you are, twat features? I'll give you a kick in the cock!'

The room went silent. I stared into his eyes, and at his pale, thin rat-face, pockmarked with acne scars and screwed up in anger, and he stared right back. His fists gripped the arm of the chair in which he sat and his body shook with nervous energy and anticipation. Already in his young life, his instinctive reaction when faced with a difficult situation was to become vocal and violent in an attempt to get his way. Sadly, I suspect it had worked often enough in the past. We looked directly at each other for several seconds, and then I turned back to the mother.

'You're the responsible adult here and you need to make the decision, not your children. What's it going to be?'

If she did not agree to return to the UK, we were going to have to inform her that her children would be taken into protective custody straight away. She didn't know that yet, and it was going to be better all round if we could avoid telling her.

The atmosphere in the room was extremely tense. She sat and thought about it for a while, looking at her eldest son, seemingly for advice or support. Just at the moment when I sensed that she might be prepared to accept the inevitable, the DCF official spoke up to encourage her.

'I think the consul is talking sense, and I think you should listen to his advice.'

The eldest boy rounded on the officer, spitting aggression. 'Fucking shut up, you,' he shouted. 'You smarmy get. Leave her alone. We'll do what we want and there's fuck all you can do about it. You need to be careful, son, or I'll fucking have you!'

This was a step too far: I couldn't allow his assault on the DCF official. I sprung up and took a sharp, menacing step towards him, which clearly he wasn't expecting. 'Right,' I snarled. 'That's enough from you. Another word and we'll have the police here straight away. You've threatened to assault me, and now you've threatened to assault this gentleman. You're old enough to go to the jail, and that's where you'll be in half an hour if you carry on. I'll arrest you myself if necessary. Do you understand me?'

I fully expected him to attack me, and whilst I was much bigger than him it wasn't what I wanted. Fortunately, he sat back and shut up.

Then I spoke again to his mother. 'As bad as things are at the moment,' I said, 'if you try to stay any longer the situation will only get worse. This trip hasn't worked out, and that's unfortunate, but there's no other choice in the matter. The only realistic decision is to get on a flight back to England tonight.'

She looked down at the floor, but nodded slowly in agreement. Then she started to cry, which had the effect of further polarising all the children against the DCF officer and me. They all crowded around to hug each other, weep and comfort their distraught mother.

I looked over at the DCF official. He rolled his eyes at me in disbelief and I shook my head in embarrassment. Then he stepped outside to make a phone call.

My staff contacted the family's holiday company immediately, and, as a favour to us, they managed to get the family on a flight to Manchester that evening and they waived any penalty fares. The DCF official arranged for an Orange County van to come and take them directly to Orlando's Sanford airport. I was pleased to see the back of them; they shouldn't have ventured across the Mersey, let alone the Atlantic.

I doubt that the mother ever flew back for her court hearing, which means she would have forfeited the bail money and she would be *de facto* prevented from entering the United States again.

Lucky Americans.

* * * * *

When holidaymaking Britons aren't stealing tat from Disney, they seem to spend most of their time beating each other up.

Here's the usual scenario: a couple comes on holiday and, after a few days of too much sun and too much alcohol, they fall into a disagreement about something or other, and then set about each other with wild abandon.

Someone calls the police and, after a short while, the sheriff's deputy turns up with his hand on his holster.

So far, so good.

Then it starts to get difficult.

Many warring British couples seem to be under the impression that, because they are on holiday and only in America for a week or two, the police won't be that interested in them.

Unfortunately, much to the surprise of the punters concerned, this is not how it works in Florida. If there is any evidence of a physical assault – a bruise or a scratch will do – the offending party is arrested and taken straight to the county jail. If both parties show evidence of having been assaulted, as they often do, they both go.

If there is credible evidence of a threat having been made (e.g. if it was witnessed by a third party), that's also enough to warrant an arrest.

Now, here's my favourite bit: once you've been arrested in Florida for domestic battery, there's a mandatory 48 hours in jail for 'cooling off' purposes. Quite different from the 'tea-and-biscuits' with the sheriff's deputy that so many holidaymakers appear to expect.

I have dealt with hundreds of cases like this, and mostly there wasn't too much that the consulate needed to do. However, if both adults go to jail and there are children with them, the Department of Children and Families takes the children into protective custody – usually they're placed with foster parents for a night or two. That leaves us at the consulate with plenty to do.

One morning I received a visit from a local official of the DCF. He had come to tell me that they had two young British girls, aged 11 and 14, in their care. They were in Orlando on holiday with their father. He had been arrested during the night and was now in Orange County Jail. The DCF officer gave me the full story over a cup of tea.

The girls' parents had separated some years previously. They ordinarily lived with their mother in west London, with their dad living not too far away and working as a mechanic at Gatwick. The girls didn't see their dad very often, but this year, as a special treat, he'd brought them to visit Disneyworld.

Unfortunately, there were some long-standing difficulties in the relationship between the dad and the eldest daughter, Caroline (ironically, in view of what transpired, this trip was intended to improve that relationship).

The previous night had been the second night of the 10-day holiday, and the three of them were having a late snack at a diner along International Drive. During the meal, an argument started between Caroline and her dad. It quickly turned nasty, and, unbelievably, the dad emptied the contents of a maple syrup container over his daughter's head. As a screaming match developed, the family was asked to leave the restaurant. Outside, Caroline's father told her, in no uncertain terms, that she was not to come back to the hotel room that night, or any other night.

I probably don't have to point out how dangerous it is for a 14-year-old girl to be wandering around Orlando alone at night, but

I will. It's very dangerous, which makes her dad a fool. The fool returned to the hotel with his youngest daughter, Hayley; at about midnight, having luckily escaped any serious harm, Caroline showed up, knocking quietly on the door attempting to wake her sister but not their father. Her plan was to get in and sleep safely. It almost worked, but when Hayley went to open the door she tripped over a suitcase and woke dad. Still in a foul temper, he made it very clear to Caroline that he'd meant what he had said: she wasn't going to be allowed in – not tonight, not tomorrow night.

She left the hotel and started wandering around Orlando, finding her way into a rough part of the city – there are actually some quite unsavoury areas in Orlando, and not far from the main tourist areas, either. At about 2am she was spotted sitting on a bench outside a brothel by two alert Orange County deputy sheriffs working on the vice squad. They stopped because they thought, not unreasonably given the time and place, that she was a crack whore. When she told them her story, the officers were astonished.

They took Caroline back to the hotel and woke her father. They tried to be reasonable, and told him that if he was prepared to acknowledge that he was wrong, apologise to his daughter and agree to accept proper parental responsibility for her, they would give him the benefit of the doubt and the matter would end there. This was an exceptionally lenient view for the officers to take – some might even argue that it was unacceptably so – and not something for which American law enforcement officials are noted. To their further astonishment, he refused. He said she wasn't going to be allowed back, whatever the cost, and that was all he had to say about it. I don't know what he thought they'd do next, but it was entirely predictable. In about three seconds flat, he was thrown up against the door and cuffed. He was then taken directly to the Orange County Jail and charged with neglect of a minor.

The girls were taken into care by the Florida DCF, and placed into protective custody overnight. Under Florida law, children who are taken into DCF custody can be held at the discretion of the senior DCF officer for up to 48 hours with no requirement to seek a court order. After 48 hours, a court order is required, which means the DCF has to make a legal case for the custody of the child. At this point the child's parents or guardians are permitted to make representations to the court, and the court can place all kinds of restrictions and instructions on how the children are supervised.

From the consulate's point of view, once this court order is in force we face some significant problems. With the order in force, for the child to be taken out of DCF custody, a new court order is required. This is a time-consuming process, which can involve requesting information from a number of sources, including the International Social Services organisation, about the child's domestic situation back in its native country. The Florida courts are reluctant to allow a child out of protective custody unless they are sure that the intended home is suitable.

Where they're dealing with British kids, the DCF usually tries to get the children back to the UK within the 48-hour time limit. This is done in collaboration with the consulate, and always involves a tremendous amount of work on the part of the consular staff, and quick work at that.

In this case, we started by trying to locate the children's mother back in England. Unfortunately, she had gone on holiday to Turkey and nobody knew her exact whereabouts, or even had a contact number. We were able to track down the children's maternal grandmother, who was deeply distressed at the situation and anxious to do whatever she could to help. She agreed to meet the children at the airport back in London, and look after them until their mother returned from her vacation. So that looked promising.

The next problem was the travel arrangements. The children had travelled to Florida on flights using staff passes issued to their father. Those passes, along with the children's passports and the travel insurance documents, were in a safe in the hotel room. Out of spite, the girls' father was refusing to provide the combination for that safe. The hotel manager refused to open the safe unless there was a court order instructing him to do so. That would have taken us too long.

The passports wouldn't be a problem as we could issue emergency travel documents from the consulate. The problem with the air tickets was going to be more difficult to resolve. We contacted the airline station manager at Orlando, a guy I knew well, and explained the problem to him. He wanted to help, but after calling his manager in New York he rang back to say that they would not carry the children without their father – the company's loyalty was to their employee, not to the children.

Luckily, the grandmother was willing and able to pay for two tickets, and the airline was willing to take the children unaccompanied. The next day, just after lunch, the DCF officer brought the two young girls to the consulate for their emergency passports, and afterwards pro-consul Viv McCulloch took them to the airport and handed them over to the airline staff. We had beaten the deadline, and the girls would get home without any further fuss.

The day after the girls left, I went to see their father in jail. He was unrepentant. He did not ask a single question about what had happened to the children, and he expressed no regret or remorse at his actions. All he wanted was some help to get his bail paid.

'At least the children are safely back home in London,' I told him towards the end of our conversation.

He shrugged.

A friend of his from London bonded him out of jail the next day and he flew straight home. I know for a fact that he failed to show up at his court hearing several weeks later, so there is now a warrant for his arrest if he ever goes back to the United States. Good job, too.

Most of these cases were depressingly similar, and quickly fade from the memory, but one – probably the wildest case of domestic violence I encountered that didn't end in murder – stays in my mind.

Roy and Eve Grey were both in their forties, and had been married for 15 years. Both from the midlands, he was an engineer by profession, and she was a designer. They had two children approaching their teenage years. I later discovered that they had started having significant problems in their marriage quite early on, and would frequently physically fight with each other. After a few years of marriage, they decided that their problems were the result of spending too much time apart with their jobs, so they emigrated to America and bought a small restaurant on the Atlantic coast where they could work together all day. This only exacerbated their problems. What a surprise! The fights became more frequent and increasingly violent, and would sometimes happen right in front of diners, which can't have been good for business. Despite this insanity, they seemed unable to live without each other. I've never been able to understand why people remain in such fractious relationships, even though I have done it myself.

On the day in question they had been arguing in the kitchen about some problem, since forgotten. Roy Grey turned his back on his wife in disgust at some comment she had made, and her response was to take a large knife from the countertop and plunge it in a downwards trajectory into his shoulder area. The blade went in a long way, piercing his lung and stopping within millimetres of his heart. He collapsed instantly, and was almost completely unable to breathe. Fortunately Eve, recognising the seriousness of the situation, called the emergency services immediately; an ambulance arrived and took Roy to hospital. When the police arrived they arrested Eve for assault. By that evening the charge had been changed to attempted murder.

The first I heard about this was the next day, when Eve's sister called me from the UK. The next morning I gave the Triumph a run out to Cocoa Beach. I visited Roy first. He was in a private ward in the hospital. He had tubes inserted into every orifice of his body and a progress chart that looked like a cross-section of the Alps; it turned out he had died twice on the operating table. He was extremely lucky to have survived, but he was conscious, if weak. He was allowed to speak to me for a while and he told me what had happened. He went on to say that this was the last straw. During all the years of fighting he said that neither he nor his wife had resorted to lethal violence before, but that she had now crossed the Rubicon.

'There is no going back now,' he told me. 'We have to break up.'

'Given that she's currently in jail facing an attempted murder charge, there might not be much choice in the matter,' I said.

'I couldn't care less about her and the trouble she's in,' he said. 'She'll just have to get on with it. I've got to worry about getting better, putting the business back on track and looking after the kids.'

He leaned forward to show me the entry wound from the knife, which didn't look much, but the operation scar was impressive and there were burn marks from where the defibrillators were used. It would probably be enough to get him a few free drinks down the pub. I gave him my business card and told him to call me if he needed anything at all.

That afternoon I went over to Brevard County Jail to see Eve Grey. At first she seemed pleased to see me, and she talked freely and openly about her situation. She said she couldn't remember what she and Roy had been fighting about, but that when he had turned his back she was so enraged that she just had this blind moment and, on an extreme impulse, grabbed the knife and went for him. She showed some remorse, and asked how he was doing, but seemed more preoccupied with her own problems. It was as if this detention business was all a little bit inconvenient. To tell you the truth, she was slightly posh, and I think she felt that jail was a bit beneath her. I think she thought I was, too. She'd probably been expecting some kind of Oxbridge FCO-type to come and see her and what she'd got was an ex-fireman from Romford. As the conversation between us progressed, she started to become slightly manipulative and almost dominating; it was as if she wanted me to show her some social deference.

'This place is fucking awful,' she said, pronouncing the 'ing' with her cut-glass accent, giving it a musical sound, like a cymbal.

'Jails are a bit like that,' I said. 'You'll just have to get used to it.'

'Some of these people are murderers.'

'If your husband takes a turn for the worse, you'll be one of them.'

She scowled at me, but there was something about her. She was really rather attractive, in an English psychopathic rose-way, and I'd started to think about the contrast between her accent and her prison issue overalls. Forty-eight hours ago, she'd been crazy enough to stab her husband in the back with a bread knife. But for some reason I found myself powerfully drawn to her. Idly, I began to wonder whether I might be a bit psychologically disturbed.

'I don't even look like a criminal,' she said.

'What do criminals look like, then?' I said, leaning forward.

She moved towards me in return, and hissed her answer just a few inches from my face. 'Not. Like. Me.'

As she leaned over, the front of her loose-fitting prison top fell forward. She wasn't wearing a bra, and in my peripheral vision I could see her breasts. She knew it, and she stayed exactly where she was, her eyes locked into mine, daring me to glance down. I didn't, but it wasn't easy. Neither one of us spoke a word, we simply looked at each other in unnaturally close proximity. We were so close I could feel her breath on my face.

It slowly dawned on me that she was trying to provoke me into doing something, and it seemed my choices were threefold.

One, divert my eyes and back away – the only sensible option.

Two, look directly down her top – foolhardy, but my conscience would have been clear.

Three, actually touch her breasts – insane, compelling, illegal.

Eventually, she made my mind up for me, slowly lifting her hand up to my chest and gently pushing me away. I think it was a draw.

I understood in that moment how insanely intense this woman was and how much trouble she would be to have in your life. I also realised that her husband would never be able to leave her. The sex must have been phenomenal. Men are sick and vulnerable. We need help.

Suddenly, things became a bit more formal between us, which was probably for the best. I asked her if she had any health issues that needed to be taken care of. She thought about it for a second and then complained that the jail had taken her spectacles away from her so she couldn't read anything. I showed her how to make a lens with her fingertips. She thought this was wonderful, and thanked me profusely. The insanity of our strange little confrontation was forgotten already. I left her studying the jail's visiting regulations whilst peering through her hand-formed pinhole camera.

Roy Grey made a remarkable recovery and went home after a couple of weeks in hospital. The months passed, with Eve still behind bars. One day, her parents came to see me at the consulate. They were a respectable retired couple, and they had travelled over from England to see their daughter. They were deeply distressed by the situation she was in. They said that everyone who knew the pair had told them that they should just separate, but they simply could not or would not do it; Eve's own father said that he could not understand why Roy tolerated her behaviour. I thought of explaining to him that his daughter was perhaps the most sexually intense person I had ever met, but I decided it wouldn't be a good idea – it's probably not what you want to hear from the British consul. Before they left my office they expressed the hope to me that she would soon be released from jail, and the charges dropped, or significantly diminished, and that she would then be deported: they thought this would be the only way to split the couple up before someone was actually killed.

Eventually, inexplicably, and, in my experience of such situations, without precedent, the charges against Eve Grey *were* dropped and she was released. She went back to her husband as if nothing had happened. A few months later I discovered that he had started visiting her whilst she was inside, and he had pleaded with the prosecutor to withdraw the charges against her: I can only assume the prosecutor agreed to this, but I was never told anything officially. Eve was not convicted of anything, so there was no deportation. Once she was back home they called me to let me know that the situation had been resolved, and they invited me to visit them if I was ever in the area. It sounded like a genuine invitation, and I took it at face value.

A couple of months later I happened to be on the Triumph returning from some business in Fort Pierce, and my route allowed for a small detour along the coast road in Brevard County. I passed the Greys' restaurant and, completely on impulse, decided to drop by and see how they were doing. They were pleased to see me, and we took tea together on the lawn. After a short while I asked how the business was doing.

'Very well,' said Eve. 'We're very happy with it.'

'No, it isn't,' said Roy, immediately. 'We aren't even bringing in enough to meet our costs. I think Eve's going to have to start doing the washing up.'

I correctly anticipated how that news was going to be received.

'I'm not going to do the fucking washing up!' she exploded. 'That's what Mexicans are for.'

'What?' he said. 'All Mexicans, everywhere, exist only to do our washing up? How dare you speak about them like that?'

'You know what I mean,' she hissed. 'They're immigrants, they shouldn't even be in the country.'

'Well, neither should you, if that's how you look at it,' he said.

'I've got a fucking visa, you bastard!' she screamed at him. She got up, and shouted right in his face. 'I'll fucking show you!' Then she ran off into the restaurant. Unsure of whether she was going to show him her visa, or fetch another knife, I made my excuses and fled.

I heard nothing more about them for a few years, and then one day an immigration officer called me to discuss a couple of deportation cases. After we'd gone through the business in hand, he asked me whether I'd ever heard the names Roy and Eve Grey. I laughed, and asked why. He told me that the Brevard County Sheriff's Department had contacted the immigration service and asked to have them deported because they were so fed up with being called to the diner to deal with domestic disputes. They weren't deported, but I was told that they would have a problem when they came to review their business visa in London the following year.

I never heard from, or about, them again; but every time I hear a woman with a posh accent use the 'F' word, ostentatiously pronouncing the 'ing' at the end, I think of Eve Grey, smouldering in her prison overalls.

Outside work, I was really settling in to Floridian life. Cheryl and I spent a lot of time together, and my flying lessons were coming on well. After a few months, I took my first solo flight. Taxiing out alone onto the runway at Kissimmee airfield that day remains one of the most exhilarating things I've done, but the nerves quickly settled as I concentrated on what I was doing. Shortly after take off, my radio failed and I lost communication with the control tower. I tried turning it on and off a few times, but it was dead. The controller, realising what had transpired, pointed the green 'clear to land' torch at me and I made a perfect landing.

Afterwards, my instructor rejoined me in the cockpit and asked me what had happened.

'The radio's packed up,' I told him.

He just punched it quite hard, and it started to work perfectly. 'Sometimes they do that,' he said, nonchalantly.

I was speechless. About two months after my first solo flight, I passed my private pilot's test and was henceforth qualified to fly a 'single-engine, land' plane under visual flight rules.

6

DEALING WITH DEATH and bereavement is probably the hardest thing that you have to do as a consular officer, and unfortunately you deal with it surprisingly often. Sometimes it's as little as processing some paperwork, and other times it means being right at the front of whatever is happening, comforting bereaved relatives or identifying corpses.

In an average year, around 80 British people die in Florida. There will be one or two from parachute jumps – occasionally a chute fails to open, but it's usually more mundane – the jumper lands on a highway and is hit by passing cars. There's the occasional suicide, and, from time-to-time, a murder. But without doubt the most dangerous thing you can do in the States – as in most places – is get into a car, or cross a road.

One Sunday afternoon, two British families from Birmingham – brothers James and Robert Braithwaite, their respective wives and five children – were in a rented minivan driving through Orlando on their way to catch their flight home.

Only the brothers, who were in the front, were wearing seat belts. The van was driving along a road that had a grass median, although there were various places where there was a tarmac area in the middle to allow vehicles to cross. As the van passed one of these areas, a car turned across the highway and into the Braithwaites' vehicle. The van fishtailed and then span into a violent rollover, throwing both women and three of the children out as it barrelled along.

One of the women was killed instantly, as were two of the kids.

The other woman was critically injured, and the remaining three youngsters were very badly hurt.

The two brothers were shaken, but, physically at least, relatively unharmed.

We didn't hear about the accident until the next morning when pro-consul John Corfield saw a TV news report about the tragedy, which mentioned that the victims were British.

We made some urgent phone calls from the office, and after locating the hospital where the survivors were being treated I left on my motorcycle immediately. When I arrived I met up with Chris Ellis, a British representative of the tour company the family was travelling with. We struck up an instant rapport and afterwards became good friends.

We went first to the private ward where the widowed husband – James Braithwaite – was sitting with his injured children, who had been getting medical treatment throughout the night; they had not yet been told of their mother's death. He told us that his brother was in a separate hospital, where his wife was, at that moment, undergoing critical surgery.

One of the hospital officials pulled Chris and me to one side.

'Can I talk to you?' he said. 'It's kind of delicate. I don't think it's appropriate to raise this with the victims, but I need to get their insurance details so that we can get approval for their medical treatment.'

Unlike in the UK, where medical treatment is free at the point of service, in the United States you are asked to provide the hospital with your medical insurance details either before they go to work, or very soon afterwards. In the middle of a crisis we find it culturally uncomfortable to talk about such things with the hospital staff, but the Americans are entirely used to it.

As sensitively as I could, I asked Mr Braithwaite if they were insured, and, if so, where were the insurance papers?

He was still in a state of shock, and appeared confused. After a few moments, he spoke. 'Yes, we're insured,' he said. 'The papers and stuff must be in our hand luggage.'

'Can you tell me where that is?' I asked.

'I assume it's still in the van,' he said. 'But where the van is…'

I called my office and asked pro-consul Vivien McCulloch to find it, which she did quickly though the Osceola County Sheriff's Department. It had been taken to a scrap yard in Kissimmee. I called the yard and explained who I was, and that I was calling to request permission to search through the van for the papers and recover them.

'You're *who*? And you want to do *what*?' said the man on the other end of the line, sounding a little sceptical.

I explained again, and eventually he relented.

'Well, I guess it's nothing to do with me. You can search the vehicle if you want to, but you're gonna need somebody to help you, 'cos it's in a hell of a mess.'

Chris and I set out in his 4x4 and by the time we reached the yard it was raining hard. It didn't take us long to spot the Braithwaites' van. The man had been right, it was in a terrible condition, with most of the roof caved in to the height of the seats and all the windows smashed. It had also been left sitting on the edge of the road outside the yard, with no protection, no cover against the elements, and some of the family's baggage just sitting on the ground beside it. On closer inspection, we saw that the interior was covered in mud from where it had rolled the day before, and that there was a great deal of blood and broken glass scattered over the seats and the floor. The rain had turned all that into a quagmire.

Since Chris was wearing a suit, and I was in my bike wear – black denim trousers and a heavy-duty leather jacket – I volunteered to clamber inside to retrieve what we could.

Only the back twin doors were at all operable, and we had to pull hard on them to open them enough for me to squeeze through. Even so, I had to take off my jacket. I wriggled along the floor trying to get at the suitcases, bags and other possessions, which were scattered around. Before long, I was covered in mud and blood, and broken glass was cutting into my hands, arms or legs. Every time I managed to dislodge a case or some other possession from where it was jammed in the wreckage, I would manoeuvre it to the rear door for Chris – soaking wet in the pouring rain – to take them from me and stow them in his car.

We were there for well over an hour, but we spoke hardly a word to each other as this grim business unfolded; just a few words of encouragement from Chris every now and then.

My clearest memory is of finding a copy of *Bridget Jones' Diary*, pages torn and soaked with blood and rainwater, with a bookmark midway through.

Wedged upside down under one of the seats, I opened the book and read a few paragraphs. It was strangely affecting: the half-finished book, the half-finished life. One moment, a couple of families chatting and laughing about their holiday as they headed for their flight home, with the chance to finish the novel on the plane if the kids were good; the next moment, everything gone. I don't think you ever get used to this interface of the mundane and the extraordinary, this sudden intervention of tragedy in normality. I left the book in the van.

We were only just able to fit everything in Chris's wagon, and by the time we'd finished he looked like a drowned rat and I looked even worse.

His staff had found a couple of rooms in a luxury hotel close to the hospital where the fathers could base themselves. More relatives were on their way over from the UK the following day, and rooms would be made available to them also; the tour company arranged all this. We decided to head to the hotel to unload the bags and clean ourselves up, before going back to the hospital.

Back at the hotel, we unloaded the bags and did what we could to clean them up. We found the insurance papers, along with the passports and air tickets, in a small bag that had been on its own under the driver's seat. There were a number of other highly personal and probably quite valuable possessions in that bag, and it upset me to think of them being left unprotected overnight.

Back at the hospital, the nurses found a quiet room off to the side where Chris could sit down with Mr Braithwaite and complete the insurance details. I went off to check on the children, who were being well cared for by nursing staff, and then found myself a seat. Just then, a man entered the corridor. He seemed dazed and bore a striking resemblance to Mr Braithwaite. I guessed, correctly, that it was his brother. I stood up to introduce myself to him.

'Hello, I'm Hugh Hunter, the British consul.'

'Hello,' he said. 'I'm Bob Braithwaite. My wife's just died.'

He said it very directly and I was speechless in response. This was probably the defining event of his life, a moment of overwhelming horror; I was the British consul, tasked with providing sympathy and assistance, but I could find nothing to say. Eventually, I managed to mumble something about being deeply sorry for what had happened, and not being able to imagine how he felt. I felt useless. I felt like a fake.

I took him in to see his brother, who was finishing up the necessary work with Chris, and we left them alone while we checked that the insurance company in England were liaising properly with the hospital doctors. As it happens, all the treatment was approved extremely quickly – it doesn't always work that way.

Chris and I ended-up staying at the hospital until gone midnight, dealing with various problems, doing media interviews and helping the families as much as we could. It was gone 2am when I got to bed, and at 4am, the phone rang. It was the consul-general from Atlanta asking me to do a live radio interview for a station in the UK. I didn't really know what I could say to them, but he was keen that I do it, so I took the number and after splashing myself to make sure I was awake enough, I called the radio station.

I remember little of what I said, but I do recall being asked 'How are the surviving members of the family feeling?'

I can understand, I suppose, why an interviewer would ask such a question, but it is ultimately a pointless one and serves only to test the respondent's vocabulary. I searched mine for something suitable, but was found wanting: I think I came up with 'devastated'. Then I put the phone down and went back to sleep.

By late afternoon the following day, the extended family started arriving from England. By that evening, Chris and I were probably superfluous, so we said our goodbyes and I headed back to the office on the trusty Triumph. After the families returned to England a few days later I heard nothing more about them, but I still think of them from time-to-time, even now: the tired, haunted face of Bob Braithwaite who had just lost his wife; the children asleep in the hospital, unaware of what had happened; and every time I go into a bookstore and see a copy of *Bridget Jones's Diary* I remember the copy on the floor of the ruined van. In my mind I can hear the rain beating down on the roof, the wind whistling through the broken windows and Chris standing outside in the mud telling me, 'Not much longer now, mate. Not much longer now.'

* * * * *

One afternoon I received a call from a man in Nottingham who wanted me to look into the circumstances of his son's death. The lad had come on vacation to Florida with some friends, and they had decided to spend a few nights in Daytona Beach, a town famous for its motor racing track – home of the Daytona 500 – and its beach, along which cars are permitted to drive and park. It never became clear exactly what happened, but late that evening the young man became split from his group. Whether through drink or drugs, an illness or seizure of some kind, or even as a deliberate act, he ended up collapsed across a railway line. Then a train came along, slicing him in two and killing him instantly. At least, I hope it was instant.

The next morning, the friends reported him missing to the police, the cops checked the description given against the railway line victim, and that was that. The police told the group of friends that they would contact the dead guy's parents and inform them of the tragedy. The remaining members of the group made arrangements to return to Orlando for their flight home the following day.

What the Daytona Police *should* have done next, according to the wording of the Anglo-American bilateral consular treaty, was to contact the consulate and pass the information to us. We would have relayed it to Consular Division in London, who would have passed it to the London Interpol office, who would have then passed on instructions to the local police force to send trained officers around to the next-of-kin to break the news.

Although this may seem a little convoluted, it ensures that, to the best of our abilities, we don't accidentally duplicate the sending of officers to a next-of-kin.

What the Daytona Beach police *actually* did was to pass the information to their force chaplain, which was *their* usual procedure, and is appropriate when a local resident has died, or if the deceased's next-of-kin was in the USA. The chaplain would then call the next-of-kin on the phone, and pass on the news. This method of informing families of deaths seems to be quite common, and accepted, in America. The Daytona Police chaplain obtained the deceased's next-of-kin's telephone number in the UK from his effects, and attempted to call them. Never having made an international call before, he did not know that it was necessary to use an international dialling code; unable to place the call after several attempts, he simply gave up.

A few days later, back in England, the victim's friends went to his parents' house to pay their respects and offer sympathy.

When the father opened the door, they said how sorry they were about what had happened.

Father's response was, 'What are you talking about?'

It was no way to learn of such a tragedy, and the parents were, understandably, additionally distressed by the incompetence of the Daytona Police.

A few days after I spoke with the father, I wrote to Gerry York, a lawyer at the Florida Department of State, asking him to look into what had happened. Daytona Beach PD undertook an investigation and subsequently wrote directly to the consulate apologising profusely; they also wrote to the victim's parents to apologise for having added to their distress.

I contacted the Daytona Beach PD and arranged to meet their chief a few days later. Whilst with him, I thanked him for having looked into their procedures so carefully, and for writing to us with the results. Oiling the smallest cogs in the international relations machine is always valuable, and often has reverberations at higher levels.

* * * * *

'Hello, you have reached the Orange County Sheriff's Department.'

'Hello, this is Mrs Sharpe. I just wanted to report my husband missing. We're on holiday from England and he went for a run along International Drive early this morning and hasn't come back. Do you have any record of any accidents today?'

'As a matter of fact, we did have a fatal road accident on I-Drive this morning,' the sheriff's deputy said. 'What was your husband wearing?'

After being given a description of the Mr Sharpe's distinctive clothing, the official said, 'Yeah, that's him. That's the dead guy.'

I cannot remember ever hearing of a call of such gravity being handled with such stupidity and insensitivity.

Soon afterwards, some deputies from the sheriff's department arrived at the hotel with Greta Snitkin, the Orange County Victim's Advocate, in tow, and Mrs Sharpe identified her husband's personal effects.

I arrived a short while afterwards, by which time Mrs Sharpe was behaving erratically, veering between lucidity, denial and great distress. Whenever she would start crying, she would rush into the bathroom so that her children could not see her. Greta had done what she could, but shortly after I arrived she was called to another fatal road accident and she left me with the new widow.

I think Mrs Sharpe was relieved to hear my British accent, and my presence seemed to help. I think most British people in trouble abroad prefer to speak to a fellow Briton, although the FCO increasingly employs local citizens as they are usually cheaper.

We sat facing each other on the edge of the two beds and talked for quite a while. I can't remember much of what we said, but I recall being tremendously impressed by her bravery and stoicism. The two children were watching the television, which had remained on largely to distract them. After a little while longer, Mrs Sharpe was, once again, overcome with emotion, and she went back into the bathroom for privacy.

I sat on the bed watching the kids, who were sitting on the floor watching cartoons. A small green mutant was moving across the screen, its electronically distorted voice threatening the destruction of the planet. The young girl, who was four, was transfixed by the drama, and oblivious to the events unfolding in the real world. Her brother, who was eight, was also looking at the screen, but I knew he was acutely aware of my presence, and of his mother's distress. He knew that something huge had happened, but he wasn't sure what to do about it. Sensing perhaps that I was watching him, he turned towards me for a moment. I gave him a half-smile, and he half-smiled back, nodded delicately and then turned back to the relative safety of pretending to watch the television again.

I began to think about how the events of this day would affect the rest of their lives. So often in moments of trauma, the overwhelming aspect is not what has just happened, but the anticipation of what it will come to mean in time. These children would have no dad to offer them love and support, or to give them confidence and reassure them. They would never see him again. I wondered if they would remember this day in 20 years? Would they think back and vaguely recollect some strange man in a blue suit, there for a few hours and then gone, never to be seen again? Who was he? Why was he there? Consular work, as with much public service work, is frequently like that – a sudden, unexpected involvement in an intense drama in which the players soon move on, and then you hear nothing more about them.

After a while, Mrs Sharpe came back and sat down. She told me she had decided she wanted go back to England soon, tonight if possible. I told her I would do what I could to help her.

Usually in situations like this, it's necessary to buy new air tickets for the journey home. The family was insured, and I called my office with the details of that policy. Consular assistant Sheila Scott contacted the insurance company and told them the situation, giving them all the names and reference numbers. She rang me back a short while later to say that the insurance company was prepared, in principle, to cover the medical, funeral and repatriation costs, but could not authorise any payments until there was a death certificate – if the death was suicide, the policy would be invalid.

I realise that insurance companies have rules and procedures, and that there may be factors that absolve them from their responsibilities, but if your business is dealing with humanitarian crises, sometimes you are going to have to be humanitarian.

We decided on a two-pronged attack on the problem. Firstly, Sheila would speak to Jim Burns, a good guy we knew at the Orange County Medical Examiner's office, to see if we could get the death certificate expedited. Secondly, she would also speak to the Sharpes' airline to see whether they would permit them to return on their current tickets. Fortunately, the Sharpes had flown with Virgin – in my experience, the most understanding of the trans-Atlantic airlines.

For the next few hours, I sat quietly with Mrs Sharpe and her children. Understandably, she was struggling to deal with her feelings and retain her composure, but she did it for the sake of the children if nothing else. She was certainly brave.

Eventually, Sheila called back. The medical examiner's office were unable to provide the certificate within 72 hours, but Jim Burns had offered to fax an interim letter, confirming officially that the cause of death was not suicide, directly to the insurance company. She'd also been in touch with the Virgin Atlantic station manager in Orlando, someone who'd been a good friend to the consulate. The station manager said that every single Virgin flight for the next two weeks was booked solid – overbooked, in fact – but that she'd see what she could do. I didn't think that Mrs Sharpe would be able to hold it all together for too much longer without the support of family, friends and a familiar environment – none of which she had in Orlando. Within an hour, the Virgin girl had called back to say that she had made room on the first flight to London that evening and were happy to take the family back on their original return tickets without charging a penalty. I'm pretty sure no other scheduled airline that I dealt with ever did that.

There were other problems to deal with. One was the Sharpes' rental car. I called National Car Rental to explain the situation, and within 30 minutes someone had arrived at the hotel to collect the car. When I handed the keys to the woman who came to collect them, I asked her to send the bill via the consulate; she waved me away, and told me that it had been taken care of, and that the family would not be charged for the rental – another rare example of corporate humanity.

By now it was mid-afternoon, so I helped Mrs Sharpe pack and we headed to the airport in a taxi. A guy from Virgin met us and took over dealing with the family, whisking us to the front of the check-in queue, where a few of the people who were waiting gave us one or two funny looks. I said my goodbyes as the family were taken off to a private lounge airside.

As I left the airport by bus, I contacted Jim Burns and arranged to go and identify Mr Sharpe's body – Mrs Sharpe having been unable to face the prospect. I took his passport, and details of some specific features by which I could identify him, and stopped by at the morgue on my way back into the city. They pulled him out on the tray for me. He was a fit man – lean, strong, and young – and he had no business being in a place like this. Life really is so unfair sometimes. I looked up at the medical examiner and nodded, and the body was slipped back into the freezer.

It was getting quite dark when I left – one of those big, late-afternoon thunderstorms was in the air. Near the office, I passed my favourite little coffee shop, and suddenly felt like a few moments alone with a brew. There was only one other person in the place: a young woman by the window was reading a magazine. As I walked by, I saw that she was engrossed in an article about finding the perfect man with whom to share your life. I wondered if she was lonely, and it made me feel sad to think she might be, that anyone was.

I took my favourite seat in the corner. The storm broke, and the rain started hard. The evening traffic rush had begun, and the headlights of the cars were reflecting off the surface water. I sat there for ages, thinking about nothing in particular. I was hoping the rain would ease off, but it didn't. Eventually the staff began to put chairs on tables, so I took that as an invitation to leave. I stepped outside under the shelter of an awning as the rain got worse. I pulled my jacket collar up around my ears, threw caution to the wind and walked the 15 minutes home to my apartment.

By the time I got home, showered and changed it was dark. I didn't want to go out on the bike in the rain to find something to eat, so I looked in my fridge. I was contemplating the prospect of a bowl of cereal with rancid milk when somebody knocked at my door. I started – nobody had knocked that door since the day I moved in – but I opened it to find Cheryl standing there under an umbrella, carrying a hamper.

'I thought you might be hungry,' she said.

'I am.'

'And I know you don't have any food in this place. Are you going to let me in?'

'Of course.'

Serendipity? Maybe. It was lovely to see her, and she looked ravishing, but I was slightly taken aback at the fact she had just arrived without notice. We were seeing each other two or three times a week by now, but she had never done that before.

She came in and took a blanket from the hamper and put it on the floor. She then laid out a spread of all kinds of food and a bottle of wine. We ate a magnificent dinner, drank a wonderful Bordeaux and afterwards we made love on the floor. It was almost a perfect evening.

Later, in bed, she asked me what was wrong.

'Why do you think something's wrong?' I said.

'Because I know you.'

'I feel bad even saying this,' I said, 'but you just came around without calling. I might have been busy with something, or I might not have even been here at all.'

'Do you mean busy with *someone*?'

'No, I don't. Why? Did you think you'd catch me with someone?'

'It took me an hour to put that food together,' she said, 'and I didn't even know whether you'd be here. I did it because I *care* about you. And don't worry, I won't waste my time snoopin' on *your* sorry white ass.'

'I'm sorry,' I said. 'That was really kind of you and I appreciate it, I really do.'

I now felt stupid and mean.

Neither of us spoke for the next few minutes.

'Honey, one of these days you're going to have to make up your mind what you want,' she said.

She got out of bed and went to the bathroom. I dozed off, but woke up when I heard the front door close behind her as she left.

7

THE WEEKEND AFTER our indoor picnic, I arranged to pick Cheryl up on the Saturday morning. I felt had to make up for my insensitivity, so I told her that I was taking her away somewhere romantic. I told her to pack an overnight bag, and that was all she could bring.

I didn't tell her that I had rented a plane from my flying club for the weekend. She had never flown with me before, and I was curious to see how she'd react.

We walked out to aircraft and I got her safely buckled in to the passenger seat whilst I did the pre-flight checks. It was a perfect day for flying: not too hot, not too windy and not a cloud in the sky.

Then I jumped in to the driver's seat, fired it up and we taxied out to the runway. I thought she was handling it well, but then she turned to me with terror in her eyes and said 'Are you sure you know what you're doing here?'

'Everything's under control,' I said. Then I passed her the aircraft operating-manual. 'Just have a quick look through there and see if you can find out what all these buttons and dials mean.'

'I don't feel so good,' she moaned.

'Don't worry,' I said, 'you'll be fine. It's safer than driving a car.'

As we left Orlando I circled a couple of times over her apartment complex, which she was thrilled to see from the air, and then we headed north-west for a couple of hours to a place called Cedar Key.

Two hundred years ago, Cedar Key was Florida's busiest port. But that didn't last long, and it's now something of a ghost town. But it's charming, in a broken down, romantic kind of way.

The island's airfield has a notoriously short runway, so landing there is never easy.

'Cheryl, if my approach isn't perfect I might have to power-on and go around to try again,' I said. 'If that happens, don't freak out

– it's nothing to worry about. It's something pilots – especially not-very-good pilots like me – do all the time.'

'I wish you'd have said you were a not-very-good pilot before you got me up here,' she said, but she was grinning.

But I got it just right and we had an uneventful landing, much to her relief. We checked in to our little B&B, and rented some mopeds to ride around for the afternoon. We explored the town, which took less than 10 minutes, and then decided to head off the island for a bit.

After a while we came to a signpost and I noticed in my mirror that Cheryl had come to a halt. I slowed down to turn around. There was nothing around us and I didn't know why she'd stopped. When I got back to her she nodded at the signpost.

'So this is where it happened,' she said. 'I always wondered.'

She paused to look about for a few moments, then turned her moped around and headed back to Cedar Key.

I looked up at the sign, which said ROSEWOOD.

I couldn't work out why there was even a sign as there was literally nothing nearby. I chased off after Cheryl. She explained it to me when we got back to our room. In January 1923, following an unsubstantiated report of the rape of a white woman by a black man, hundreds of whites from the nearby town of Sumner descended on the black town of Rosewood. In what became known as the Rosewood Massacre, six blacks were killed and the whole town was razed to the ground. It was an atrocity for which nobody was ever arrested or charged, and although it was not the only such event to have occurred in the United States during that period it has earned a special infamy in the civil rights movement and in African-American consciousness.

By the time we had sat down to dinner, the mood of the trip had completely changed. Cheryl had asked whether we could head home that evening, but I told her that I wasn't confident taking off from the island after dark – the airstrip is surrounded by water and the absence of any light around it means there is no horizon for the pilot to work with. For a pilot without an instrument rating, like me, that's more dangerous than it sounds.

We didn't talk much over dinner, and she didn't even finish her meal. I couldn't comprehend her melancholy. Had I failed to be sufficiently outraged about the atrocity? Had I underestimated her reaction to visiting the place? Was it something else I'd said or done?

I was starting to feel pretty fed up, too. I had flown her up here, to what was probably the last undiscovered romantic hideaway in Florida, we were staying in a Victorian B&B with lace everything and trinkets up the yin-yang, and now she was sulking.

'Did it upset you today, finding that place?' I asked.

'Yeah, it did.'

'It seems to me like a long time ago,' I said. 'Does it really still cause that much pain?'

'It wasn't that long ago. My grandparents were alive at that time.'

'Yes, I suppose that's true,' I said. 'Mine were too.'

I tried to think of some parallel in my own life or culture that might help me to understand this. At first I was lost, but then I remembered my own overwhelming emotional reaction to visiting the war graves in the Somme valley in France, and it made a little more sense to me.

'You know, what makes it worse for me is that it is still unresolved,' she said.

'How can you ever resolve something like that?' I asked.

'I have no clue,' she said, which didn't seem particularly helpful.

So much for the romantic weekend! We had a long, serious discussion about American politics, the civil rights movement, injustice, reparations and forgiveness. We didn't agree on everything and we spent an uncomfortable, silent night on opposite sides of the mattress.

The next morning we had an early breakfast, got a ride over to the airfield on a golf cart and were soon flying back towards Orlando.

About 25 miles out, we over-flew Leesburg airfield – a small place with no control tower, popular with Orlando-based pilots for practising take-offs and landings. I tuned in to Leesburg's radio frequency so that I could monitor the traffic using the airspace whilst I was passing through. There were two other aircraft in the vicinity, both doing circuits, and I checked in with them so that we all knew where we were.

The next radio communication gave me a shiver.

'Leesburg traffic, this is Delta-November-Five inbound for landing. I'm three to the south-east, and heading straight in for runway 31. I have engine problems, and I'm not sure I'm going to make it. Please keep the field clear.'

I could hear fear in the pilot's voice. I scanned the horizon to locate him. It took me a while to find him, and when I did my heart sank: he was at a much lower altitude than he should have been that far from the airfield. I pointed him out to Cheryl.

'That's him over there. He has a mechanical problem, almost certainly he's running out of fuel, and at that altitude he won't make the runway if he loses the engine.'

One of the other two pilots in the airspace contacted the distressed plane.

'Delta-November-Five, this is Papa-Six-Zero, Leesburg traffic reads you. We will keep clear of the field for your approach. Other Leesburg traffic please acknowledge that.'

Each of us in the airspace confirmed that we had heard and understood the instruction. Papa-Six-Zero then radioed to the troubled plane to ask how many were on board. He replied that it was just himself. I slowed my plane down a little. I wanted to see this. I couldn't take my eyes off it.

The radio remained clear for a short while, but you could just sense the tension building. The silence was broken when Delta-November-Five radioed in again.

'I've lost the engine. I'm not going to make it to the field.'

He sounded terrified. Normally, when you hear a transmission from a pilot, you can hear the engine loudly in the background. This message was notable for the ambient silence.

The approach to runway 31 at Leesburg is across a large lake, and a light aircraft landing on water is highly likely to be a fatal accident. The water fully arrests the speed of the landing gear almost immediately. The subsequent force on the occupants of the plane is tremendous, and usually knocks them out or causes serious internal injuries. The plane quickly sinks, drowning the passengers. He would have known that, and we knew it too. I felt that I had just heard the last words of a dead man. I had to remind myself to retain proper and full control of my own aircraft, as I was becoming transfixed on the troubled plane. A few seconds after the pilot told us that his engine was out, Papa-Six-Zero came on the radio for a second and simply said: *'Good luck, my friend.'*

We all watched as the plane descended lower and lower, and eventually it hit the bank of the lake, about 400 metres short of the runway, and only a few metres short of a small wood that filled the gap between the lake and the runway. The plane somersaulted over twice, and came to rest on its roof. To my surprise, it did not immediately burst into flames, but surely, I thought to myself, it would at any moment: residual aviation fuel would be leaking from the vents in the wing, and as soon as those fumes touched the exhaust the whole thing would go up like a firework. Nothing moved down there for about 20 seconds, and then we saw the pilot climb out from the door. He stepped away from the plane and then waved to show us he was okay. I felt an enormous sense of relief, and decided to head back to Orlando and leave the area clear for the emergency services. The Lake County Sheriff's Department helicopter was on its way, so they would need the airspace.

As we left the Leesburg area, Cheryl said to me 'Safer than driving?'

'Well,' I said, 'it does depend who's driving.'

* * * * *

At around the same time as I took Cheryl to Cedar Key, a small group of Saudi Arabian nationals were learning to fly in the area. I've often wondered whether I shared airspace with any of them, maybe even exchanged radio communication; it's unlikely, but not impossible. But these people weren't much interested in the finer details of pilotage and airmanship. If only we had known.

I was working in my office on the morning of Tuesday 11th September 2001, when my brother called me from Canada to tell me that a plane had just crashed into the World Trade Center in New York. He was watching it on the news, and from the pictures he could see he said it looked like a commercial jet.

'Is it foggy or cloudy there?' I asked, groping for the remote.

'No, it looks really clear,' he said.

I realised immediately that this was a deliberate act, and I turned on the television in my office to see what was happening. Moments later I watched as the second plane crashed into the south tower.

Within minutes, the consular desk officer in London called me.

'Hugh, didn't you work in the New York consulate?'

'Yes.'

'Is it anywhere near the World Trade Center? We can't seem to get any calls in or out to them.'

'It's about four miles away.'

'Okay, let's stay in touch. I'll catch you later.'

I knew things must have been chaotic if they'd lost all their communications so quickly. The rest of my staff came through to my office to watch events unfolding. The planes crashed, the towers fell and then all air traffic over the United States was suspended indefinitely. I don't think we had a single phone call from a member of the public all day: the great British travelling public quickly understood that any problems they had were going to take a back seat. A few people coming to the end of self-arranged holidays faced being turfed out of private villas, but the British pub on International Drive, The Cricketer's Arms, acted as a clearing house for available accommodation, and the authorities and local population rallied round. As far as I know, no Britons in Orlando found themselves without a place to stay.

Of course, in New York things were very different. The two senior consular officers up there were out of the country on vacation. I couldn't get through to the NY office, but I guessed they could use some help, and soon. I decided to drive up. Around 7pm, I left Orlando in a rental car and drove until the early hours. I stopped at some little motel in South Carolina at around 2am, and by 8am I was back on the road. As I approached New York City on the New Jersey Turnpike that evening, signs warned that vehicular access to Manhattan was impossible, but I decided to keep going. I could always park the car in New Jersey and walk across the George Washington Bridge and make it to my mate Chris's apartment on the Upper West Side. I decided to take a chance on the Lincoln Tunnel, fully expecting to be turned away, but as I crested the hill leading down into the tunnel itself, I caught my first sight of the devastation where the World Trade Center had been.

It was dusk on Wednesday September 12, and in the half-light I stopped the car where I could overlook the Hudson River and just looked at the enormous column of smoke that was rising from downtown. I was overwhelmed by the sheer physics of it. It didn't seem possible that it could have actually happened; it didn't seem real until you saw it with your own eyes.

There was almost no traffic at all by this point, and the tunnel was open and clear. I was at Chris's apartment within a few minutes and there was even parking on the street outside the building – I had once lived in this building, and that had never happened before. I went into the lobby and spoke to the doorman, who told me that, as far as he knew, nobody from the building was missing. I went up into the apartment, which faced north over the Upper West Side. Chris, who was a doctor in Manhattan, was on the phone, so I went out on to his balcony for a few minutes. From there, everything looked absolutely normal; yet, a few miles away, buildings at the WTC site were still collapsing.

Later that evening, we went downtown to Chris's hospital to see what was going on. When we arrived there were lots of people congregating outside, posting photographs of their missing loved ones along the fences around the hospital. There was an uneasy quietness on the street, but at one point the piercing sound of two F-16s patrolling the skies caused everyone to look up.

'What the hell do they think they're going to be able to do?' someone shouted in anger.

It did seem incongruous. I suppose they were there to make us all feel safe, but New Yorkers are a bit too cynical for that.

Outside the hospital we chanced upon a small group of doctors and nurses that Chris knew, taking a smoking break. He started talking to a couple of colleagues whilst I stood aside a little. One of the doctors from the group was standing next to me. I looked at all the people milling around the place, and all the posters of missing people pinned to the wall.

'Are there really that many casualties inside?' I asked him.

He took a drag on his cigarette.

'We've got almost no patients at all from downtown,' he said. 'For the most part, you either lived or you died. There wasn't much in between. The few people we did get yesterday were relatively minor cases. Most of them went home by last night.'

Chris was on a week off, and it was clear he wasn't needed so eventually we went for a coffee and headed home. The next morning I called and spoke to the consul in New York.

'I can probably use you, Hugh,' he said, 'but not for a day or two. We're still trying to assess where we are on this. Could you call by tomorrow morning?'

Chris and I decided to go downtown to see what became known as Ground Zero. Surprisingly, there had been no public announcements about access to the site, so we didn't know how close we'd be able to get to it. The subway trains were still running as far downtown as 14th Street, and from there we walked the last mile or so. Once we got within a few blocks of the site, there was a casual police line – some people were being allowed through, some turned away.

At the cordon Chris showed his doctor's identification and I showed my federal consular card: neither was checked properly and we were waved through. We were able to get quite close; all around were cars, vans and emergency vehicles that had been close to the buildings when they had collapsed, and had been towed the short distance away from the site. Some were completely crushed or badly damaged; all were covered with a kind of damp, grey dust-cum-plaster. I looked closely at the debris and realised that this was, among other things, the emulsified remains of people. We were touching this stuff and breathing it into our bodies.

We didn't stay long. I had felt compelled to see the scene, as had Chris, but being there felt voyeuristic and profoundly emotional; neither of us wanted to prolong the experience. As we were leaving, we passed a large group of onlookers. The atmosphere was fraught with tension – the stunned, silent mood of the last 48 hours was turning into anger. Some people in the group were taking photographs and someone else in the crowd became confrontational with them.

'This is a grave,' he yelled. 'Show some respect to the dead. Stop treating it like a fucking tourist attraction!'

Most of the people stopped taking pictures, but not all of them.

The next day I went to the consulate in New York and spoke to some of my old colleagues there. I met with the consul; he said that they had had an overwhelming response from the employees at the consulate, and that he didn't think he would need me. I wished them all luck. It had already become clear that hundreds of British people were missing and were probably victims of the disaster.

That evening Chris and I went out for dinner to a little Indian restaurant in his neighbourhood. At the table just across from us was an English guy, eating alone, and at the table behind him were a New York couple. Somehow the English guy had started talking to the American guy about the attacks. They were agreed on how horrific it must have been to be aboard one of the hijacked planes, and the English guy said, 'I'd like to have seen them try to seize control of a flight from Glasgow to Ibiza, especially after the drinks trolley had been round.'

I said nothing, but the thought of a couple of dozen drunken Glaswegians resisting a hijacking brought the first smile to my face since it had all happened.

There was still no sign of when domestic US flights would recommence. I was checking in with the office in Orlando several times a day, but there was nothing happening in Florida so I decided to wait it out in New York until the flights resumed. I had a strange, almost surreal weekend in the city catching up with friends and hearing their 9/11 stories. There was the sense that something of great significance had happened, and that it would precipitate something of even greater magnitude.

After several days there was an announcement on the radio that domestic flights were going to recommence the next day. I booked myself onto the first flight back to Orlando and it cost me less than 30 dollars. I flew on a 737, and there were precisely five passengers on board, including myself. We were all taken up into first class and given a meal. Understandably, the only talk amongst the cabin crew and the passengers was about the events of the previous week.

I flew commercially frequently during the next few years, and a routine seemed to develop amongst the passengers during that time. After everyone was seated on the flight and the cabin doors were shut, almost all of the men would consciously look around at each other and assess the threat level. I realised that Americans were beginning to notice and interpret their environment in a way they had never needed to before, and I wondered what they would make of it.

* * * * *

Back in the consulate, the fun was about to start. Although Florida itself had not been affected directly by the terrorist attacks, thousands of British tourists had been trapped there when the flights had been suspended. They were all anxious to get home, but there were only a couple of flights per day. Crowds of frustrated Britons were gathering at Orlando International Airport, and the airline staff was having problems dealing with them.

I took a couple of my staff with me and went to the airport to help however we could. I set up a temporary consulate in the airport, complete with a desk and a Union Jack, opposite the Virgin Atlantic and British Airways desks. I had a briefing with the Virgin and BA staff, and then we took on the responsibility of moving among the waiting throngs to let them know what the situation was. The airlines were doing what they could, but some people were going to have to accept that it would still be several days before they could get on a plane home. Priority was given to those most in need: those requiring urgent medical care back in the UK and those with young children – which in Orlando is many people – were put to the front of the queue. As consular staff, we did our best to placate people and explain to the most frustrated ones what the problems were. One man was livid that his journey home was going to be delayed for a few days. I tried to put it into some kind of perspective for him. 'Look,' I said, 'there are people in New York and Washington who have lost people they love. This is really nothing in comparison.'

His reply took me a little by surprise. 'It's a statistical certainty that many of those firemen and policemen that died have been giving money to the IRA for years. It didn't worry them when our soldiers, policemen and firemen were being killed, so why should I care about them?'

'I think that's a bit harsh,' I said.

But by now other passengers were listening to him, and many of them were nodding in agreement.

'The only good thing that might come out of this is if the Americans start taking a bit of a closer look at themselves for a change,' said one.

'That's as may be,' I said, 'but for the time being, some of you will have to wait a few days for a flight. I'm sorry, but that's just how it is.'

They calmed down, but it wasn't the last time during the next few days I heard that kind of sentiment.

The problems experienced at the consulate in New York were, of course, far greater – 9/11 remains the largest loss of British life to a terrorist outrage – but they at least had hundreds of FCO staff available from other departments (including many from the British delegation to the UN). Their combined efforts were remarkable, and they received deserved praise for their response. But it had all been reactive – there had been no contingency plan for an emergency on this scale, no FCO or treasury budget set aside, and it quickly became clear that these were needed.

Unfortunately, it wasn't in place by October 12, 2002, when a bomb detonated in a nightclub on the island of Bali. It killed 202 people, 24 of them British. This time the FCO response was rubbish, at least according to the collected opinion of the British media. In fairness to the staff in Bali, only one consular official was on the island, and he was a part-time volunteer. But it took several days for other consular officials to arrive from Jakarta, and by then it was too little, too late. The Australian consular officials had managed to arrive within 24 hours, why hadn't we?

It was clear that consular staff couldn't just muddle through in the age of Islamic terrorism and new media. Consular work had always been an FCO backwater. No diplomat with career ambitions would have gone anywhere near a consular section – it was considered dirty and low-brow. But now journalists were asking difficult questions of FCO ministers, and things had to change. Consular work was about to come in from the cold, but it was going to be a slow, painful process; the jury's still out on whether it would have been better off where it was.

The Bali debacle accelerated the changes being introduced to the FCO's consular operation, but they weren't the changes some of us had been expecting.

Up until this point, consular work had been under the management of Consular Division, a largely neglected side street in the map of command. The FCO now announced that Consular Division was about to become Consular Directorate with its own corporate director – the widely respected Paul Sizeland – and with the ability to bid for its own budget priorities and set its own strategy.

The first thing they did was to recruit 170 new staff. Those of us at posts around the world where our resources were stretched anticipated that we would get most of these new people, with probably the majority going to posts where there was a higher likelihood of terrorism.

We were incorrect. All but 10 of the new staff positions were located to the headquarters in London. Many of them were assigned specialist roles, such as child abduction cases, death penalty cases, forced marriage cases and so on, where we were told they would be available to give us advice and explain policy decisions.

I had a gut feeling that this wasn't going to work quite as I had hoped.

8

A MAN CALLED PETER PALMER was slung in a cell in Orlando one night for resisting arrest.

He'd been spotted 'jaywalking' – crossing the road other than at an approved crossing place, or against a red light. It's something the Orlando Police Department are quite strict on, particularly during the hours of darkness, because so many drunks get hit by cars.

Palmer had been pulled aside by the patrolman and had remonstrated fiercely. He was told to calm down, but persisted and was then arrested. Funnily enough, the officer had no power to arrest him for jaywalking itself, but he *could* arrest him for resisting being arrested for an offence he couldn't be arrested for. No, I don't understand it either.

We were told what had happened that evening, and I wrote Palmer a letter at the Orange County Jail the following day informing him that I would visit him soon. Two days later, I called to arrange the visit, only to be informed that he was no longer there. No other information was available on the computer, so we assumed that he had been released. That was a pretty routine occurrence, especially for such a relatively minor offence. We filed the case in our archive section and forgot about it.

About 10 months later, I received a call from an attorney in the Orange County's Public Defender's office.

'I'd like to meet to discuss a case I'm dealing with concerning a British national,' he said. 'It's just kinda unusual.'

'OK,' I said. 'And the name of the defendant?'

'It's a Peter Charles Palmer.'

The name meant nothing to me, but I arranged to meet him the next morning. That afternoon, I checked our files and found the few notes we had on Palmer from his arrest almost a year before, showing that he'd been released. I assumed he must have been arrested for something new, but I took our notes from the file so that I would have them with me.

When I met the public defender (PD) the next morning, I asked what Palmer had been re-arrested for.

'Well, here's the thing,' said the PD. 'My client wasn't actually released in January. Under advice from the Orange County Jail medical department, the prosecutor referred him to be assessed for his mental competency to face the charge. He was taken to Chattahootchee [this is a secure psychiatric institution in northern Florida] and detained there for observation. He's been there for the last 10 months. They eventually decided he could face the charges, so they sent him back to Orange County Jail two weeks ago. I got assigned the case last week and we're now awaiting a court date.'

I was alarmed at this news: 10 months is a long time to be locked up for crossing the road at the wrong place.

'Tell me,' I said. 'What kind of sentence would he get for the original charge – the resisting arrest?'

'It's not straightforward. He was arrested for resisting arrest without violence, which is a misdemeanour and carries only a fine. But I think they realised they screwed up, and they later changed the charge to resisting with violence, which is a felony and carries up to five years. He refuses to plead guilty, which is his prerogative, but the main problem now is that he refuses, or he can't, pay bail. It could be months before we can get a trial date.'

The PD was as concerned at the situation as I was. He told me that he was going to meet with the prosecutor and seek to have the case resolved quickly,

'I'll go over and visit Mr Palmer tomorrow,' I said.

'Before you do,' he said, 'two things. The first is that I have his British passport, which I'll give to you now. The second: I should tell you that whatever they say up at Chattahootchee, this guy is nuts.'

The next morning I was sitting in a cell at Orange County Jail when Palmer was brought in wearing the regulation orange jump-suit. He was escorted in by a guard, but he waited by the door until the guard left before checking to make sure he wasn't listening outside the door. He then moved across the room towards me like a stalking cat, as if I might make a threatening or evasive move. I was disconcerted: already there was a strange atmosphere in the room, a tension, as if anything could happen. Apart from his feline movements, there was nothing physically remarkable about him; he was about 5ft 9ins tall, brown hair in a non-descript style, medium complexion, average build. Even after our meeting, I would have struggled to pick him out at an identity parade.

Because I had his passport in my office, I knew the following facts about this man: his date-of-birth (he was 36), his place of birth (Calne, Wiltshire), the date his passport was issued, and the date he entered the United States (about four days before his arrest). I also knew the date and place of his arrest, and his charge. That was it.

He sat down gently and fixed an unnerving stare on me.

'I'm Hugh Hunter, the British vice-consul,' I said, by way of an introduction.

'I know who you are. You're late.'

'Am I? I'm sorry, I thought I was here in good time.' I was actually early.

'Don't worry about that now; have you swept the room for wires?'

It's always difficult to know how to deal with these situations. I suspect most consuls would simply terminate the interview as quickly as possible, but I could never resist the opportunity to see where it might go.

'No, I didn't bring the equipment with me,' I told him.

'All right,' he said, rolling his eyes, 'but be sure to bring it next time. We'll just have to talk low, we should be okay.'

'I just have a few routine questions for you,' I said.

'Shoot.'

'Were you on holiday in Orlando?' I asked.

He looked at me as if I were an idiot, and I heard him mutter underneath his breath 'Oh, for God's sake.'

'I'm sorry, I didn't hear that?' I said.

'Of course I'm not on bloody holiday! You should know that.'

'OK,' I said. 'I'm sorry, but I don't know what you mean?'

'I was working,' he said.

'What kind of work do you do?'

He sighed in despair at my ignorance. 'I was on an undercover operation.'

'What was the nature of the operation?' I said.

'I can't tell you that!' he snapped in hushed tones, looking around the room and checking for Americans.

I thought about ending the interview at that point, but I was in too far now. Checking for Americans myself, I leaned in closer and asked to which 'branch' he was attached.

'Army,' was his terse reply.

'Oh, right,' I nodded.

'Special Air Services,' he added – superfluous, really.

Not quite sure what to do with this new information, I decided to write it down.

'Don't write it down, you idiot,' he hissed, checking the otherwise empty room again for hidden Americans. I crossed it out.

'So, what happened after your arrest?

'They took me to a military establishment for interrogation.'

'Did you crack?' I was now completely absorbed in it.

'No. Name, rank and serial number, that was it.'

'What is your rank and serial number?'

'Under the Geneva Conventions I'm not obliged to tell you that, only the enemy.'

I wasn't really sure where to go from here, but I thought a return to earth might be a good start. This is more easily said than done, as the consular guidelines for dealing with persons showing signs of mental illness state that you should not contradict their reasoning, nor should you display a sense of disbelief or amusement. Their truth is their truth, and it should be respected. I decided to try a different tactic to see what I could discover.

'Do you have a name and address for your father?' I asked.

'My dad is Moses Israel. He works for Mossad and MI6, but he is currently planted undercover with the Edinburgh Police Force. Mounted Division.'

My further efforts to get more information about his background were rebuffed. He told me that he intended to plead not guilty to the charge against him. He also stressed his need to get back to his regiment as soon as possible. He told me that he had no money left, and he wasn't sure how he'd get back to the UK, but I assured him that we would do all we could at the consulate to help him.

When I got back to the office, we started to investigate Peter Palmer. Pro-consul John Corfield was expert at cases like these. Given just a modicum of information to start with, he could usually discover a great deal. We obtained a copy of Palmer's passport application form. There was an address in Yorkshire, listed as his home, but when we investigated that it appeared that Palmer had lived there briefly years before, but had soon moved on and was otherwise unknown there. Predictably, our inquiries with the Army came to nothing, as did our inquiries with the Edinburgh Police Force. We didn't bother to contact Mossad. Despite the fact that Palmer had listed a Mr Moses Israel as his father on his passport application form, we were unable to trace anyone with that identity in the UK who even knew Palmer. There was nothing. No missing person report, no address or information from the Department of Health and Social Security, no previous convictions in the UK. Who was this guy? He was certainly British: his Yorkshire accent was strong and authentic. We had his passport, and it was legitimate, but beyond that we were unable to discover anything else about him. This was the only occasion that happened – a real mystery man landed on me – during my time in Orlando.

A few days later I met again with Palmer's PD, and we both went to meet with the prosecutor, one of those lean, ambitious, thrusting young lawyers – the type you see on television.

'Look,' he said to the PD, shaking his head, 'I can't completely drop the charges against your client after we've had the guy in custody for so long – it just wouldn't look right. But, if he pleads guilty to a misdemeanour "crossing the road other than at an approved crossing" and also "resisting without" he can be on his way immediately.'

'Okay, I can't see a better solution at this point. I'll do what I can to get my client to accept the plea,' said the public defender.

The prosecutor looked at me. 'I'm not happy at the prospect of this guy walking around on our streets. Can you assure me that he will leave the United States immediately on release?'

'I'm not in any position to guarantee that,' I said. 'Once he's released he's a free man and it's up to him what he does. But if he comes to my office and he wants to go home I'll do whatever I properly can to help him.' He shifted a little uncomfortably in his chair. 'To be honest,' I said, 'if you want him gone for sure, you'll have to deport him.'

The prosecutor didn't want to get involved in anything like that, so he let it go. Provided the public defender could persuade Palmer to accept the guilty plea, we had a deal.

The public defender was confident as we left the building, and said he'd be in touch again soon

A few days later the public defender called me.

'Did he leave?' he asked.

'Did who leave where?' I said.

'Did Mr Palmer leave the United States?'

'He's out of jail?' I said, surprised at the news.

'Yes. He was released yesterday morning. I didn't get a chance to call you and let you know, but he said he was coming directly to your office.'

'Well, I haven't seen him,' I said.

'Damn. I hope he's OK. Call me if he turns up?'

It wasn't long before he did.

A few nights later two US immigration officers were patrolling Cocoa Beach on the Atlantic coast at about 2am. They were looking for any small craft that might come ashore with illegal immigrants.

Although it was dark, behind some boulders on the beach one of the officers noticed the pale, moonlit glimmer of a human face appear from above a rock, and then quickly disappear. With guns drawn they approached the suspicious character and asked him to identify himself. He explained that he was a British special forces officer who had recently completed a mission in America, and was waiting for a submarine to rendezvous with him at 'zero-three-hundred-hours local time' and return him to the UK. He gave them a name, rank and service number. The name, of course, was Palmer.

He missed his submarine rendezvous owing to his detention by the immigration officers at the local county jail. The next morning we got the call that he'd been picked up, had been identified as having overstayed his visa and would be processed for deportation, a process that would normally take, at the least, a few months.

Later that day, I met the immigration officer handling the case – a good contact of mine – and explained to him everything that Palmer had been through. I said that I thought it would be extremely unjust if he now had to spend even more time in custody awaiting a deportation. The officer agreed and we discussed some options. Eventually, he said that, provided we could supply an air ticket back to the UK the next evening, and provided that Palmer agreed to go, he would bring him to my office to collect the ticket, and then take him directly to the airport and ensure he left. It was a generous offer. I told him that I thought we could do that.

I contacted Consular Directorate in London later that day and asked for permission to buy Palmer's air ticket from official FCO funds. There is a procedure whereby this can be done; it involves confiscating the person's passport and issuing an emergency passport to facilitate the journey back to the UK. The person concerned must also sign an official undertaking-to-repay (UTR), and Consular Directorate must approve the whole thing in advance. It is rarely agreed to in London – mostly because the recovery rate for the money is spectacularly poor (less than 20%) even though, technically, the person owing the money is prohibited from obtaining another British passport until the debt is paid – but I thought this was a case that warranted exception. I had never asked for this procedure before, so I thought my request would carry extra weight.

London refused my request out-of-hand. They argued that because Palmer was of unsound mind, he could, after returning to England, claim that he did not know what he was doing when he signed the UTR, perhaps thus invalidating the legality of the agreement. I was furious.

'Are you telling me that there are legions of mentally-ill British people around the world, trying to borrow money from us to get home, knowing that, because they are mad, they will probably be able to avoid paying it back?' I said. 'Are these people retaining the services of experienced, expensive, specialist lawyers to challenge the FCO in the High Court with the intention of avoiding a £300 debt?'

'That's not the point.'

'You're quite correct, that's not the point,' I said. 'The point is, we have a mentally unwell person who needs our assistance. He doesn't have the means or the ability to help himself. Furthermore, we don't know what this guy might be capable of doing to himself or someone else if he goes back into jail. How is it going to look in the press if it goes pear-shaped and they find out we refused him help for the sake of a couple of hundred quid? Besides, the US immigration service has agreed to co-operate with us on this and I need it to work, or we're going to look foolish.'

'Shouldn't you have thought about that before you offered to help?' was the response.

'All right,' I said, 'thanks for all your assistance.'

In the early days of my time in Orlando, the London desk officers would have acted as my voice back home and tried to get me whatever I needed to solve the problem. But the London office was becoming overrun with advisors and policy wonks who would look for every reason why a particular course of action might be open to media criticism or legal challenge. It made problem solving extremely difficult. Of course, you can't blame the desk officers themselves: they were now answerable to the advisors and managers in a way that they had not been before. But whilst the desk officer can dispense with a problem by stating the policy, for the officer abroad dealing with the actual situation the problem remains and will probably deteriorate.

Without the money from London, we had to devise another solution. The next day, we bought Palmer a ticket to Manchester from a small charitable fund that we had available for such occasions, and which we often topped up from our own pockets. By lunchtime, he was in our office with two US immigration officers. I gave the passport and the ticket to the officers, and thanked them for their kind assistance. I turned to Palmer.

'Looking forward to going home?' I asked.

'Me? I'm straight off to Kosovo,' he said, jangling his handcuffs at me.

'Stay safe,' I told him.

'Carpe diem,' he said, and with that Peter Palmer, international man of mystery, was gone.

* * * * *

London's refusal to authorise money for Palmer left a bad taste in my mouth, but those kinds of problems were becoming gradually more frequent. During a conference at around that time, the then head of Consular Directorate, Paul Sizeland, told the attendees that this strict adherence to policy was necessary because the public was becoming increasingly aware of the type of service British citizens were receiving from the FCO. Therefore, to avoid a legal challenge – one person suing, for example, because another had received a better level of service than he had – there was a big drive to ensure a defined standard of service across the board. I can understand the theory behind this, but it meant that the level of service to be offered devolved fairly close to the lowest common denominator, it being far easier to bring the best people down to the lowest level, rather than the other way around.

But how do you compare a Briton stuck with no passport and no money in Port Moresby with someone in the same predicament in Paris? Flexibility, enterprise, local knowledge and common sense should be the order of the day, and those approaches had now become politically incorrect.

With the legions of new advisors in London, actually getting something done there was, paradoxically, becoming more difficult. That was bad enough, but, even more perversely, whilst they would not be prepared to risk the loan of a few hundred pounds to help a mentally unwell person get safely back to the UK, they would be prepared to spend thousands on vacuous high-profile, media-friendly policy initiatives.

In 2000, the FCO announced, with much fanfare to the public and to Parliament, that it had enrolled a panel of eminent British lawyers to assist consular officers around the world.

These lawyers would be available to review various criminal convictions sustained by British nationals abroad, provided that certain criteria were met, in order to address possible abuses of human rights; these might include cases heard against minors in adult courts, prisoners suffering from mental incapacity or mental illness, or serious physical illness and so forth.

If we felt that a given case fell within the necessary parameters, we could submit it to one of these hotshot British lawyers for a legal opinion and, possibly, challenge the case legally, or seek a compassionate pardon.

A circular was sent to all FCO posts, for the attention of consular sections. We were asked to search our records and identify cases that matched the given criteria. Having done so, we were requested to send that information to London for consideration by the lawyers.

During the first year that this panel existed, five cases worldwide were submitted to London: three were from the USA, and two of those were from Orlando.

In Florida, it's not that uncommon for a minor to be tried, convicted and sentenced in an adult court. If the prosecutor feels that the crime is heinous enough, he can make an application to the judge for adult proceedings which can mean children as young as 10 being tried in a full criminal court, amenable to the same terms of imprisonment as an adult might be. Most alarmingly, the minor could then serve this sentence in a prison full of adults.

You don't need the imagination of Shakespeare to see how terrible it might be for a young boy to wind up in a Florida prison; as we've seen, the guards are there to ensure that nobody escapes; what the prisoners do to each other is largely left to the inmates themselves to organise.

As soon as I'd read the circular announcing the new development, I thought of two of my cases that might be eligible.

Both involved British nationals who had been minors when they were tried and convicted as adults, and both were serving their sentences in adult prisons. I wrote up both the cases and submitted them to London for consideration.

The first concerned one Daniel Muller. Born in London, his parents had broken up acrimoniously before he was three. His father moved to the States, remarried and started a new family. Daniel stayed in London with his mother and his brother, but as he grew older he started to become a problem child. After several brushes with the police, and a short spell in a juvenile detention facility, his mother was unable to exercise any meaningful control or influence over him. Desperate for a solution, she talked with Daniel's father in Florida. The father's new wife was reluctant for them to become involved, but eventually agreed to accept him in America for a while to see if they could help.

It did not go well. Daniel, now 15, was out of control, and the more his father tried to bring him into line, the worse Daniel fought and rebelled against his authority. The situation deteriorated quickly, and before Daniel had been in the States for six months, he was spending time with the wrong people. He was in a gang, and he had access to drugs, knives and firearms.

One fateful afternoon, the most awful thing that could happen, happened. It was as sudden and shocking as it was inexplicable.

Daniel, a small, weedy boy, went to his home with a lad of 20, who was 6ft 2in tall, and strong. They were armed with knives and a pistol. They lay in wait for Daniel's father to arrive at the house, and they planned to kill him and steal his money. But Daniel's father worked late that day, and the first person to arrive in the house was Daniel's 10-year-old half-sister, home from school.

For some reason known only to Daniel and his partner-in-crime, they attacked her instead. The bigger boy held the small girl down whilst Daniel stabbed her repeatedly and then, as a *coup de grâce*, he forced the gun into her mouth and blew her brains out.

When the detectives investigating the case asked him why he'd done it, all he said was, 'I hate my father.'

Like so many other utterly shocking stories, this case did not make the news in the UK; in fact, it only merited a few paragraphs in the Florida newspapers.

Daniel was tried as an adult. Taking into account the circumstances of the offence and the mindset of a typical Florida jury, he was lucky to escape the death penalty.

Instead, he got a mandatory life sentence with a recommendation that he serve at least 40 years.

I read through his file the night before I first went to visit Daniel at Glades Correctional Institution. Besides a detailed account of what happened, it mentioned a couple of other interesting points.

The first was that he had twice tried to escape from the prison by going 'over the wire'. Most Florida DOC prisons don't actually have walls; instead they have wire fences, usually around 10 metres high, and there are usually two or three of them between the prisoner and the outside. The wire is thick, and the fences are topped with a further layer of vicious razor wire. One of the fences, normally the inner one, is electrified. Additionally, the gap between the two outer fences is known as the death zone. Armed guards sitting in corner towers watch the fences, and if a prisoner sets foot in that space the guard is under orders to shoot to kill. Even if you *could* clear the wire, most Florida prisons are in the middle of nowhere – you'd have to traverse miles of swamp or open land, across which the dogs would chase you down; in the darkness, there would be helicopters with night vision capability.

Daniel's two escape bids were clearly actually suicide attempts. That he had not been killed was either fortunate, or unfortunate, depending on your viewpoint.

He had been tried and convicted both times of attempted escape. He was sentenced to a further 15 years imprisonment for each, to run consecutively to each other and his original sentence.

The second point was that Daniel had a long list of health and psychological problems. To survive in a Florida prison, you need an angle. Probably the best angle is to be freakishly big, extremely aggressive and fearless, but even such a man would struggle to repel two or three smaller, determined men. Being intelligent can sometimes help, as there's a shortage of brains in prison and you might be able to get a reputation writing legal arguments for the other inmates. Daniel was neither of those things, so he needed his own angle. According to the report I read, he had submitted to older, bigger men for sexual favours in exchange for protection. Over the years, this had become a lifestyle for him. As a direct consequence of this he had contracted HIV.

My meetings with him – and there were several over the years – were always difficult.

He would almost completely avoid looking at me, and was unresponsive and surly. When I once questioned him directly about his attitude to me, he told me that I represented authority to him, and he hated all authority. But he never once refused to see me, which he would have been perfectly entitled to do. I was, in fact, the only person who ever visited him in prison as his mother was unable to travel from London, and his father had, unsurprisingly, disowned him.

This case appeared to me to match the criteria for a legal assessment in London on at least two counts. Firstly, he was tried and convicted as an adult, despite being a minor at the time. Secondly, he was now suffering from a serious illness. Arguably, his mental capacity was also a matter for concern. I knew that the state of Florida would be unlikely to take a sympathetic view of any submissions a bunch of namby-pamby lawyers in London might make, but that was hardly the point. Daniel Muller's was the first submission I drafted.

The second was for Mike Shepherd.

Like Muller, Shepherd had been born in London. He had moved to Florida with his mother when he was about 11 after his father abandoned them. She'd wanted to be closer to her wider family who had settled in the States, but Shepherd did not take well to America. He had something of an awkward and withdrawn disposition, and did not make friends easily. Some of his peer group at school made fun of his English accent, and his response was to become quite a solitary figure.

Late one night, three years after arriving in the USA, he pulled a leather mask over his head, grabbed a steak knife from the kitchen and broke into the apartment next door, which was home to a young single mother and her two small children.

In the darkness – he knew the layout of the apartment as it was the same as his own – he found his way into the woman's bedroom, where she lay sleeping. He woke her by placing his hand over her mouth; threatening her with the knife, he told her that her children were also in danger. In a state of absolute terror, she acceded to his demands. She was repeatedly raped, assaulted and brutalised for several hours.

Shepherd wasn't the brightest of rapists. He had known the woman for a couple of years: she was a friend of his mother's and a frequent visitor to his home. Obviously, she recognised him immediately, irrespective of the mask; his voice alone gave him away. But she realised that if he knew that she'd recognised him, that would place her life in jeopardy, so she made a point of saying to him several times during the ordeal, 'Who are you? Where are you from? Why are you doing this to me?'

Maybe that saved her life.

As soon as the assault was over and he left the premises, she called the police. Shepherd was arrested a few minutes later and taken to Dade County Jail.

He was just 14, but like Muller he was charged and detained as an adult.

He was assigned a public defender, who did not, from the records I have seen, provide him with much of a defence. Admittedly, there doesn't seem to have been much of one to provide, but he didn't even mention Shepherd's age in mitigation.

Eventually, under guidance from his counsel, Shepherd accepted a plea-bargain of 40 years' imprisonment.

He was subsequently admitted to the Florida DOC as an adult, which is where he has been for the last 20 years.

I wrote his case up as well, and sent them both to London.

Three months later I'd heard nothing, so I chased them up.

'Someone will get back to you in a few weeks,' said the woman on the other end of the phone, after 20 minutes spent searching for my reports.

Nobody did.

Three months later, I chased it up again. They were still unable to give me a response.

A year after I'd first sent the paperwork and after several more attempts to get a resolution, I decided to press for a decision.

I rang London one afternoon and asked my desk officer for a decision. 'OK,' he said, after I'd explained the situation. 'I'll find out the latest on it.'

He called me back about 30 minutes later. 'There's nothing we can do in respect of these two cases,' he said.

'Why?' I said.

'Well, it's just... the thing is...' He prevaricated for a few moments, and then got to the point. 'Firstly, Muller's crime was too serious, plus he tried to escape. And Shepherd has already had an appeal and it was rejected.'

'Whose opinion is that?' I asked.

'Mine,' he said, slightly embarrassed, but at least he was honest with me about that.

'Have any lawyers seen those papers?' I asked.

'Not that I can see, although the file hasn't been managed very well and it's difficult to know what's happening exactly.'

'So what's been going on with this for the last year?'

'I'm afraid I have no idea. As you know, I only started on the desk a few months ago, and this is the first I've heard of it.'

I was getting nowhere. As far as I could tell, not a single thing had been done on these two cases since the day I submitted them. Despite the blaze of publicity during the launch of the legal panel, it was, apparently, a PR exercise. The Government gets to look like it's taking a stand on human rights, with positive press, TV and radio interviews accompanying the launch. But when it comes to action? Not so much. The media have long moved on to the latest policy announcement, and it's left to people like me to deal with the reality on the ground.

Precisely a year to the day after the legal panel was announced to the world, I took a red pen out of my desk. On the front of the file copies of the applications I had sent on behalf of Muller and Shepherd

I wrote 'No Further Action' and put them away again. As I did so, I was embarrassed to think that I had actually believed something might come of it.

As it stands today, Muller and Shepherd are both still in Florida prisons: Muller with no realistic prospect of ever being released, and Shepherd only just over halfway through his 40-year sentence.

9

'HUGH, WE'RE ALL frantically looking for Koo Stark, and you've got to help us!'

I recognised the voice of one of the consular desk officers on the other end of the phone.

'What on earth do you need her for?'

'She's gone on holiday to Florida with her children.'

'Surely that's only a case of poor judgment – it's hardly a crime.'

'No, you don't understand. She's involved in a child custody dispute with the children's father, Warren Walker – he's an American, but he lives in London.'

'What's this got to do with us?'

'The court in London gave her permission to take the kids to visit her family in Florida for 10 days, but it's been over two weeks and she's still not back. The newspapers are saying she's abducted the children and we need to brief a junior minister on the situation.'

'Don't any of you have anything better to do?'

'It's the newspapers, Hugh. They're going bananas for it and we have to respond.'

I shook my head in disbelief. I had a mountain of real work sitting on my desk, yet I was going to have to drop it all for the next few hours to look for a retired adult movie star and her offspring, just to placate the press.

'Is she even British?' I asked.

'Er... I hadn't thought of that. I have no idea. I just assumed she was.'

'What about the children? Are *they* British?'

'I don't know that either.'

'What *do* you know?'

'Only that the newspapers are going berserk and that the FCO press office needs information now.'

Journalistic interest in a consular case tends to set off alarm bells with FCO officials. If the case goes wrong, which can easily happen and often does, there is scope for public humiliation and career ruination. As the media interest in consular cases intensifies – especially if there's any blood or guts involved – FCO ministers and senior officers in London and at posts occasionally overreact, and, in their panic to mitigate criticism, they sometimes tailor their response according to media-dictated priorities. Occasionally this is a good thing – if the FCO is getting it wrong, it should be subject to scrutiny from the press and public. But other times, as an officer on the ground, you find yourself being instructed to do unimportant stuff simply to tick a box when there are other more pressing but less glamorous jobs in hand. In the years following 9/11, the FCO's press office in London grew in size. Not only did it develop a voracious appetite for information from posts, it increasingly started telling the rest of us what we could and couldn't say about a particular case. This was entirely understandable when the intention was to protect bereaved family members and so forth, but it was less forgivable when we were protecting FCO incompetence.

'Leave it to me,' I said, as reassuringly as possible.

As far as I could tell about FCO best practice from observing senior colleagues, the injunction 'leave it to me' means that you must immediately delegate the task to someone junior to you. Accordingly, I asked pro-consul John Corfield to look on the internet to see whether we could find out Ms Stark's nationality, her children's nationality and their whereabouts.

Now, the FCO's computer system is set up in such a way that access to things like pornographic sites, chat sites, social networks and anything else that might actually be useful is prohibited. If you try to access such a page, a big red computerised hand appears referring you to the system administrator, and you are then required to file a report to the FCO security department in London, explaining why you were attempting to access a prohibited site.

Virtually every page that John attempted to access to find out more about Koo Stark was pornographic. We did manage to discover that she was American-born but there was no information about whether she had naturalised as a British citizen, though I can testify that, physically, she appears to be in excellent working order. It all turned out to be a false alarm anyway – within a few hours of our first call from London, Ms Stark was on a plane back to London with the children, and we didn't need to pursue it any further; but John spent the next three days filling in official forms explaining why he was looking at photos of naked women on an FCO computer.

'I don't mind the paperwork,' he told me, 'but just don't tell my wife.'

As it turned out, this obviously wasn't the 'child abduction' case it was first feared. But we do get lots of these cases, and they can take many forms: the most traumatic being the snatching of a child from its parents' custody by a complete stranger, such as happened to little Madeleine McCann in Portugal in 2007. Fortunately, such incidents are extremely rare. I never had to deal with a case like that, although we once came close.

A girl of seven was staying with her family in a hotel in Orlando, when a man tried to grab her as she left an elevator on the ground floor. Her brother, a 12-year-old who was in the lobby, cried out the alarm, and the stranger abandoned his attempt to take the chid and fled. The girl's father and uncle, who were close by, chased the man into the car park. The villain managed to get into his car and lock the door, but before he could drive off the uncle, a police officer from Ulster, punched through his window and hit him several times in the face. He managed to get away and was never caught.

The kind of abductions I dealt with were almost exclusively part of a parental custody dispute after family breakdown. They usually occur when one parent has no confidence in the outcome of a child custody court hearing, and decides to remove the child from the process. Some of the most heated discussions and arguments I've had are with parents in dispute about custody of their children. A few of them became desperate or even ferocious. One I remember well, and it all started with a phone call.

'My name's Steve Harvey,' said the voice on the end of the phone. 'I'm in a really tight spot and I need your help.'

'I'll do what I can. What's the story?'

'I'm British, I'm from Southampton, and six years ago I had a child with my girlfriend. We never married.'

'Is your girlfriend British?'

'Yes, and our son was born in England too, his name is Toby.'

'Okay.'

'She's a qualified nurse, and early last year she took a job with a hospital in Houston, Texas. She got a three-year work visa, but as we weren't married I didn't qualify for one. I came over on a tourist visa and looked for work, but as I didn't have a work visa I was pretty much at home taking care of things and relying on her money.'

'That must have been hard.'

'It was. Anyway, late last year I told her I'd had enough, that I wanted to go back to the UK and I wanted to take Toby with me. She wanted to keep him here. I said, "How are you going to be able to look after him if you're at work all day, and sometimes all night?" but she didn't want to hear it. Cut a long story short, we went to court in Texas to try and resolve it.'

'What was the outcome?'

'The judge decided that, as we were British and were only over here for three years max, we should take the custody dispute to a British court.'

'That's an interesting decision. Did you do that?' I asked.

'We did. The judge in Southampton awarded me custody of the boy last year and I have the court order with me.'

'I'm sensing it didn't end there.'

'No, it didn't. She went back to Texas and I stayed in England with Toby, but a few months after the court case she started calling me and saying how much she missed us both. She asked me to bring him over on a holiday, which I did.'

'When was that?'

'That was about three months ago, and that's when it all went weird. We arrived at Houston airport, and she was there to meet us. It was all smiles and laughter. I left Toby with her while I went to get a rental car. When I got back there was no sign of either of them. They'd just vanished. I looked everywhere. I put out an announcement on the airport PA system, I reported it to the police. I was frantic.'

'I can imagine.'

'So, a few hours later I drive over to her apartment, and there's no sign of life. The place is empty, and the guy next door tells me she moved out a few weeks ago. That's when I realised that she'd done a runner with the kid, and that she'd planned the whole thing. So, I was in a bit of a fix. I spent a couple of days in Houston asking around for her. I went to her hospital, but she'd left there the month before, and there was no forwarding information. None of her friends knew where she was, or if they did they weren't telling me. So, I gave up and took a flight back home, but before I did I hired a private detective to try and find them.'

'Did he have any success?'

'Yes, he did. He called me last week. He traced them to an apartment in Sarasota, Florida. They're living there under a false name.'

'So what do you plan to do now?'

'I've already done it. I went to my son's school this afternoon, and when he came out for his lunch break I took him away with me. I've got him here in Orlando and I have two tickets to London for tomorrow evening. All I need at this point is a passport from you so I can take him with me.'

'Does his mother know where he is?'

'I very much doubt she has the slightest idea, and I would prefer it to remain that way for the time being.'

'She must be freaking out.'

'That's her problem. She wasn't worried when she did it to me.'

I appreciated this man's honesty about the situation, and I told him so. Experience has taught me that most people in his position would have simply contacted the consulate, told us that his son had lost his passport and asked us for a replacement, without mentioning the full story. He wouldn't have got away with it if he'd done that.

'You'll need to give me 24 hours on this one, Mr Harvey,' I said. 'There are obviously legal aspects to it, and I'll need to take advice. In the meantime, can you please fax me that court order?'

'Okay,' he said, 'but our flight's tomorrow evening, so that's cutting a bit fine. I'll send the fax in the next few minutes. I'll come in to see you after lunch tomorrow.'

As soon as I hung up, I called the consul in Washington for advice. His name was Graeme Wise, and he was responsible for the passport section, among other things. Once Graeme had heard the story he asked me to contact the court in England to confirm the decision about custody of the child. He told me he'd make some inquiries and get back to me.

Just before I left work that afternoon I received a phone call from an extremely distressed woman.

'He's taken him! He's stolen my son!' she was yelling, taking great gulps of air as she tried to speak through the sobs. 'He went to his school and he's taken him away.'

I realised immediately who this was, but it was hard to understand her when she was crying so hard. I asked her to try and calm down and tell me the situation.

'I'm English. I live in Sarasota, and my son was kidnapped from his school today. His father has taken him, and he'll try to get him back to England. I've reported it to the police and they told me to call you. You mustn't give that man a passport for that child. I absolutely forbid it. You have to find him and get him back to me.'

'Is there any background to this case?' I asked her. 'Are there any court orders, or anything like that?'

'No,' she shouted. 'He's my son and he lives here with me.'

Her failure to acknowledge the existence of the court order, a copy of which I had in my hands as I spoke, did her no credit. 'Decisions about passports are taken at our embassy in Washington,' I said. 'You'd better call there and ask for Mr Wise, who will be able to give you more information.'

As soon as I put the phone down, I called Graeme and warned him to expect the call.

'What will you tell her?' I asked.

'As little as possible. We'll stall for time until we know where we stand.'

The next afternoon, Steve Harvey came into the consulate. We left his son in the waiting area with Viv McCulloch and we went into my office.

'What's the decision?' he said, before we'd even sat down.

'We're going to respect the court order. We'll be giving you an emergency passport to fly home this evening.'

'Thank you for that,' he said, looking almost overwhelmed with relief. 'I really appreciate your assistance.'

'I'll check for confirmation of your flight's departure this evening,' I said. 'Once I know you've gone, I'll have to call the boy's mother and let her know exactly what has happened. I hope you can understand.'

'Once I'm out of this country, you can do whatever you want.'

Later that evening I called the boy's mother to tell her what the situation was. I expected her to be angry, but I did not expect the hysteria.

'You fucking bastards!' she screamed. 'You fucking bastards! What have you done to my son! You don't know what that man's capable of! You can't do that, it's against the law. He's my son! I'll sue you. Call the airport and get them to turn that plane around. You have to get him back here, you bastards!'

She was screaming and hyperventilating so much that I expected her to pass out. I entreated her to calm herself down and to discuss the matter properly, but she just became worse. The screeching went on for many minutes, without any real exchange of conversation.

'You've done it now! You don't know what he's like! I'll never see my son again! I'm going to kill myself, and it will all be your fault!'

'Please calm down. There's a proper way to deal with this and move forward, but you must be reasonable.'

'I'm going to kill myself,' she shouted, and then it sounded as if she dropped the phone onto the floor and all I could hear were repeated, gut-wrenching screams. 'Aaaarghhh! Aaaarghhh! Aaaarghhh!'

After a minute or two of that the phone suddenly went dead. This was difficult. Although she was hysterical, I thought she was unlikely to attempt suicide. But you can never be sure, so I called the police and told them what had gone on. They called me back a few hours later. She was fine. They had calmed her down and they were satisfied she would be safe.

'You did the right thing to call us,' said the sheriff's deputy. 'You never know with someone like that.'

In cases like that, you rarely find out the eventual outcome. It's a fact of life as a consul that once you've dealt with your part of a case it moves on to someone else's desk, perhaps even in another country, and that was the last you hear of it. But this case had a strange twist in the tail.

Several months after the hysterical phone call, I got a fax from a number in the UK. The fax was an order from a court in Southampton giving custody of Toby to his mother, with permission to bring him to live in the USA. There was no covering letter, no request for assistance. I could see that it was a fuck-you-fax.

A week later, I got a call from Toby's mother.

'I've got him here with me and there's nothing you can do about it,' she said.

'I'm happy for you that it worked out well,' I said, and I meant it.

'You're still a fucking bastard,' she hissed and slammed the phone down.

* * * * *

The first principle of child custody arrangements between civilised countries is that a court in the couple's country of normal residence should make the decision about custody. This is enshrined in the Hague Convention on Child Abductions, to which the United Kingdom and the United States are both signatories. Disputes between British/ American couples are well regulated by the courts in both countries, with established laws and precedents. There is ordinarily no need for them to become unnecessarily difficult. But child custody disputes are seldom ordinary. The parent from the USA could sometimes leverage certain home advantages, creating circumstances outside those anticipated by the Hague Convention. I've seen it happen and it isn't pretty.

A lady called Beverly Curtis telephoned me from Nottingham. She was softly spoken, although I sensed that her calmness masked a deep sadness. As she told me her story, I understood why.

'Three years ago, I went to the States as a visitor and got married to an American man I'd known for a while,' she said. 'We had a little girl less than a year after the wedding, and I thought it was going champion, like. But once we'd had the kid he changed a lot. He started slapping me around and stuff. He were a right nasty piece of work. We lived in the same street as his brothers and cousins, they all knew each other and everyone took his side of things, if you see what I mean. Then he threw me out, so I had to go and live in a motel in another town about five miles away. When I went back to see my daughter the following weekend, they'd gone and nobody would tell me where they were. I spoke to an attorney, and we filed for a court hearing to get custody of my daughter.'

'That's a sad story,' I told her. 'What's the latest situation?'

'Oh, it gets worse,' she said. 'Although we were married, I never filed papers to get my green card. About three weeks after he threw me out, the US immigration service came to my motel room and arrested me. They deported me a few days later. They told me I'd overstayed my tourist visa by two years, and now they won't let me back in.'

I was upset to hear this. The US immigration service was legally obliged to inform us of this, yet had failed to do so. Mrs Curtis had not thought to contact the consulate, so I had not known about her deportation until now. If I had known, there might have been something I could have done to help her remain in the USA – at the very least I could have found an immigration lawyer prepared to look at the case – but now she was back in England, it did not look good for her. She had applied to the US consulate in London for a visa to go back to the States to appear in court for a custody hearing, but, because she had been deported, they denied her a visa.

I knew the US consul in London – we'd met a couple of times. I wrote to him about Mrs Curtis, saying that I thought it would be manifestly unjust if she were prevented from being able to petition the court for custody of her child. He called me a few days later saying his position was difficult, but that he would agree to a visa permitting Mrs Curtis a short stay visa for the purposes of appearing in court.

A few weeks after the visa was granted, Mrs Curtis attended a court in Florida. She was unable to get legal representation. She was on a low income, so could not afford her own lawyer. There was no legal assistance available for her in Florida, and she did not qualify for British legal aid because the case was in a foreign court. She was there alone. Finally, when the day came, there was no custody hearing. Mr Curtis's lawyer requested a month's delay, and the judge granted it. Beverly Curtis returned to London, her visa lapsed and she was unable to get another one.

The following month, in her absence, the court gave custody of the child to Mr Curtis. Mrs Curtis was granted visitation rights, but only in the United States. Owing to her deportation, she was unlikely to be allowed to enter the USA for 10 years, perhaps longer, so the visitation rights were meaningless. Mr Curtis soon moved to an unknown location with his daughter, and Mrs Curtis has not heard from either of them since.

The last time I spoke with her she was disconsolate. She had spoken to Reunite, the British agency developed to provide support and advice to parents whose children have been abducted, and civil servants at the Lord Chancellor's Office, the government department with responsibility for such things, but, strictly speaking, Beverly Curtis's daughter had not been abducted, so they could only offer limited assistance.

It doesn't seem fair to me. Heartbreaking and unjust is a better description.

Meanwhile, I had begun to encounter some child-related problems of my own. Cheryl and I had been together for over a year by now, and the subject of kids had reared its downy head on more than one occasion. It seemed a bit too previous to me, but she very much wanted progeny and would take any half-reasonable opportunity to remind me of it. Not wishing to jeopardise my carnal visitation rights, I would be vaguely encouraging yet uncommitted.

One weekend I decided to take her to the Bahamas for a couple of days, just to get away and relax. She wore a beautiful white silk top, perfect for a few days on a subtropical island, and looked immaculate; she had the stature of a model and she walked with the confidence of a movie star. As we made our way through the terminal at Orlando airport, I could sense the eyes of both men and women following her across the concourse. I wondered how I'd managed to get to here from my greyer, slightly less glamorous beginnings in Romford, and felt like an extremely lucky bloke.

When we boarded our plane I took the middle seat and let Cheryl sit by the window. But a woman arrived to sit in the aisle seat with her young baby, just a few months old, and Cheryl asked me to change places so that she could play with the kid. I was happy to distance myself from it, but Cheryl promptly struck up a conversation with the mother. Mostly, from what I could hear, it was about the joys of being a parent.

At 29,000 feet, Cheryl turned to me and whispered 'I want one of those.'

'They're expensive,' I whispered back.

'But they're so gorgeous.'

'Yes, sometimes they are,' I had to admit.

'We'd have a beautiful one, don't you think?'

'Yes, probably we would.'

'C'mon, you have to want one too, don't you?'

I was about to point out a few of the downsides when the baby's mother asked Cheryl to hold the kid whilst she went to the bathroom. Cheryl clutched that thing to her breast like it was her own, and I could see how deep these feelings were within her. It frightened me, to be honest.

After about a minute of holding on to this thing, she held it out in front of her and cooed, 'You're so beautiful. You're such a beautiful baby, aren't you?'

At that moment the baby's face changed colour and it projectile vomited a jet of bilious green slime all over Cheryl's front. I had never seen so much fluid exit a living creature before, especially at such velocity. Cheryl was completely motionless, as the pungent mucous dripped all down her face and her expensive shirt. I just stared and waited to see what might happen next. The baby began to cry, at which Cheryl sat it on her lap to comfort it, but then the baby did a poop. Not a regular one that creates a bit of a smell and requires a nappy change, but an atomic one. Gallons of liquefied shit oozed out of its nappy and all over my girlfriend. As Cheryl herself would have remarked if she'd been able to speak, it was awesome.

Moments later the baby's mother arrived, and in a flood of apologies she whisked the kid off to the bathroom to clean it up.

Passengers around us started to make noises and movements of discomfort. I think one of them dry-retched, and a few of them got up and moved to other seats.

Then, for the first time in the minutes since this catastrophe unfolded, Cheryl turned her head slowly to look at me. I hadn't done a single thing to help her or the kid, and the disgust in her face was evident. She looked at me for a long time, just daring me to say something stupid. The longer she stared at me, the more I felt a deep, uncontrollable urge to laugh. I could feel my shoulders start to shake, so I bit the inside of my mouth to try and stop myself from losing control. She intensified her stare at me, and I knew I had to say something, anything.

'You were magnificent,' I said, and then I just collapsed into uncontrollable laughter.

Wordlessly, Cheryl got up and went to the loo to try to clean up.

That night we went for a stroll along the beach. Normal relations had resumed and we were enjoying the warm breeze. We walked without speaking for a while, but then Cheryl, who obviously still had children on her mind, broke the silence.

'You do want kids, right?' she said.

'I don't know. It's a big commitment.'

I think she was slightly dismayed by my lack of enthusiasm about the idea, but she looked for a positive angle on the whole thing. 'But you're not ruling it out?' she said.

'No,' I said, 'I'm not ruling it out.'

'Can we talk about it a little bit?'

'All right,' I said. 'Let me start by asking who would have to clean up the puke and the shit?'

'We would take turns at that.'

'I thought we might.'

'It's only fair,' she said.

'Yes, it's only fair,' I said, 'but that's what I'm afraid of.'

10

IN 2003, THE FOREIGN and Commonwealth Office released its first-ever strategic priorities document. It was called 'UK International Priorities: a strategy for the FCO'. This was an attempt to bring much sharper focus to its work. By stating its eight priorities, the senior management team wanted all staff, and the public, to have a clearer understanding of what we were supposed to be doing. The foreign secretary stated that its intentions were to 'clarify our priorities so we can concentrate our efforts where they are most needed and respond flexibly to unexpected events'. Personnel in London and around the world were instructed to tailor all their efforts to projects that dealt with the strategic priorities, and anything that wasn't on that list should be marginalised or disregarded altogether. The objectives of the senior management team were supposed to cascade down through the ranks so that everybody, from the permanent secretary down to the filing clerks, would be singing from the same hymn sheet. It was supposed to improve our performance – whatever that means.

When I saw the list of priorities, I was astounded. Consular work was not mentioned once; in fact, none of the FCO's public services were mentioned. For me, the message could not have been clearer: despite the rhetoric of how important consular work was becoming, and how valued the efforts of consular staff were, it actually meant nothing to the people running the show. They had either taken a conscious decision to make consular work a marginal activity, or, worse still, simply forgotten it.

I was disheartened, as were my consular colleagues around the US network, and I was perturbed about the message it sent to the British public: serving and protecting you whilst you are abroad is an inconvenience to the mandarins; we would prefer to be negotiating about the European Union, or governing our dependent territories, so please don't get into any problems on foreign soil – if you do, helping you isn't that important to us.

Consular work is the shop front of the FCO. For 95% of Britons, the only contact you are ever likely to have with the FCO is with someone like me. How your problems are dealt with is therefore extremely important. The FCO brass had shot themselves in both feet. Firstly, they'd offended the public by failing to acknowledge their duties and obligations to them. Secondly, they'd upset the consular officials, who are largely overworked and underpaid despite having pretty poor career prospects. Most consular workers are motivated by the desire to help others and a wish to serve – commitments that were not really acknowledged.

The mistake was soon noticed and the next strategic priorities document specifically mentioned consular work. But the damage was done. Most of my consular colleagues had long believed their work was unappreciated at senior levels, but now it was official.

Actually, the document made no difference to me. At the start of the next year, I was asked to define my personal objectives for the year, in line with the strategic priorities, and to require my staff to set their own targets accordingly. At first I refused. I told the consul general in Atlanta, to whom I answered on such matters, that nothing I did, or that my staff did, could possibly be tied to the FCO's stated objectives. I proposed to carry on as I had been doing without reference to the document.

I was told to *imagine* that consular work was a strategic priority, and set targets in line accordingly. So that's what I did; I imagined some priorities, imagined some objectives and imagined some targets, and I made sure they would all be easy to achieve. I wrote them all down and sent them to Atlanta, who sent them to Washington, who sent them to London. Job done! Everybody above me was happy, and nobody subordinate to me could have cared less one way or the other. Back in the office we were just getting on with the job, one problem at a time.

I always tried to provide the best help I could and to be the best ambassador for my country on every occasion. I also encouraged my staff to see their work in the same light. When someone comes into the consulate, for any reason, whether they're British or not, there is an opportunity to make an abiding impression and that opportunity will never come again. Personally, I enjoyed the contact, and casual visitors to the consulate could be one of the most interesting parts of the day.

Whilst I was working away at my desk one morning, consular assistant Sheila Scott popped her head around my door.

'There's a dishevelled middle-aged Scotsman in the waiting room,' she said.

'Is there any other kind?'

Sheila, herself a Glaswegian, was unamused. 'He's wearing an eye patch and he claims to have detailed plans for a new submarine,' she said. 'Do you want me to get rid of him?'

'Don't be ridiculous,' I said. 'I wouldn't miss this for the world.'

I went out to see him out in the reception area.

'Smith,' he said, by way of introduction.

'Hunter,' I replied, shaking his hand.

'I grew up on the banks of the Clyde, overlooking Faslane,' he told me, still shaking my hand.

'I grew up in Romford, overlooking the dog track,' I replied. 'What brought you to the United States?'

'Work,' he said. 'I was for many years with Bassett's.'

'Marine engineers?' I asked.

'Liquorice Allsorts,' he said.

We sat down together at the coffee table. He immediately unfurled his plans and spread them out over the table in front of us. It looked something like a submarine to me, but what do I know?

'My submarine has one major advantage over all other underwater craft currently available on the international market,' he said, dramatically. 'Cost!'

'It's cheap?' I said.

'It is constructed entirely from Tupperware,' he told me.

I turned and looked at the plans again. The components did now seem to resemble generic kitchen containers of various kinds.

'Do you really think it is going to be up to the job of underwater warfare, Mr Smith?' I asked him.

'No question,' he responded, in a shocking Glaswegian accent. 'There will be some limitations on speed and depth of operations, but my calculations leave no ambiguity. There will, in addition, be significantly less susceptibility to detection.' He moved his eye-patch from one eye to the other. Both eyes appeared to be working perfectly well.

Looking again at the plans, I saw that he had written along the bottom, in ostentatious calligraphy, 'To Scale'. It occurred to me that a man would not fit in this craft. Frankly, a man's foot would not have fitted. I was considering the wisdom of pointing this out to him, when he spoke first.

'There is, however, one problem that I have not yet been able to overcome.'

'Which is?' I asked, assuming that he would mention the size of the craft.

'Tupperware doesn't make anything that would function as a conning tower.'

Looking at the plans again, I noticed the lack of a conning tower. How had I missed that?

'I had expected,' he continued, 'that a new sugar container in their EveryHome line would resolve the problem, but it is too tall and too thin.'

'That's unfortunate,' I said, using my favourite FCO euphemism.

'Very,' he said.

'Have you been to speak to anyone over at Tupperware?' I asked him. (The world headquarters for Tupperware is in Orlando.)

'Yes, I was there last week.'

'And what did they say?'

'They threw me out.'

I nodded and there followed a bit of a reflective silence, before he asked me the question that I knew he'd been burning to ask me since his arrival. 'Do you think the Royal Navy would be interested?'

'Well, it isn't really my specific area of responsibility,' I said. 'But I think we're developing a new generation of nuclear submarines in conjunction with the French.'

I knew perfectly well that we weren't, but it was the best I could come up with on the spur of the moment.

'Ah, yes, the French,' he said. 'I had forgotten all about them.'

I assured him that this was perfectly understandable.

'Have you tried the Americans?' I asked.

'Yes, but they need something bigger.'

'Well, they do have a larger budget than us,' I said.

Another long silence followed and we both looked again at his plans for a while before I realised that the initiative had fallen to me.

'I'm afraid I must get back to my work.' I said. 'This has been very interesting.'

'Okay,' he said, 'thanks for your time. I'll get busy with this conning tower and let you know how I get on.'

'Excellent. Good luck, and keep in touch.'

He did occasionally come back to see me again, and, if time permitted, I would go and sit with him for a short while. One time he had developed a missile silo from a stack of plastic coffee mugs that he'd melted together. 'Very portable,' he assured me, 'and impossible to see from a satellite.'

Another time it was a series of kitchen buckets attached together in what appeared to be a random fashion. 'What is it?' I asked, after studying it for while.

'I have absolutely no idea.' he said.

One day he left, and he never came back again. I don't know what became of him, but I hope he is okay. I think people whose perception of reality is so different to our own enrich our lives immeasurably, unless they're actually Members of Parliament.

Consulates do seem to attract quite a lot of people like that, and, when circumstances permitted, I was always happy to give them my time. This, to me, is at the heart of what the FCO calls 'public diplomacy', which is the dark art of raising and improving the image of Britain throughout the world. The FCO has devised many policies designed to achieve this, but I think that if you want to persuade the world that your nation is a wonderful place, the best way to do it is one person at a time. Ten minutes of genuine human contact is worth a thousand pages of policy waffle.

On one occasion I had a visit at the consulate from an FCO colleague who was slightly senior to me. Whilst he was there, I went and spent five minutes with the Tupperware man. When I returned to my office, my colleague said, 'Do you really think that is a good way to spend your resources?'

This from a man who spent most of his time either eating lunch at the taxpayers' expense, or sleeping off his prandial excesses at his desk.

'What do you mean?' I asked him.

'Talking to crazy people from the street? Is it really what we should be doing? Might it not be construed as a waste of time?'

'Don't be absurd,' I said. 'Ninety per cent of the FCO's activities are a waste of time. Why would speaking to the public, God forbid, be considered less productive than talking to colleagues? The only real difference is from a safety point-of-view. Some of these people can be quite unstable, prone to irrational actions, sexually deviant or even physically abusive. But, then, so can members of the public.'

* * * * *

Later that year I had a visit from a senior consular policy person from Consular Directorate in London. She had come all the way from England to speak to me about our telephone system.

'What's wrong with our system?' I asked.

'When someone calls the consulate in Orlando, a member of staff here picks up the phone and speaks to the caller.'

'Yes, that's right.'

'Well, that won't do at all.'

'Really? What are we supposed to do?'

'All the other British consulates in the United States now have automatic call-filtering systems, whereby callers can select the options according to their specific question. Most of the questions can be answered by pre-recorded messages. You must install such a system here so that the standard of service is the same across the country.'

I was hostile to this suggestion, for a couple of reasons – mostly that the last thing a Briton in real trouble wants to hear when they call a consulate is series of irrelevant questions from a machine inviting you to press one for English, two for Swahili, or three for Vulcan. You want to talk to the consul, and, in my case at least, the consul wants to talk to you.

But my main issue with it was that it was another case of (to slightly abuse a metaphor) the bureaucratic tail assessing the dog's problem and coming up with the wrong solution. The problem was that, by some margin, most of the calls to British consulates in the USA were from foreign people who wanted a visa to travel to the UK. The visa issuing operation had been centralised to New York some years before, but the visa office in New York never – and I mean *never* – answered the telephone to callers. I know that for a fact as when I worked there nobody answered the phones, which rang constantly: there were simply too few of us and we were too busy dealing with personal callers and other pressing problems. The visa office continued to be badly organised and badly managed. As a consequence of this, people unable to contact the visa office in New York would call other British consulates around the US attempting to speak to a human being. The proper solution to this problem was to resolve the issues at the visa office; the problem at the other consulates would then naturally disappear. This was too simple for the FCO.

'While we're at it, there's something else,' added my visitor.

'What now?'

'You're open from nine till five,' she said.

'Yes, regular office hours.'

'We want all consulates worldwide open for no longer than five hours a day,' she said.

'Why?'

'The extra time away from the public can be spent doing back office work, such as preparing statistics and writing reports,' she said.

'It would be hard for me to turn away someone in need.'

'They can use the emergency number. So, five hours a day is the standard.'

The next day, and with a heavy heart, I ordered a new phone system with lots of buttons to press, and a sign for the door reading 'Office hours, 9am to 2pm'.

We had another regular caller to my office during my time there. When he first showed up, he frightened the life out of the receptionist. She came into my office in a state of some anxiety.

'There is a huge man in the waiting room,' she squeaked, 'and he wants to talk to the consul. I think he might be crazy. Shall I call the police?'

'What's he done?' I asked, somewhat alarmed.

'Well, nothing. But he's just very big.'

'You can't call the police just because someone's big,' I told her. 'I'll come and see him.'

I hate speaking to people through the bullet-proof glass, so I went out to the reception area to talk to him. He was African-American, and I would say he stood at least 6ft 4in; he was probably in his 40s, and he was dressed in the attire of your average Orlando homeless person.

We shook hands, and I invited him to sit down with me. He told me his name was John.

'So, how can I help you, John?' I said.

'Yes, sir,' he said, his voice a low, booming, southern drawl. 'If you please, sir.'

'Please call me Hugh,' I said.

'Yes, sir. If you please, sir.'

He began emptying various pockets of his jacket and trousers. Foolscap scraps flew everywhere. Crumpled pages, covered for the most part with indecipherable script, cascaded to the floor. Other pages appeared with diagrams containing arrows pointing all over the place.

'This looks interesting,' I said.

'Yes, sir. You see, the thing is that I am the illegitimate son of Her Majesty Queen Elizabeth the Second. Prince Charles is my older brother.'

He passed me a piece of paper covered in writing that was barely intelligible to me. I perused it closely and nodded. 'I see,' I said, though I didn't.

'It's all written down there, sir. I have all the documents.' He pointed to another scrap of paper. It looked a bit like a birth certificate, except it was entirely in his own handwriting. 'This shows that I am second in line to the throne of England.'

'Well, I must confess, this kind of thing has been known to happen before,' I said.

'There is a definite resemblance between me and my brother, Charles,' he said, looking straight at me.

Before I could express any doubts, he turned his head 90 degrees to give me the profile.

'You could be right,' I said.

'It's all down there.' He pointed at the various papers lying around on the table.

'These are some obscure documents here,' I said. 'Do you mind telling me where you got them?'

'Yes, sir. I got them from the Orlando library, sir.'

'It is a good library,' I said.

'Very good library,' he agreed. 'They got everything in there.'

'Have you tried their little coffee shop downstairs?' I asked as a matter of interest.

'Yes, sir. They knows me in there, sir.'

He then gave me a letter in an envelope simply addressed to HM The Queen.

'It's for mommy. I just want to let her know that I miss her,' he said.

'I understand,' I assured him. 'I'll make sure it's dealt with appropriately.'

'Appropriately' meant filing it in the office archives, but there was no reason to explain this to him. We said a cheerful goodbye and parted almost as old friends, except that as he was about to turn away, he checked himself, drew himself up to his full height and saluted me. He caught me unawares, and not knowing quite how to respond, I saluted him back.

He would return to the office periodically over the years, and each time he would bring a new letter for his mother. He never once acted in an angry or threatening manner, and, despite his imposing physical presence, the women in the office soon lost their fear of him. In fact, they became rather fond of him and began to look forward to his occasional visits. If too long passed between his calls, they would become concerned for his safety. Sometimes, if time permitted, he might even get a cup of tea, which he loved. Occasionally I would see him at the library, and whenever I did I would always come to attention and throw him a smart salute, at which he would come to attention and salute me back. I cannot imagine what the public made of it all.

In February 2002, Princess Margaret died. Whenever a senior member of the royal family dies, there is a protocol followed at British consulates around the world. A rather grand, leather-bound condolence book is placed in the visitors' room. Local dignitaries and members of the public alike are then invited to attend the consulate and add their condolences to the book. After a period of time, usually a week or so, the book is closed and then sent by diplomatic bag to Buckingham Palace. When Princess Diana died, many thousands of people in New York queued around the block to sign the condolences book. Of course, Princess Margaret was a slightly different kettle of royal fish and when we placed the condolence book in the waiting room on the morning after her death and opened the door of the consulate at 9am, there was only one person waiting outside.

He came in and sat down very solemnly, before writing an entry. After he finished he stood-up and remained in front of the book with his head bowed for a few moments before leaving without speaking to the staff. I went to see what he'd written.

'Dear Aunty Margaret, I am so very sorry that I have not been able to see you for so long. I am still waiting for mommy to write, but I think she is probably too sad right now. I shall miss you a lot, and will always remember our times together long ago. Prince John.'

The condolence book remained open for a week, but nobody else came to sign it. Afterwards we had a discussion in the office about what we should do with it. We could simply file it away in the office archives for a suitable period of time before destroying it, or we could surgically remove the first page with a scalpel, and use it again after the next royal bereavement; or we could send it to the Palace as it was.

We sent it to the Palace.

11

REGARDLESS OF THE RELATIVE unimportance of consular work to the FCO management, it remained important to me and I'm sure it remained important to the British people in need of my help. Sometimes, that help did not take the form you might expect. Most of the people I visited in jail wanted my assistance to try to get out as quickly as possible. Unfortunately, there was almost never anything I could do to help them with that. Occasionally, however, someone would want my assistance to try to keep them *in* jail for a while longer, but there wasn't much I could do about that either!

Many of the prisoners I visited were not serving time for criminal convictions, but were detained in deportation centres by the US immigration service, pending removal from the USA. Some of these people had simply been caught living and working in the US illegally, but most of them were people who had been convicted of a crime and then, after having served prison time, were amenable to deportation.

Up until the early 90s, the US immigration service had some latitude over whether an individual foreign criminal would be deported. In 1996, the US Immigration and Welfare Reform policy passed into law. It stipulated *inter alia* that non-citizens convicted of certain crimes, including aggravated felonies, would be subject to mandatory deportation (*nota bene*, if you're planning a trip, that the term 'aggravated felony' now applies to shoplifting, drunk driving and other relatively minor offences); soon many foreigners in the United States, some of whom had been there for a long time, found themselves being thrown out. For many of the Brits I visited who had been in the USA for a while, the deportation was more daunting than the criminal sentence; but most, once they were in deportation proceedings, wanted their situation resolved quickly so that they could get out of detention and back to Britain to get on with their lives. However, that wasn't always the case.

Richard Walters was born in Wimbledon, London in 1965. His parents had arrived in the UK from Jamaica the year before looking for work, but things hadn't really worked out for them in England so they had moved to New York City in 1976.

They'd settled in the Bronx – a pretty tough place for anyone to grow up, but particularly difficult if there's anything unusual about you. There were two unusual things about Walters: he had an English accent and he wore an eye-patch over his right eye. He needed the patch after an accident as a young child, in which his eye was punctured by glass and became disfigured and useless.

To make matters worse, not long after the Walters family arrived in America, Richard's father deserted his mother and she was left to raise him as a single parent. But he had struggled through and, by the mid 1980s, despite – or perhaps because of – his tough childhood, he had become involved in the emerging New York hip-hop scene. Initially, he was known locally for his work with a guy called Doug E. Fresh, who pioneered the art of making vocal noises that sounded like a beat-box, but in 1988 he became celebrated throughout the United States and elsewhere after the release of his first album entitled *The Great Adventures of Slick Rick*. The record went to No1 on the American R&B/Rap chart, and number 31 on the US Billboard chart. It eventually went platinum, meaning it shifted more than a million units and was considered a seminal hip-hop work; it's still widely available in record stores around the world.

Within a few months, Walters was wealthy. He did not, as he subsequently admitted, deal with this situation well. The man known to his fans as, variously, 'Slick Rick', 'MC Ricky D' or 'The Ruler' began living 'The Life', which included draping himself in jewellery and driving around in expensive cars. Realising that his status and wealth now made him a target, he took the dubious precaution of hiring bodyguards, and carrying firearms himself.

At about this time, one of his cousins, Mark Plummer, arrived from Jamaica, where he was known as violent and habitual criminal.

Walters employed Plummer as a bodyguard, but it quickly became apparent that Plummer was more interested in dealing in drugs than working as a hired hand. Worse, he began demanding more money from Walters and became aggressive when Walters declined to pay. Sensing that the situation was going from bad to worse, Walters tried to pay him off, offering him $3,000 and a van. Plummer was having none of this, and stepped up his campaign of intimidation, threatening Walters' mother and other members of his family.

One day, some men broke into Walters' apartment and tied him up, beat him, pistol whipped him and robbed him, before making off in a hurry. There was no doubt in Walters' mind that Plummer was behind this. It was becoming a nightmare, and it had only just started.

At about 3am one morning in April 1990, Walters was sitting with two friends in his Nissan Pathfinder outside a Bronx nightclub. A group of men approached and shouted, 'We're looking for you!' before opening fire. Twenty shots were fired in all; three of them hit Richard Walters, and his passengers were also shot. Fortunately, although they all required hospital treatment, none of them suffered a life-threatening injury.

Walters had recognised the attackers as being associates of Plummer, and a few days later he confronted his cousin about the shooting.

'Yes, I arranged it,' Plummer told him, 'and I gonna do it again 'less you pay me more money.'

If nothing else, it was audacious.

On the evening of 3 July 1990, Walters was out driving with his girlfriend, Lisa Santiago, who was seven months pregnant with their child, when he spotted Plummer leaving a corner store. He pulled a Davis .380 automatic pistol from his waistband and, as he drove by Plummer, he shot at him. The first two rounds missed their intended target and hit a bystander, Wilbert Henry, an unemployed taxi driver, in the ankle. The next three shots did hit Plummer: two of them in his leg, one in his arm. Plummer fled back into the store, and Walters drove off at speed.

The police were called, and a patrol car soon spotted Walter's car on the Bronx River Parkway. A chase ensued, during which Walters weaved in and out of traffic before trying to exit the highway at high-speed. He failed to make the turn successfully, his car left the road and hit a tree. Both of the pregnant Santiago's legs were broken, and Walters suffered serious lacerations. They were both taken to hospital under arrest.

At trial in 1991, Walters was convicted of assault, use of a firearm, possession of a weapon, and two counts of attempted murder. He was sentenced to between 40 and 120 months in prison, which was an astonishingly light sentence for such a conviction, even in the notably liberal state of New York.

Whilst inside, he settled a civil lawsuit with both Wilbert Henry and Plummer, though Plummer never had a chance to spend the money: in 1992 he broke into an apartment in the Bronx and raped a young boy. The boy's father went looking for Plummer, found him, and shot him in the head, killing him instantly.

After spending two years inside, during which he had an exemplary disciplinary record, Walters was placed on a work release programme. This allowed him to live at home, albeit under curfew, and work. He began to record an album – eventually to be released as *Behind Bars* – for the leading rap record label, Def Jam. He also mentored vulnerable youths about the dangers of crime. He was, he claimed, a changed man.

He was, however, still British – something most people had missed. 'Most people' did not include the US immigration service. By the end of 1993, when Walters had been out of prison for six months on work release, he got a knock on the door. It was a couple of immigration officers, and they served him with a notice of intended deportation. As part of the deportation process, he was required to go back into the New York State prison system until his case was resolved. He immediately retained the services of an immigration attorney, and began to fight the deportation notice.

In 1995, he appeared before federal immigration judge called Alan Vomacka, seeking relief from deportation. The courtroom was packed with fans and supporters, and a petition asking the judge to allow Walters to stay in the United States was signed by almost 6,000 people, including Def Jam founder Russell Simmons. Several people appeared in person to give testimony on Walters' behalf, including New York State Senator David Paterson and Wilbert Henry, the man Walters had shot by accident five years before. After praising Walters' character, Henry crossed the courtroom floor and tearfully hugged him, crying out 'I forgive you! I forgive you!' Walters himself then broke down.

Judge Vomacka was evidently persuaded by the case, and granted Walters relief from deportation. The US immigration service immediately appealed the decision, accusing the judge of 'abusing his discretion', but the Board of Immigration Appeals ruled that he could stay. There followed a further appeal by the immigration service on a legal technicality, and this time the decision went against Walters.

Walters finished his prison sentence and was paroled as his lawyers continued with further attempts to appeal the deportation order.

For the next few years, he lived quietly at home in the Bronx with his new wife, Mandy Aragones, and their child. He spent most of his time looking after the two apartment buildings he had bought in his neighbourhood, and was renting out. He made the occasional public appearance and did a little community work with troubled youngsters.

On 11 September 2001, the attacks on New York and Washington occurred. In the fallout from this tragic day a number of security measures were implemented. One of these was the integration of the computer systems used by the immigration service and the FBI; this was to have a significant effect on Walters.

In the summer of 2002, he took a Caribbean cruise. On the final night, when the ship docked back in Miami, immigration agents boarded the vessel. Walters was arrested in his cabin, in his pyjamas, and told he would not be permitted to re-enter the United States. The customs and immigration personnel at the port had run his name through the computer as a matter of routine, and discovered that he had an outstanding deportation removal order.

He was taken from the port, in handcuffs, to the US immigration service's Krome Detention Center in Miami. After a few days there, he was taken to the immigration service detention centre in Bradenton, Florida.

The first I heard of this case was when pro-consul John Corfield came into my office one day and asked me whether I'd ever heard of a British rap singer called Slick Rick.

'No,' I replied, 'I've no idea who he is.'

'Neither have I,' he said, 'but he was arrested by the US immigration service at Miami a few days ago, and now he's at Bradenton awaiting deportation. We've just had the request for a travel document.'

John and I sat down and read through the paperwork sent to us by the immigration people. Walters didn't seem to have a leg to stand on: he was under a notice of removal, and by taking the cruise to the Caribbean, he had, essentially, deported himself. He seemed to have absolutely no legal right whatsoever to re-enter the United States.

A few days later I took a ride over to Bradenton to meet Richard Walters.

Before I went I purchased the album *The Great Adventures of Slick Rick*. Rap music isn't really my kind of thing – I pretty much only listen to jazz these days – and the album was full of blatant misogyny and foul language. Consequently, I expected to meet a recalcitrant rapper with a haughty attitude and a vocabulary laden with profanities. I couldn't have been more wrong.

Walters was an intelligent and charming man: softly-spoken, articulate and sensitive. I warmed to him quickly, and we spent a long time talking about various things, ranging from his singing career to his family, from his views about the deportation ('terrified') to his feelings about England ('depressingly limited choice of television programmes').

'Look,' I said. 'I'll do everything I can to help you, but I don't think you stand much chance of beating the deportation. I certainly don't know of anyone else in a similar situation who managed to avoid it.'

He nodded thoughtfully. 'I want to stay,' he said. 'I have a good immigration lawyer, and I'm just hopeful that something can be resolved.'

'At least you probably have the money to fund a proper legal challenge, and some influential political contacts. Maybe you'll be able to pull something off.'

'I'm going to try,' he told me. 'But the only thing I'm concerned about is that they deport me before I get an opportunity to appeal my case all the way to the top. Can you stop them sending me back to England?'

'No I can't do that. I might be able to buy you a few days, or a couple of weeks at best, but I've confirmed to them that you're a British citizen and if they have a removal order from the judge I have to cooperate with them. I'm sure you can appreciate my position on that.'

'I understand,' he said.

I wished him luck, but when I left him that day neither of us had any idea what would happen next. I warned him that he could be in the detention centre for months or even years. Either way, he seemed prepared.

Within a few weeks, the federal immigration judge in Bradenton ordered him to be deported, a judgment which was quickly appealed by Walters' attorney, Alex Solomiany, who argued that because the federal courts in New York had been dealing with the case before Walters went on the cruise, the decision should be made there.

Solomiany's tactics were these: the 11th federal circuit, which covers Florida, Alabama and Georgia, is a conservative region, whose judges were far more likely to side with the government than the traditionally more liberal 2nd federal circuit in New York. Justice shouldn't really work that way, but I suppose that's what comes of having politically-appointed judges. Solomiany managed to get a stay of deportation whilst this argument was being prepared and presented.

I went to the Bradenton deportation centre every few weeks on average, as there was a regular turnover of British nationals there. (While more Mexicans are deported from the USA than any other nationality – unsurprising given Mexico's proximity, and the disparity in wealth between the two countries – Britons are the eighth most-deported nationality.) Most of the immigration detainees in Bradenton are held in large cells, containing dozens of inmates. As you walk past the cells to the interview room, hundreds of detainees, mostly speaking little or no English, scream at you to help them. Because you're in a suit, they think you're either a senior immigration official or a lawyer, and they want you to save them from deportation. It is hard to ignore them – it seems inhumane – but there's nothing you can do, so you try to pretend they're not there.

Each time I visited Bradenton, I spent a while with Walters, trying to help keep his spirits up.

After about six months, the 11th district handed down a decision in the case permitting the immigration service to deport Walters. He was actually taken to Orlando airport and was about to be put on board the plane when a judge in the 2nd district allowed a petition delaying the removal. Walters was driven back to Bradenton that night. It was his closest call yet.

Around that time, I had a heart-to-heart with Walters, whom I'd grown to like.

'You're wasting your life sitting in jail waiting for this to be resolved,' I said. 'I hate to see that, especially when I don't think you have any realistic chance of avoiding deportation. I think it's only a matter of time. Living in England wouldn't be so bad and it has to be better than four walls in Bradenton.'

In his position, knowing he could be stuck in Bradenton for years, I'd have thrown in the towel and gone back to London as soon as possible, perhaps to fight again another day. (Although if I were from Afghanistan I have to admit that I might not feel the same way about going back to Kabul.) But he saw it differently.

'I'm grateful to you, Hugh,' he said. 'But I'm not ready to give up this fight. I feel as if I'm an American. I've lived in New York nearly my whole life that I can remember. It's my home. I ain't about to leave unless they drag me out.'

'Well, I admire your resolve,' I said. 'It's up to you, but if you ever change your mind you know where I am. I can get you on your way back to London within a few days if you want to go.'

Eventually, in 2003, a federal judge in the 2nd judicial circuit found against the immigration service. Judge Wood ruled that they had acted unlawfully in seeking to overturn the order of relief from deportation granted to Walters by the Board of Immigration Appeals back in 1995. Because that error pre-dated the current action, it took precedence. (Incidentally, that judge was Kimba Wood, who was nominated by President Clinton for the position of US Attorney General but failed to get confirmed in that post when it was revealed that she had hired an illegal immigrant as a nanny.)

In 2003, on the day after her ruling, Walters was released from Bradenton, just like that, and told he was free to travel back home to the Bronx. It was a startling development, and although I was pleased for him that he was free again, I was surprised when I heard about it. I certainly didn't think it would end there, and I was right. The immigration service immediately appealed Judge Wood's decision, and eventually found another judge in New York prepared to rule in the Government's favour. The case was remitted back to the 11th judicial circuit on the grounds that Walters was arrested there when he sought to re-enter the United States after his cruise. It was beginning to look as if it could go on indefinitely.

On Friday 23rd May 2008, though, this case took an unexpected and dramatic turn.

Governor Paterson of New York, who had only been in office for two months, pardoned Richard Walters. The governors of all the States of America have it within their gift to pardon any convicted criminal, for any or no reason at all. The American president has a similar power.

This meant, effectively if not actually, that the original crime – for which he had been facing deportation – had never happened. The federal government now had no basis upon which to remove Walters from the United States. That meant – 18 years after he had tried to kill his cousin – he had finally won his fight to remain in America. Provided he is never again convicted of a criminal offence, he will likely be able to live in the USA for the rest of his life.

12

IF YOU'RE an international coke dealer, how do you get your 'product' from the jungles of Colombia to the streets of British cities?

First, you find your 'mule' – a swallower or stuffer (more on these in a moment) – who is prepared to secrete your drugs about his or her person and carry them across the Atlantic for you.

Of course, if you send them direct to Heathrow from Bogotá, that makes it rather too easy for the customs officers: passengers on flights from known hotspots are scrutinised carefully on arrival in London, and anyone who has been anywhere near Bogotá is getting the third degree.

To avoid this, you speedboat the cocaine to a nice tourist destination – Jamaica is a favourite – and have your intermediary collect them *there*, in the hope that he will end up getting lost among the general holidaymakers.

But then, because the Caribbean islands also have something of a reputation for drugs, you might prefer to have your mule break his journey somewhere – like, say, Miami, Fort Lauderdale or Orlando. You'll probably have them fly on separate tickets: one from Kingston to Orlando, say, and a different one for the Orlando to Gatwick leg, in an attempt to disguise the fact they ever even visited Jamaica.

The major problem with all of this is that your mule will be required to clear US Customs, laden with drugs, on his return journey.

Undeterred, many people try to do exactly that, and often they get caught.

And that's where I come in.

Most British people in prisons around the world are there because they have committed drugs offences – either the possession, distribution or trafficking thereof. The Orlando consulate is a bit of an exception to this rule but it still deals with a significant number of people facing drugs charges.

So: swallowers and stuffers.

Swallowers place small amounts of drugs into large numbers of condoms – dozens, to make it economically viable – and swallow them. They follow this up with anti-diahorreal medication to produce constipation for a period of about 48 hours. Once safely at their destination, they're taken to a safe house and given an abundance of laxatives until they have expelled their cargo. They're running more than just the risk of jail time, by the way: if even only one of these small packages breaks open inside the carrier it can prove fatal.

Stuffers – as the name suggests – insert small packages of drugs into their bodily orifices. There's much less chance of a medical emergency when drugs are carried this way, but there's the disadvantage of a limited capacity. Additionally, drugs hidden in an orifice can be quickly detected by an invasive search by a customs officer wearing rubber gloves.

Both stuffers and swallowers can be detected by x-ray machines, and their body odour often attracts the interest of sniffer dogs.

I dealt with hundreds of British nationals arrested for carrying drugs through Florida. Their profiles were almost always the same: they'd be between 18 and 25 years old, from an urban council estate, uneducated and unemployed.

Usually they would be carrying just less than 2.4kgs of cocaine. The reason for this is simple: under US federal sentencing guidelines, the maximum sentence for carrying more than 2.4kgs is significantly higher than for anything less than that. (In my experience, if someone was carrying 2.4kgs or less, they would probably get away with three to four years in prison. Anything over that would push the minimum sentence up to around seven years.)

The most surprising thing was how little they earned – especially in view of the medical dangers and the risk of jail time they were running. I don't think any that I interviewed was earning more than a thousand pounds. I understand that a grand-in-the-hand is not insignificant if you're on income support, but you can earn far more by taking a minimum-wage job for a few weeks, without the threat of prison or death hanging over you.

Not only does such behaviour transgress the laws of economics, though; it frequently offends the basic tenets of humanity. The following case is a good example.

Sharnell Sharman, a heavily pregnant British woman in her early 20s, was travelling from Jamaica to London via Miami. She was with her cousin, a woman two years her junior. Something about them must have seemed wrong to the US customs officials at the airport, because they took both girls aside and x-rayed them during their transit. The x-rays showed that both had swallowed significant quantities of cocaine. Sharman must have thought that nobody would suspect that an obviously pregnant woman would swallow an enormous quantity of a lethal drug and put her child in danger. Ironically, her plan was predicated on the idea that the customs officers would not imagine that anybody could be as callous as she was, in fact, being. Unfortunately for her, customs officials around the world have seen it all before, and worse.

Both women were immediately taken under armed guard to a hospital. The standard procedure in the USA is for the doctors to administer laxatives, but if the drugs are not expelled within a few hours of arrest the medical team prefers to operate and remove them, rather than risk a fatal overdose. Sharnell Sharman was far along enough in her pregnancy that the doctors had to perform a Caesarean section at the same time as they removed the drugs.

We followed this closely in the consulate, of course – not least because we knew we would soon have a baby to deal with. Luckily, the birth went well and there were no complications, but there was a degree of resentment in the office – especially from the women – that Sharman had endangered her unborn son by such a selfish and reckless adventure. I was surprised to learn at this time that over 75% of women in American jails are single mothers.

Months later, Sharman and her cousin pleaded guilty as charged and were sentenced to 48 months' imprisonment. By that time Sharnell's new baby son was already long gone; within hours of its birth, Sharman's mother had taken custody of him and taken him back to London. She raised the little boy for the next four years, whilst her daughter was serving time in Florida. The poor woman was already raising another young grandchild as a second daughter was in jail in England.

Once Sharman had been sentenced, I went to visit her in prison.

'How're you feeling?' I asked, as a polite opening question.

'Don't be a fucking div,' she snarled. 'How do you think I'm feeling?'

'I don't know, that's why I'm asking,' I replied.

'I'm well pissed off, is how I'm feeling.'

'Why's that?' I asked, trying to ignore her rudeness.

'I wanted a natural birth for my son, and these bastards have given me a scar right across my stomach. I'll have to live with that for the rest of my life.'

'I don't think they had much choice about that,' I said, feeling my own temper rising.

'Whose side are you on? I pay my taxes so that you can come here and take care of my rights,' she said.

I doubt she had paid much in the way of taxes during her brief years of adulthood, nor would she ever be likely to, but she seemed depressingly well-rehearsed in demanding her civil rights, and not much inclined to accepting any personal responsibility. For the next 30 minutes she complained about everything she could think of, from the food in the prison to the long sentence she'd received, and I had to sit there and listen to the whole thing. It wears you down, this kind of thing, but you're paid to be there so you listen and you learn what you can.

* * * * *

It's not just swallowing condoms and inserting packages into your darkest recesses: people try all sorts of other enterprising methods to smuggle drugs, and are sometimes so creative that I often think that if only they applied their talents to legitimate industry they'd be roaring successes.

One British woman of Afro-Caribbean descent arrived at Miami airport with the most magnificent beehive hairdo – it stood fully 18 inches tall, and amazed the customs officers, who had never seen anything so grand in their lives. They took a closer look and discovered that a bag of cocaine was glued deep within the plumage.

She remained adamant that she had no idea how it had got there, and would be having strong words with her hairdresser the next time she saw him; unfortunately, that wouldn't be for at least another three years.

Rhona Herbert was a striking young blonde from Glasgow who tried to foil the sniffer-dogs by packing half a kilo of coke inside a large, raw halibut carried in her luggage. This is a surprisingly common strategy, and one which never, ever works – while it may disguise the smell of the drugs, the odour of rotting fish drives the dogs crazier still. Herbert landed at Orlando airport on a flight from Jamaica, and was immediately pulled aside and taken to a small interview room, where she was shown her unopened suitcase.

'Is this your case, ma'am?' she was asked.

She made a great show of checking the name and address in the plastic window on the case and then confirmed that it was.

'Did you pack it yourself?'

'No,' she said, 'it was packed by a fishmonger near my hotel in Montego Bay.'

The investigators raised their eyebrows at this slightly unlikely tale, so she expanded. 'I met him a few days ago and he told me he was very good at packing suitcases,' she said. 'I had loads of stuff to take back to Britain so when he offered to help I let him.'

Er, right. They opened the case and found the coke-stuffed halibut, itself wrapped in an unwashed pair of Marks & Spencer's knickers.

As they were putting the handcuffs on, she was cautioned and asked if she had anything to say. In her report, it said she thanked the officers for finding the drugs, as otherwise she would have just thrown the fish onto the barbecue when she got home.

Another Briton, Tommy Bannister, took the fish tactic to the extreme. He lived in Jamaica, and owned and operated a fishing boat out of Kingston. From there, he exported his catch around the Caribbean and North America.

That wasn't all he exported, and he came to grief near Fort Lauderdale. He'd travelled there to meet a consignment of fish that he was exporting to the US. It had been unloaded off his boat into a refrigerated lorry and was *en route* to its destination when US Customs Service personnel intercepted it. It turned out they had been watching Bannister's boat since it had entered American waters, and on the night before it had docked they had secretly boarded the vessel and established that it was carrying cocaine – 200kgs of the stuff.

They arrested three people in the lorry and two others, including Bannister, in a car that was following. They were charged with trafficking and, given the amounts involved, Bannister was facing a lifetime in jail.

I went to see him a few days after his arrest, and he protested his innocence to me. I told him it didn't matter either way to me, but that he'd better have an extremely good explanation for the judge or he wasn't going to be seeing either the Caribbean or the UK ever again.

For a while, he continued to protest his innocence, claiming that as far as he knew this had been just another delivery of fish, but that defence gave him two hopes with a jury, and Bob Hope had just left town. So he made a deal with the federal authorities: although he claimed to be clean, he knew a number of people back in Jamaica who were involved in trafficking drugs into the States. He would give the DEA names, numbers, addresses and other inside information that would help them secure convictions.

The Americans went for that deal and he got off with five years – a very light sentence indeed. He had to give evidence in court against those he had named, though, so he became a marked man. His wife and two children had to flee Jamaica immediately, and he joined them in the UK when he had served his time. To this day, there are some extremely unpleasant men looking for him: I hope for his sake he's never found.

I was never convinced by Tommy Bannister's protestations of innocence, but I dealt with quite a few people who probably weren't guilty – or were at worst naive about the company they kept.

One Friday morning I took a call about a girl of 18 called Leona Murray who had been arrested at Miami airport for smuggling cocaine.

I went to see her at the Federal Detention Centre in Miami later that day. She was a young slip of a thing and probably the most hysterical person I ever interviewed in person as a consular officer. She was alternately screaming, crying and hyperventilating – at one point I was concerned that she might lose consciousness – and was only able to tell me her story through a waterfall of tears and with convulsive breaths.

Leona was from London, and she had many school friends with family connections in Jamaica. She had been invited to visit the island by one of these friends, who had offered to pay for her air ticket and provide her with a hotel room for the duration of her stay. On the last night she was there, she had been entertaining some people in her hotel room when one of them 'accidentally' sat on her suitcase, breaking it irreparably. 'Don't worry,' he'd told her, apologising profusely. 'I'll get you a new one.'

The next day he arrived with a new suitcase – problem solved and no charge.

Like I say, naive.

She packed her things and flew off to London via Miami that evening. At Miami airport the customs officials examined the case and found a false panel hiding a compartment containing 6kgs of cocaine.

Several times while I was with Leona she got up and ran out of the interview room, slamming the door closed behind her, only to come flying back in again seconds later crying that she wanted to go home. My attempts to calm her down were futile, and eventually the guards came and escorted her back to her cell.

One of the things I *was* able to do for her was find her a good lawyer, paid for by her distraught parents. Miami-based attorney Sydney Smith was a Londoner who had moved to Florida many years before and who now specialised in criminal defence. He could be an abrasive character who sometimes unsettled even his own clients with his direct and perfunctory manner. He wasn't the right lawyer for everyone, but he was known for one thing: if he believed in his client, he would fight hard for them.

About three months later this case went to trial.

Smith had recommended to Leona that she turn down the deal the prosecution was offering – six years in jail if she pleaded guilty. This was not a bad deal for six kilos, and I doubt there were many attorneys in Florida who would have gone to trial – if convicted, she was looking at 15 years in a federal prison. But Smith had testicles of titanium. The trial lasted several days, and at the conclusion Leona Murray was acquitted – I'm pretty sure that, during my tenure in Orlando, this was the only drugs case in Florida involving a British citizen that went to trial and ended in an acquittal.

She was released from prison that day and flew home to London the next night. I never saw her again, and she never contacted the consulate after her return to the UK. I suspect that her family never made a better investment in their lives than Smith's legal fees.

Peter Walsh was slightly less innocent, but he was certainly naive. He was a young guy from Blackpool who was also found with drugs concealed in his suitcase. He was happy to put his hands up to the 2kgs of marijuana, which was wrapped up in his clothing; what he wasn't happy about was the further 1.4kgs of coke that was stuffed inside the handles.

When I went to see him he was furious.

'Listen, man,' he said, 'I've been stitched up here. Yes, I knew I was smuggling drugs, but I was told that I was bringing back a couple of keys of dope. Fair enough. When I was stopped I knew I'd get caught for that, and I was expecting six months. I didn't know they'd put that coke in the handle as well, I swear.'

When I left him, he was talking about helping the authorities to track down the people who had double-crossed him in order to lessen his sentence. But when push came to shove he was unable to remember their names. Maybe he didn't know them – nicknames are common in such circles for obvious reasons – but I suspect he'd realised discretion was the better part of valour; if he had helped with the arrest of his contacts, he might well have come to a sticky end. In the end he took his three-year sentence, and phoned me at least twice a week to complain about it the whole time he was there.

One of my favourite stories concerned another London man, Terry Shaw. Someone in the East End had offered Terry a free cruise from Miami to the Caribbean islands plus a thousand pounds in spending money if he would just collect a package onshore at Antigua and bring it back to America. This package turned out to be a hand grenade-sized chunk of cocaine packed in bubble wrap, which he simply took back on board the liner as casually as if it was a souvenir woodcarving.

Terry was in his late 30s and should have known better, but he was pretty unworldly. He hadn't realised that on arrival back in Miami he would need to pass back through customs to get back into America – he'd imagined that because the cruise had started there he'd simply be able to disembark and drop off his delivery before blowing his loot in an establishment of dubious repute.

When the ship arrived back in Miami, he started to walk down the disembarkment gangplank and suddenly realised to his horror that there were a dozen customs officers waiting at the bottom, searching people's bags. He panicked and froze, forcing all the people coming down the gangplank behind him to come to a sudden halt. By doing this he drew attention to himself. Then, in full view of everyone – all the customs officers, the ship's crew, the dockside workers and the other passengers – he reached into his bag, took out the brick of cocaine and tossed it over the side into the sea. Everyone watched it fall down the gap between the ship and the berth straight into the water. To the delight of the customs officials, and thanks to the bubble wrap, it floated!

Result: four years in prison, and a fine of $800.

There are many more tales like this, but I'll finish with Scott Benson.

I once needed to visit 15 British inmates at the Federal Detention Center in Miami, and I decided to see them all in one day. Just getting inside the prison could easily take an hour, so you didn't even want to leave for lunch, let alone spread it all out over two days. I started before 9am, and I just saw one person after another after another – each time going over the same information and recording details of their situation and taking instructions from them about what they wanted me to do on their behalf.

I broke for 15 minutes at 1pm to get a sandwich and a can of apple juice from the vending machine – hardly the protracted, champagne lunches you might imagine diplomats enjoy – and by mid-afternoon my head was spinning and I was starting to get a pain in my neck. I vowed not to see so many prisoners in one day again.

Around 4pm, a new prisoner came into the room, and as I was looking for his case notes, he said, quite cheerfully, 'Hey, Hugh. How you doing, dude?'

'Have we met before?' I said.

He went on to explain that he had been arrested for dealing in cocaine in Fort Lauderdale five years earlier, and had subsequently been deported. I had visited him then and assisted him during the deportation process. He'd been born in England to British parents, but the family had emigrated to the USA before he had reached his first birthday, so he had grown up in America and never really considered himself to be anything other than an American. All his friends and family were in Florida and he knew nobody back in England, but after deportation he'd gone to Luton to live with a distant cousin.

'I got kinda bored there,' he said.

'That's entirely understandable,' I said. 'Luton is boring.'

'So, after a few months I left England and travelled to Mexico,' he said, 'and my girlfriend drove down from Fort Lauderdale to meet me. So we lived in Mexico for a few months before her money ran out and then we just drove to the border and I told them I was an American, I'd been to Mexico for the day and I'd lost my driver's licence.'

You can exit and enter the USA via this border using only this form of ID, and with his strong American accent and knowledge of American life, he was easily able to persuade the immigration official to allow him in. What a fantastic stroke of luck!

But he couldn't help himself. Within weeks of moving back to live with his girlfriend, this Bohemian Tartar started dealing cocaine again. He was arrested and prosecuted by the state of Florida for the dealing offence and after he had served his sentence for that, he was passed into federal custody to face the charge of illegal re-entry to the USA. He faced quite a long prison sentence for that, but he cut a deal with the federal prosecutors whereby he gave evidence against drug dealers in Southern Florida for a reduction in his own sentence.

'So what are your plans after deportation?' I said.

'Well, I guess I'll go back to Britain and stay there and try and make a go of it,' he said.

'Do you think you'll like it any better this time?'

'I don't have much choice,' he said. 'If I ever come back to Florida, the motherfuckers I testified against will saw my head off, impale it on a flagpole and parade it through Miami.'

Fair enough.

13

WILLIAM MCCORKLE WAS the infomercial king, and Chantal was his queen.

They seemed the embodiment of the American dream: both were under 30, and they were attractive, glamorous and wealthy. They lived in a huge Orlando mansion, had a fleet of luxury cars and had money to burn.

That money had come from infomercials – TV ads that usually run for half an hour and are vaguely disguised as a regular programme. They offer anything from jewellery to medical services and everything in between, and William McCorkle's speciality was selling video packages, books and personal tuition, which purported to show you how to buy repossessed real estate and sell it for a handsome profit.

He himself claimed to have made a significant fortune using these techniques. He certainly worked hard to give that impression. During one infomercial he alighted from a private jet, which bore the name 'McCorkle' on the side, and later in the programme he was seen sitting on the prow of a luxury yacht, which bore the name of his beautiful young wife, Chantal.

At the lower end, McCorkle charged $69 for his 'Fortunes in Foreclosures' package, basically a booklet and a video. The 'Whole Enchilada'– a weekend's intensive tuition, along with videos, literature and the US government's own auction package – cost around $4,000.

He guaranteed you would make money from following his methods, offered to underwrite financing for clients with poor credit rating and promised you your money back if you were unhappy with the product. The company sold many thousands of these packages.

One thing William McCorkle omitted to mention in his infomercial was that he was a registered bankrupt who had been barred by the US authorities from operating any company. Undaunted by this minor inconvenience, William simply had the company registered in his wife's name.

The US Internal Revenue Service (IRS) and the FBI had been watching the infomercial industry for some time, and were wary of the sharp practices employed by some of the main players. They decided to have a closer look at McCorkle's operation, and it didn't take them long to find interesting things.

Whilst you could, ostensibly, use the McCorkle technique to buy and sell property for profit, there were some fundamental problems with his claims. Firstly, he had personally made absolutely no money whatsoever from buying and selling property. The aircraft in the infomercial had been leased for the day, and his name temporarily sprayed on the side in removable paint. It was returned, clean, to the owner later that afternoon without having so much as having taxied to the runway. Much the same thing happened with the multi-million pound yacht. The 'satisfied customers' interviewed by William and Chantal during the infomercial were paid actors reading from a script. The chances of ordinary people – his customers, in other words – getting finance to buy repossessed properties was almost zero, and the promise of underwriting by McCorkle himself was an empty one. The investigation also discovered many disillusioned customers, often poor and elderly, who had requested a refund and been stalled for months. In fact, the investigators were unable to locate a single person who'd actually received one.

Significant irregularities were also found in the company accounts.

In May 1997, a team of armed federal agents from the IRS, the FBI and other agencies searched the McCorkles' magnificent house in Orlando. As they were led away in handcuffs, past the luxury cars parked in the driveway, television reporters were there to record the couple's embarrassment. They were taken to the federal court in Orlando and arraigned on charges of money laundering, mail fraud and tax evasion. Bail, which was set at $300,000 each, was paid within hours.

Over the following months, as the government was preparing its case, the couple continued to run their business much as before. However, they also squirreled money – seven million dollars of it – out of company bank accounts to personal accounts in the Cayman Islands.

When the US authorities discovered this money was missing, they tried to get it back. After the Cayman Islands authorities refused to co-operate, the prosecutors convened a court hearing in Orlando to discuss the terms of the bail. They explained to the judge that, by having such a large amount of money secreted away in overseas accounts, the McCorkles were a high flight risk. They asked the judge to raise the bail amount to three million dollars each. The judge agreed to this request, so, in order to retain their pre-trial liberty, the McCorkles paid the money from their Cayman Islands account a few hours later.

The case finally came to trial many months later at the federal courthouse in Orlando. The prosecution offered up evidence in 129 specimen charges of obtaining money by deception, alleging that the customers had been deceived by the infomercials, and an equal number of charges of money laundering.

As the McCorkles and their attorneys left the federal courthouse after the first day of the trial, a throng of press and television reporters accosted them on the steps. They were asked many questions, most of which were answered by the indomitable William, whilst his lawyer basked in the attention. At one point, though, a TV reporter turned to Chantal McCorkle and asked her if she had anything to say.

She gave a short, one-sentence answer denying their culpability in any crime: it was all a big misunderstanding, and she was certain they would be acquitted.

It was big news locally, and the report, featuring her comment, was run and re-run on the news throughout that evening. Although I didn't see it, pro-consul John Corfield did.

'Did you see that couple in the big fraud case, the McCorkles, on TV last night?' he said, sipping from a morning cup of coffee. 'The wife was asked a question and I don't know but I'd swear she was English.'

I sat up immediately. This might turn what was previously just an everyday story of enormous greed, colossal hubris and media millions into something of more direct interest to us.

I looked into her background and it turned out John was right; as was so often the way, the US authorities had failed to inform us of her arrest – even though they were required to do so by treaty law.

Chantal McCorkle (*nee* Watts) had been born in Taplow, Buckinghamshire, and grown up there in a typical, loving English family. At 19, she had travelled to the USA to work as a nanny for an American couple who were family friends. In Florida she met William and was bowled over by his charm and energy; she was a very attractive young woman and it's not hard to see why he fell for her. They married shortly afterwards – she had only just turned 21 – but she had never become an American citizen.

She was free on bail, so we just kept a watching brief. The trial was long – it lasted for a couple of months – but the press coverage was comprehensive and it made headline news on the local TV station's bulletins every evening, so I was able to follow the developments closely. I didn't attend until the last day.

From the media coverage, it seemed to me from the start that the McCorkles were in trouble. Just before the jury returned with its verdict, a contact of mine from a local newspaper called me at the consulate to let me know the court was being reconvened and I headed over to Orlando's federal courthouse to be there.

I took a seat in the public gallery, surrounded by friends and family of the accused and also people who had lost money on their scheme.

The verdict: guilty on all counts.

Immediately, an incredible commotion erupted. Journalists and TV crews all dashed for the exit to file their reports as sobbing and shouting and cheering broke out all around me. The bailiffs and the judge demanded order and William McCorkle passed out – he was taken from the court to a hospital on a stretcher.

Eventually, calm was restored and the judge ordered the defendants to return to court for sentencing a few weeks later. Again, I was there; this time, the place was packed to the rafters with no spare seats in the public gallery and people standing around the walls and sitting on the floor.

I collared the court bailiff, showing him my consular identification.

'I was hoping to observe the sentencing,' I said. 'I don't suppose…?'

He led me smartly around the throng of people and through a little wicket gate into the front few rows of the court, which was like a kind of private area. There was a long bench seat, and only one person was sitting on it, a sharply-dressed middle-aged man who I quickly realised was the federal district attorney himself.

I introduced myself by name, and said I was there to observe the sentencing. Throughout the morning's proceedings, he gave me a whispered running commentary, throwing in plenty of comments and opinions for good measure; for a couple of hours he was like my new best friend. At one point, the lead prosecution counsel was searching for some papers whilst making a submission to the court. He wasn't having much luck finding what he was looking for whilst continuing to talk, but his colleague sitting next to him, the female federal prosecutor, made no attempt to help him. 'Pay attention you dumb bitch,' hissed the DA. 'You're part of a team, give him some help.' He was totally absorbed in the proceedings, like the manager of a football team playing in the FA Cup final.

Two co-defendants of the McCorkles, both other senior figures in their venture, were sentenced first. One, Brian Higgins, read a statement from the dock. He said that he had joined the company at a time of enormous growth, and it seemed like a wonderful opportunity for him.

'I was a young man with a new family, and this job appeared to offer me great prospects. I quickly came to realise that things were not what they should have been. William McCorkle was asking me to do things that were not ethical. I should have left, but I was making so much money that I found every reason I could to stay.'

He described what it was like working at the company during the peak of its operation by saying that trucks full of applications for the packages would arrive every few hours. Each envelope contained a cheque. It sounded surreal.

'During my time with the company, William McCorkle has never once spoken a civil word to me. He is a cold and detached man, fixated on wealth and appearances.'

He then came to the hardest part of his speech, and he began to cry as he delivered it. 'I did wrong,' he said. 'I know that now, and I knew it then. I became utterly greedy, and my greed deprived many poor and elderly people of their money. I will never forgive myself. I understand that I will be punished, and I will take my punishment. What is harder to bear than anything else is the fact that I have let down my family – my parents, my wife and children.'

At this point he lost his self-composure completely, and two court officials rushed forward to assist him as he became unsteady on his feet. Just across the courtroom were the man's parents and his wife. I could not help but be moved by their evident pain. Beside me sat the district attorney, impassive.

Higgins was sentenced to the minimum sentence permitted under the guidelines: 60 months in a federal prison. He was told to go home and get his papers and clothes in order, and to report to his designated prison in one month.

After a rather less dramatic presentation, Herman Venske was also sentenced to 60 months.

Now for the ringleaders.

The lead prosecutor spoke first, only to say that the government sought a sentence at the lowest point of the sentencing guidelines.

Both the McCorkles' attorneys made representations about their clients, though William's lawyer seemed to me to be taking the wrong tack: instead of mitigation, he droned on about his client's innocence, and how the court had erred in its findings. This line of argument didn't go down very well with the judge.

Chantal's lawyer tried to paint her as a minor player in the operation, suggesting to the court that her charismatic but scheming husband had manipulated her. At this suggestion, the DA next to me started to hyperventilate. 'That little bitch is the brains in that outfit,' he said, *sotto voce*. 'William McCorkle couldn't scratch his ass without her!'

The McCorkles sat impassively throughout, making little eye contact and seeming somehow detached from the events, as if they were casual spectators at someone else's hearing. Finally, they were asked if they wanted to say anything. Neither did – Chantal looked directly ahead and appeared to be in shock.

After the mitigation, the judge sat for a long time consulting legal books and making notes. Eventually, she looked up and began speaking to the couple. She told them they had instigated a scheme of great cunning and greed, targeting many vulnerable people. She found them to be equally culpable, and had seen no real signs of remorse from either. The sums involved were large – tens of millions of dollars from many thousands of often unidentifiable victims. The sentencing guidelines for crimes of such magnitude were onerous, she said, and she had no discretion to sentence outside those indicated terms: she was required to award them each a term of incarceration of between 24.3 years and 30.4 years.

'This case is troubling,' she remarked. 'The defendants are young. They have no prior record. This is a very stiff sentence and it gives me great pause. But my duty is clear.'

She passed the minimum permitted sentence of 292 months each: with the maximum possible reduction for good behaviour of 15 percent, they would still have to do 20 years in prison. They would both be over 50 before they saw the streets again.

What they had done was wrong, but I felt these were harsh sentences. Compare it with rogue trader Nick Leeson, who defrauded the stockholders of Barings Bank out of $817 million: he got six years in Singapore, and served three.

The US Marshals led the prisoners from the dock in handcuffs. As they reached the door of the courtroom, family members and friends of the couple surged forward mobbing them and shouting words of love and encouragement. Once again the scrum of photographers and camera crews were pushing and shoving for a good view, and the bailiffs were trying to keep order.

I was one of the last to leave the courtroom. As I walked back to the consulate I reflected on the prospect of 20 years in jail. I did not think that I would be able to face it. I stopped off in a diner on the way back and sat down with a coffee. It was cool winter's day, and there was a heater on in the corner. I could smell the coffee pot and the bacon on the griddle. At one point, someone walked in and a breeze came in and blew across my face. It felt so beautiful. I did not think that all the riches the McCorkles had aspired to would have made them any happier or more content than I felt at that moment, knowing that I was at liberty to go wherever I wanted, at any time I wished with whomever I chose. It does you good every now and then to remind yourself what it means to be free.

* * * * *

I first visited Chantal McCorkle at the Lake County Jail in Tavares a few days later. She was being held there before being transferred to the federal prison in Tallahassee, Florida. I made the mistake of going during general visiting hours and the lobby area of the jail was teeming with family members and friends of the inmates. The atmosphere was high on volume and low on manners: everybody was pushing and jostling to get to the head of the queue, and at the front, controlling access to the facility, was a solitary guard. I was the only one there in a suit and tie, and the guard beckoned me forward. I gently pushed my way through the throng.

'Are you a lawyer?' He asked me.

'No, I'm the British consul. I'm here to see a British citizen.'

'You're from the British government?'

'Yes,' I replied.

'I was in the US Marine Corps,' he said, 'and I fought with your guys in Iraq. God bless you and God bless your country, sir.'

As soon as he said that, he ushered me away from the masses, through the door and into the jail without further ado.

I mention this incident as it was the only time, during my years in Florida, that anyone in an official capacity, other than a politician, made a point of praising the United Kingdom to me or treated me with special respect on account of my nationality. This ground level experience didn't square with the constant talk I heard whenever I was in our embassy in Washington, where British diplomats would bang on about our 'special relationship' with the Americans, about how at senior levels we had unique access to the US State Department and knew before anyone else what the Americans were thinking. I always wondered if they knew what it was like for the rest of us; as any ordinary Briton knows – and I count even those who, like me, love America and the Americans – there is nothing very special about our relationship at all.

It was, as I mentioned, the first time I'd met Chantal and she was, as one would expect, deeply distraught. We talked for while about her family in England, her life in America and her desire to have a family.

'I'll be too old to have children by the time I'm out of here,' she said, tears in her eyes, and it was hard not to feel some compassion for her.

She was bitter about her husband, whom she blamed for her predicament.

'I can't believe we turned down the deal,' she said.

'What deal?' I asked.

'During the build-up to the trial, the prosecution approached us and said if we pleaded guilty to some specimen charges, and forfeited all our assets, they would go for a maximum of 18 months in jail for each of us. We discussed this with Lee Bailey' – a charismatic, well-known but bullish US attorney – 'but he advised us against accepting the deal. He said what we were doing was normal business practice, and that he could get us acquitted, plus if we did accept he would withdraw as our counsel.'

On the basis of this terrible advice, the McCorkles proceeded to trial, and ruin.

Before I left Chantal that day, I told her something about the international prisoner transfer agreement between the USA and the UK, which would permit her to apply for a transfer to a British prison to complete her sentence.

'You will need to complete your appeals process and be free of any other legal obligations in the US before you can apply,' I said.

She knew this would take some time and that there was no guarantee of success, but the possibility – however distant – of returning to the UK raised her spirits a little.

Her case soon turned into a *cause célèbre* in Britain. She was featured in many British magazines and newspapers, and her family, friends and supporters also started a website to publicise her situation. Chantal's mother was unsurprisingly distraught, and regularly flew to the US to visit her daughter and work on the case. Several times she visited me for discussions, but she never seemed fully satisfied with the limited assistance I could offer. She seemed angry that the British Government was unable to instruct the US federal authorities to release her daughter. Her frustrations were occasionally vented on me. All I could do was sit and take it.

In 2002, the McCorkles appealed their convictions and sentences before the federal 11th Circuit Court of Appeals in Atlanta.

In terms of the convictions, they alleged that there had been juror misconduct and outside influence on the jury. Specifically they said that one of the jurors had a personal animus against the McCorkles, which made him biased, and that a court bailiff had also told the chairman of the jury that they would have no trouble convicting the pair 'if they knew what he knew'.

The court was having none of this and dismissed that part of the appeal.

They were more successful with the sentence: the appellate court confirmed that the trial judge had erred in sentencing, and remitted the case back to the federal court in Orlando where the jail terms were reduced to 18 years apiece. This was still tough, but better than 24 years.

Chantal spent five years imprisoned in Florida before she was transferred to a federal prison in California. During that period, I visited her at least once or twice a year. I always enjoyed talking to her, and I hope that my visits were able to lift her spirits a little.

Over time, however, I sensed her becoming defeated. The failure of her appeal was a crushing blow, and her resilience started to break afterwards; her aspirations changed.

Our conversations were always easy and flowing; in fact, they were almost intimate. We were almost the same age, we'd both grown up in south-east England, and we shared many cultural references. We laughed at the same kinds of things, and had been to many of the same pubs and restaurants in London. Her family came as often as the cost and distances allowed, but other than that I was the only person from the outside – more importantly, from home – that she saw. Over time, as her trust and affection for me grew, she shared more, and we laughed more; not something I suspect she did much over the course of an average day.

During my flight home from what was – although I didn't know it at the time – my last visit with her, I reflected on the changes I had seen in her during the five years I had known her. From a physical point of view, the dyed blonde hair she had so glamorously worn at her sentencing had long since disappeared and had been replaced with her natural dark brown colouring. Her face, so alive and vivacious during the television infomercials, was now lined with anxiety and destitution. Her strong, athletic body – she had been a triathlete – was now looking weaker, and her shoulders were a little slumped. Yet she was still attractive, with something of an ethereal quality about her. Years of imprisonment would take their toll on anyone, and Chantal showed all the physical, mental and emotional signs of being institutionalised. Where once she had talked about being free and having a family, she now talked about getting a job in the laundry room of the prison, which she thought would be easier than the kitchen. Hope was slowly draining from her formidable character.

Within a few months of that visit, she was transferred to a federal prison in California. This was another setback for her. She had petitioned several times for a transfer to the women's federal prison in Danbury, Connecticut, as it would be easier for her family to get there from England; going to California made her family's visitation problems worse. With the transfer her consular care passed to my colleague in the British Consulate General in San Francisco and I never saw Chantal again. But I did follow her situation on her website.

Her requests for a transfer to a British prison were repeatedly refused, but in 2008 her lawyer petitioned for a presidential pardon. There was reason to think that President Bush might look upon this matter favourably; he was close to former Prime Minister Blair, and his wife, Cherie Blair, had been supportive of Chantal's plight. But those hopes came to nothing. In October of 2008, Chantal's lawyer received a letter from the US Department of Justice's lawyers, containing the following sentence: 'The application for commutation of sentence of your client, Chantal McCorkle, was carefully considered in this Department and the White House, and the decision was reached that favorable action is not warranted. Her application was therefore denied on August 28, 2008.'

For those of us working in the cesspool of international relations, it was yet more evidence that that so-called 'special relationship' does not filter down very far.

It very much looked at that time as if Chantal would remain in an American prison until at least 2014, but, in 2009, when she could have been excused for having given up hope, her request to transfer to a British prison to complete her sentence was approved. In September of 2009, she arrived back on British soil for the first time in many years and was taken directly to HMP Holloway in London. Within weeks she was transferred to an open prison, where she will, barring unforeseen circumstances, serve out a sentence that should allow her to be a free woman by the end of this year.

I was watching television in American recently, and some of the channels were showing infomercials of the type the McCorkles used to make – infomercials that are, as far as I can see, no different in form, content or veracity than theirs. It reminded me of an article by Greg Dawson in the *Orlando Sentinel* during the time of the McCorkles' trial. In it he described feeling some sympathy with the defendants. He wrote: 'Is McCorkle's vision of instant wealth really more outrageous than the promise of salvation and answered prayers from bejewelled televangelists with (freephone) number donation lines? Is it as desperately bogus as the homemade signs tacked on to power poles telling you that you can "Stop Smoking in One Day"? It can't possibly be as ludicrous as the infomercials for spray-on hair.'

What the McCorkles did was morally wrong and it was illegal – as Chantal herself admitted unequivocally in her own blog from prison on May 6, 2007: 'After much soul searching and self-examination, I must place full responsibility on myself for blindly working with my husband to take advantage of people through fraudulent marketing schemes and false claims of potential profit.'

Nevertheless, that initial 25 year sentence, on a first-time, non-violent offender, seems to be draconian. But it was certainly a warning to others. She refused, when charged, to accept the will of the US Government, and the consequence of that was direct and overwhelming. This response to dissent seems particular to American authority on both the macro and micro levels, and it is pervasive in popular American culture, where morality is frequently seen in clear, unambiguous terms. Morality has a much more ephemeral quality in Europe, and, for better or for worse, it is impossible to imagine anyone being sentenced for such a long time for a similar crime in the United Kingdom.

14

IF THE ACTIONS of the McCorkles seemed little different to those of others who went unmolested by the law, with many other people there was nothing equivocal about their intentions.

British conman Kevin O'Leary was arrested in Florida for an entirely greedy, spiteful and callous crime.

His *modus operandi* was to rent a villa somewhere in central Florida for a few months, pass it off as his own place and advertise it for holiday rental. People would send him deposits of hundreds of dollars, but when they turned up at the house O'Leary would be long gone, leaving behind the unsuspecting owner or some other legitimate renter. The families would be out of pocket and left desperately looking for somewhere to stay, with their vacations ruined.

He moved all over the state over the course of a couple of years, always one step ahead of the law. He must have thought he'd covered his tracks pretty well, but he was out of luck on that score.

The way he was eventually caught was actually quite brilliant in its simplicity. The police officer investigating this case felt that O'Leary would continue with the same method until he was caught. So he arranged for one of the Briton's previous victims to sit with him in an office for a few hours while he went through the local newspaper advertising sections and called each vacation rental house in the area asking for information about prices and availability. The victim, who was confident that he would recognise O'Leary's distinctive voice, was listening on the speakerphone. It was a potentially painstaking method, but, as luck would have it, on their first afternoon the fraudster answered the phone. He was arrested within the hour.

I went to visit him at Osceola County Jail a few days later. Usually, I wait until someone has opened their mouth to speak before I take an instant dislike to them, but in O'Leary's case I took against him the moment I set eyes on him. It wasn't because he was ugly, although he was, but the way he sprawled across the table in the visiting room as if it were in his own lounge, ostentatiously scratching his testicles and wearing the most inauthentic smile-cum-sneer since Larry Grayson hosted *The Generation Game*.

'Good morning,' I said. 'Are you Mr O'Leary?'

'All right, son?' he replied, laying on a Cockney accent far too thickly. 'How you doin'?'

'I'm fine, thank you. And you?'

'Yeah, alright,' he said, with a dismissive wave of his hand. Then – before I could even introduce myself – he began lecturing me. 'Now, listen to me, old cock, I'm innocent of this. They've got the wrong bloke, see what I mean?'

'Well, if they've got the wrong bloke, you shouldn't have any problems proving it in court. It should be pretty straightforward.'

'Yeah, but they're gonna frame me for it. They've got all these witnesses, apparently, who are going to say it was me what did it. See what I'm sayin'?'

'Well that's outrageous,' I said. 'You must explain all this to your attorney, and he'll take care of it all in court.'

Sensing my sardonic tone, he realised that he wasn't going to be able to bring me onside. He sat back and regarded me with dead eyes for a few moments, picking his teeth with his dirty, mangled fingernails.

'This place is a fuckin' dump,' he said.

'I've been in worse.'

'So have I, but that's not the point.'

'What's the point, then?

'My human rights are being infringed upon,' he said.

'How so, exactly?'

He had to think about this for a few moments.

'They make me eat grits for breakfast,' he complained.

Grits, or corn porridge, are an American staple; I quite like them.

'I hardly think serving you grits is an abuse of your human rights,' I said. 'Apart from anything else, they're good for you.'

'Tastes like shit.'

'Put some jam on it,' I said.

'There's no jam.'

'No jam?'

'Not a scrap.'

'That's too bad, but I'm not sure a lack of jam constitutes a human rights issue either.'

He heaved a sigh and threw himself back in his chair. The conversation wasn't going in the direction he'd hoped for, which is to say that we weren't discussing a plan of action that would lead to his imminent release from jail.

I decided to try and move the conversation on.

'Have you had any problems other than the food since you've been here?' I asked.

'Yeah, as it 'appens, I 'ave. A couple of the guards in 'ere tried to give me some serious grief the day before yesterday.'

'Serious grief?'

'I've had to give one of 'em a slap, and then I picked the other one up and threw him through a plate glass window. That'll learn 'im. They're all scared of me now, so I won't have any further aggro, know what I mean?'

I smiled at this. O'Leary was morbidly obese, and if he had so much as thrown a punch at someone he'd have had to sit down afterwards for a rest. Besides, if he really had assaulted an officer in that jail he would have been manacled by his balls to a concrete post at the bottom of a septic tank, not talking to me now. I looked closely at him. A few strands of lank, unwashed hair drooped down across his forehead, and his round, piggy cheeks and greedy little eyes made his fat face look like Bernard Manning's backside. Although he was sitting there doing precisely nothing, he was struggling for breath.

He was a heart attack waiting to happen, and I idly wondered how I might be able to help it along.

The thing that most struck me about him was the fundamental fecklessness of his character. He led his life as if he had an entitlement to take whatever he wanted, regardless of the consequences for others. He saw no relationship between his contribution to the world, and his reward from it. In his whole life, I doubt that he had undertaken a single act of generosity or benevolence for anyone outside of his immediate family. If he had chanced upon some humanitarian disaster, he would have looted the pockets of the dead and dying, and in doing so his conscience would not have been in the slightest bit troubled; afterwards he would boast to his friends about how much assistance he had given to the emergency services.

Later that day, when I got back to the consulate, I began some research into his background. I soon discovered that his name was not O'Leary at all – it was Callaghan, and, unsurprisingly, he had a long criminal record in the UK. Six years before his arrest in Florida, he had absconded from an open prison in England. He still had a year left to serve on a sentence he'd been given at Snaresbrook Crown Court for fraud. Although I met him several more times during his incarceration, I never revealed that I knew this.

O'Leary spent over a year at Osceola County Jail before he was eventually convicted, sentenced to time-served and then deported back to the UK. The police were waiting for him at Gatwick airport, which must have come as a shock, and he was taken straight to Belmarsh prison.

That'll learn 'im.

O'Leary was not an intelligent man, nor was he ambitious. His bogus home rental scheme could have been invented and executed by a 10-year-old. He just wanted an income without having to work for it. Others are more intelligent, and more ambitious.

One day I received a fax at the consulate to inform me that the FBI had arrested two British men, Alan King and Peter Barron, in a hotel room in Palm Beach. Barron was still in a local jail and King had been transferred to the pre-trial Federal Detention Centre in Miami. They were being held separately to prevent them from communicating, which is standard procedure for co-defendants. All I knew about the case before my visit was that they had been charged with fraud.

A few days later I flew down to Miami. King, who was in his 60s, came into the small interview room unshaven, unkempt and unimpressed, although he managed a polite half-smile. I went through my standard introduction, and we briefly discussed his health and welfare. After a short while he said, 'Do you mind if we discuss my case for a minute?'

'No, I don't mind at all. What's the problem?'

'This is a very bad thing that's happened, and something's not right about it – there's something strange going on.'

'What's not right about it?'

'It's a long story, and I'll admit right-off-the-bat that I've been a naughty boy, but... look, I have to go back to the beginning.'

He told me his story. He and Barron had, for some years, known an Irish US resident named Patrick Quinn. The three of them had been involved in a number of illegal activities together over the years. Unbeknown to Barron and King, Quinn had been arrested by the FBI in Miami many months ago and charged with quite serious offences. (I never found out what those charges were.) He was bang to rights and facing a significant period of imprisonment, so was quick to seize upon a fairly standard offer of co-operation from the FBI: if he could supply information about ongoing criminal activity which led to an arrest and conviction, his sentence would be significantly mitigated.

Unfortunately, Quinn had no such info. Unfazed, the FBI simply adjusted the terms of their offer: if he was prepared to assist the officers in the creation of an illegal enterprise involving criminals he knew, even if they were not in the USA, the offer stood.

This would never be allowed in the UK, but America is a foreign country and they do things differently there.

Quinn snatched the offer with both hands. He and the investigators came up with a scheme whereby he would set up a bogus investment bank in South Africa, offering highly attractive interest rates to investors and a promise of exemptions from tax liability. He would do this in conjunction with Barron and King.

'To be honest,' said King, 'we'd pulled off a similar scam in Zimbabwe a few years ago.'

Quinn called his old chums and set the ball rolling, with the FBI taping the whole conversation. He and the investigators then produced some glossy brochures, purporting to be from a South African bank and advertising ludicrously attractive investment opportunities. They also created a website and provided an email address and a telephone number in South Africa, which was re-routed to the USA. Investors were to be provided with an account number into which they would simply wire their funds, with a promise that their interest would be paid quarterly.

In fact, what would have happened if the fraud had been genuine – if that's not a contradiction in terms – is that the money would build up over a period of a few months before the crooks withdrew it and disappeared.

'I know it sounds crazy,' said King, 'but you'd be surprised how many people will go for something like that.'

To help the scam along, Quinn had been released on bail to live at home. He was fitted with an electronic ankle-brace to prevent him absconding, but he could make and receive calls – all of which were recorded – without raising any suspicions.

'Once the brochures were complete, Quinn sent a couple of them to us for our approval,' said King. 'They looked great, really professional. Peter (Barron) wanted a couple of minor amendments made – spelling mistakes, that sort of thing. But when he pointed these out to Quinn he said he was pressed for time and had to ring off. He said, "Just sketch any suggestions on a spare leaflet and post them back to me in Florida so I can sort them." We agreed, and that was that.'

A few days later, Barron and King separately wrote some changes on spare brochures and posted them to Quinn. That one simple action proved to be their undoing.

'A couple of weeks later, Quinn called and said he'd made those changes,' said King. 'We were going to have to fly over to Cape Town to run the operation down there, so we had a chat about that. Then he says, "Why don't you come via my place, we can have a few beers, catch up, and plan stuff." That sounded like a good idea, but we were short of cash so said we'd give it a miss. But he said he'd really like to see us, and that he'd pay for our tickets. So we said we would.'

A few days later Peter Barron and Alan King slid into two business class seats for the flight to Miami, courtesy – if only they had known it – of the FBI.

Quinn met them at Miami airport and drove them up the coast to Palm Beach, where they checked into their hotel. The three men went up to the hotel room for a celebratory drink, and had scarcely popped the champagne when a team of FBI agents barged into the room from an adjoining suite and arrested Barron and King at gunpoint.

'At first, with all the confusion, I couldn't work out why they weren't cuffing Quinn,' said King. 'But it dawned on me fairly quickly. I couldn't believe it – I'd known the bastard for 30 years, I was a friend of his family. As we were led out of the room, he just looked at us, shrugged his shoulders and said, "Sorry, lads." I could have punched his face in.'

The two men were charged with 'mail fraud' by virtue of the fact that they had posted the brochures back to Quinn via the US Mail. Because of the way the federal sentencing guidelines are structured, they both potentially faced 15 years in prison.

'Look, Hugh,' he said, 'I'm no angel, and I've done some bad stuff in my time. I'll be straight with you: I would have done that crime and taken the money, no worries. But there *was* no crime. Nobody was ever at risk of losing anything in that scheme. It was an artificial exercise, created by the FBI for the sole purpose of getting

Peter and me. It wouldn't be legal in the UK, or anywhere else in Europe, or the rest of the civilised world. Where do I stand on it here in the States?'

'Can you afford a good lawyer?' I said.

'I haven't got a penny to my name.'

'Well, I'm not an attorney,' I said, 'so I can't give you the exact situation in law, but without any money you'll end up being represented by a court-appointed lawyer, and you're unlikely to get much information from him about where you stand. In fact, other than a brief introduction at your arraignment, you probably won't see him again for around six to ten months. When you do, he'll almost certainly come to you with a deal offered by the prosecution. If you decline the deal and go to trial it will probably be another year before your case gets into court, and you'll be lucky to see your lawyer again until a week before the case. I'll let you work out how comprehensive your defence will be on the strength of that.'

'Oh, that's just fucking great,' he said.

'In my experience, entrapment is a grey area in the United States,' I told him. 'Under certain circumstances, they seem to be able to get away with it in court. Let me ask you, do you have any previous convictions?'

'Yeah.'

'For fraud?'

'Yep.'

'Then I would have to advise you that you would be running an enormous risk by fighting this in court. If they offer you a deal, I suggest you consider it carefully. If you go to trial on this it will really piss them off and if you go down, with your previous form, they'll send you away for a long time.'

He nodded as the full gravity of his situation dawned on him. Tears came to his eyes. 'I'm sorry,' he said. 'My first grandchild is on its way, back in Canterbury, and I had thought I'd be there for that. That'll be hard.'

'It's okay,' I told him. 'I understand.' I've seen many grown men cry in jail, and it never gets less uncomfortable to witness.

'So there's nothing you can do about it?' he asked, after he'd pulled himself together a bit.

'No, there's nothing. I've already done more than I should by telling you all that.'

'Thanks,' he said, 'I appreciate it.'

After my first meeting with King, I went for lunch at a small restaurant out on Calle Ocho in Miami's Little Havana. I found myself thinking about him whilst sipping a Cuban coffee. It seemed to me that, like O'Leary, his life had been defined by his greed. So much so that he didn't care how he came by his advantages or who he harmed on the way. I thought it would be a horrible way to live, and I couldn't imagine how any of the fast cars or big houses he aspired to could have blinded him to the pain he had caused others. For all his indignation and tears, he had a mercenary soul. Strangely enough, this led my train of thought to something closer to home. During the previous few months we had started to hear whispers from Washington that the FCO was going to move us all on to performance-related pay, with bonuses to high achievers, whoever they might turn out to be. The rumours had persisted and I began to wonder whether they might be true. We had certainly been told that some staff would be awarded discretionary payments for successful, specific projects. Bonuses are unpredictable animals, and from what I could see they frequently failed to lead to the results they were intended to produce. I had no idea how they could be implemented in the Foreign Office, which in no way could be described as a business. If they were, I was sure the senior managers would put themselves in line for large payouts, whilst the people at the bottom, like me, would be lucky to maintain their standard of living even if we performed well. As it was, the LE staff in the US had been on a pay freeze for months anyway, because the government had apparently run out of money. I couldn't help but notice that the DS staff had been paid their cost-of-living raise and their annual increments, so the money can't have been that scarce.

Whilst I recognise that fraud is theft and illegal, and bonuses are approved and lawful, it's clear that they both endorse financial advantage as a primary motivating factor in people's lives. Financial security is important, but this seemingly ubiquitous grab for cash leaves a nasty taste in my mouth. If I were making or selling widgets, I might work harder to make more money; but the idea that I'd do more to help someone in trouble for some shabby change is offensive to me. How much of your integrity would you sell for £500? How about £5,000, or even £50,000? What price would you be prepared to pay for a bigger house, just to impress your neighbours?

A year after they were arrested, Barron and King made a deal with the prosecution and each went to prison for 36 months.

15

I'D HAD A LONG DAY. Two gentlemen from Salford had overstayed their fortnight's vacation in Key West by around five months and had, the previous day, spent their last few hundred dollars on a flight back to Manchester. They had changed planes in Orlando, but as their surprisingly small jet taxied out on to the runway they were astonished to hear the pilot estimate their flight time at around three hours. They summoned the air hostess to check they'd heard right.

'Yes,' she assured them, 'three hours to Manchester.'

'Only three hours to England!' one of them exclaimed in amazement.

'What? Are you crazy?' she replied. 'We're going to Manchester, New Hampshire.'

The pilot promptly taxied back to the gate and dropped these two hapless individuals off, leaving them to their own devices. Unfortunately, their only device was me.

I had spent the whole day trying to sort that one out as they had no money left and the travel agency that had booked the flight denied any liability for the error.

That evening I called Linda in Atlanta, as I so often did, just to share my day.

'You won't believe this one,' I said. 'The two guys I was dealing with didn't have quite the day they were expecting.'

'How come?' she asked.

Once I'd finished my story, she said, 'Well, if you think they had a surprise, let me tell you about the chap I was dealing with.'

Linda went on to tell me about someone called Dave Weaving. 'He's from Norwich,' she said, rhyming it with Shoreditch.

'They have a reputation up there for marrying within the family,' I told her, for no particular reason.

'Oh, really?' she drawled, in her Georgian accent. 'You have that in England too? I thought it was just in Alabama. That might explain it.'

'Explain what?' I said.

'Well, how can I put this? He isn't the finest fir in the forest, if you see what I mean?'

'I do.'

'He was telling me that he hasn't had a lot of luck with women in his life. He was 40 last year and he got so desperate that he turned to the internet '

'Did his luck change?'

'Well, yes and no.'

To Mr Weaving's utter amazement, Linda explained, he had quickly hooked up with an extremely attractive American woman called Bunty. They did the email correspondence thing, and after a week or two they sent each other some photographs.

'He showed me one of the photos,' said Linda. 'It had like a sepia effect on it, but she looked real pretty. Said she was 35 so the ages worked out about right. So after a couple of months, he decides to fly over to here to meet her.'

He had arrived in Atlanta a couple of days earlier; Bunty was there to meet him, but Dave hadn't recognised her at first.

'Had she put on a few pounds?' I said.

'No, her weight wasn't so much of a problem as her age: she's 77. The photos she'd sent him were taken in the 1960s.'

'My goodness, he must have been furious with her?'

'Well, you'd have thought so,' said Linda, 'but he was really quite understanding and actually felt sorry for her. She apologised to him and she was crying and deeply distressed; so much so that when she invited him back to her house, he went.'

After a few cups of tea, the ageing Bunty told Dave Weaving from Norwich that he was her closest friend and confidante. She said that now she'd found someone she wanted to spend what was left of her life with she didn't want to begin by being underhand or telling any lies. Or any *more* lies, anyway. She told him she had a deep secret she needed to share with him and took him downstairs to the basement. In a corner was a large chest freezer, secured by a lock. She undid it, opened the lid and revealed the frozen body of her late husband.

'That must have frightened the life out of him,' I said to Linda.

'Well, I guess it must have, but he handled it calmly. She said she hadn't killed the old guy, he just died in his sleep a couple of years back and she didn't want to lose his pension payments. Mr Weaving persuaded her to call the police and get the whole thing straightened out. He made a statement yesterday, and the authorities are happy that he's done nothing wrong. He flew home earlier today. I don't think he'll be back anytime soon.'

I had to laugh; that was one of the strangest stories yet. The gap between what we expect in life and what we get is known as reality. Like love, taxes and gout, reality hurts. As a consular officer, you soon learn that whenever hopes fail to match an outcome, it's a problem. A big part of the skill of the job is trying to manage expectations, sometimes retrospectively. The FCO's rule of thumb in these things is 'let the buyer beware'. Sometimes, as in the case of the Key West couple, there's clearly neglect or plain stupidity on the part of the victim. Other times, as with poor old Dave Weaving, you have simply been deceived, and there's little you could have done about it. But, as a consul, you do what you can to help either way.

Over the last 10 or 15 years, more Britons have looked to emigrate to the USA, particularly to Florida. Residency is hard to come by for an ordinary Joe, but one way to get it is by buying into a business. The US Government, keen to promote the country as a good place to invest your cash, created the 'E' class of visa. This confers residency, and is available to foreign investors who were prepared to invest a given sum of capital into an American business. In order to attract as many investors as possible, the qualifying requirements for the 'E' visa were set quite low: anyone able to invest a little over $100,000 could potentially qualify (the qualifying sum has since been raised to $1 million).

Many British nationals use the 'E' visa as a backdoor way of getting into the States and they sometimes don't think too hard about the businesses they are getting into – they just want to get to the USA.

Unsurprisingly, this leads to problems – which is where people like me come in.

As the equity in British homes soared through the 1990s and into the 21st century, many Brits suddenly found themselves sitting on enough cash to qualify for an 'E' visa. It became a relatively simple deal: often using a business broker, they would find a company for sale in America, usually for just over the qualifying amount of investment. Normally these are small outfits – restaurants, pubs or maybe a property management business, looking after the rental of vacation homes.

Having bought their way in, soon the happy emigrants have sold up, flown across the Atlantic and are living the American dream.

Only, sometimes they aren't.

America is a strange and foreign place. Yes, they speak our language (kind of), and, yes, we watch their TV programmes; millions of us have soaked up their sun on their sand. But living there is a completely different thing from a two-week holiday, and in my experience a lot of people find it tough to settle in. This can be exacerbated if they're also trying to run a business for the first time in their lives.

Let me tell you about a couple of cases that illustrate how badly wrong things can go.

Steve Smithers and his wife Lucy had always hankered after a life in the sun. They had two daughters, and one of them was disabled: the warm weather would offer health benefits to her. They'd also dreamed of running their own restaurant. In 2004, they decided to go for it. Steve quit his job as a dental assistant, they sold their house in Cardiff and used their $120,000 profit to buy a small family-owned diner in Fort Lauderdale.

It was doing well and, on paper, it looked a good buy. But its popularity largely stemmed from the gregarious proprietor, who was born and grew up in the neighbourhood and was well-known and liked. Shortly after Steve and Lucy started trading, another similar bistro – with a curiously similar name – opened up a few blocks away. The chef, coffee maker and chief bottle-washer was none other than the seller of the old place, and the customers quickly transferred their allegiance to his new diner, leaving the original one struggling.

The British couple felt swindled, and it's hard to argue that they hadn't been: their contract for the business had contained the usual clause prohibiting the seller to open another restaurant within 20 miles. They hired an attorney – not cheap – to look at the situation, but it turned out that the new diner was owned by the bottle-washer's brother-in-law. The non-competition clause was questionable, at best. At around this time, Steve and Lucy had a fire-and-safety inspection. This revealed a series of expensive problems, which needed to be fixed immediately or the place would be closed down.

Bear in mind that they were also a normal family, with two kids to feed and mortgage payments, car-loan bills and medical insurance costs to meet, along with other relocation expenses.

The months went by, and the situation deteriorated. Eventually, Steve called me at the consulate and told me the whole story.

I listened with genuine alarm and sympathy, but I realised very quickly that there would be nothing I could do for them.

'I hate to say this,' I said, 'but if you have any recourse anywhere it's going to be through the courts, not through us. We just can't get involved in this sort of thing. I'm sorry.'

The phone went quiet for a few moments. Trying to get a judge to enforce the non-competition clause might cost tens of thousands of dollars, with no guarantee of success.

Finally, after a long sigh, Steve spoke. 'What would you do in my situation?'

This is always a hard question to answer and one a Foreign Office employee like me was probably best avoiding – if I offered advice and it led to trouble, I'd inevitably be blamed. On the other hand, I always felt that if I could offer a disinterested insight into a tough situation, something constructive and tangible that maybe the people actually embroiled in the emotion of it couldn't see, that had to be a good thing. Not all of my consular colleagues would agree with that, but it was my way. In this case, I could see only one option.

'Personally, I'd cut my losses and go back home to Britain.'

'I can't do that,' he said. 'What about my daughter? The climate really helps her. We can't take her back to that terrible weather. Plus we sold everything we had there, and invested it in our new lives here. We've got nothing to go back to.'

'Look,' I said. 'I really feel for you. I think you got a very bad deal out of this, but I need to make you aware of something that you might not have considered. Your visa expressly prohibits you from working in the USA other than for the purposes of running your business, and it's a requirement that your enterprise remains viable. If your business fails, you must understand that not only will you have no source of income, but you will be in breach of the terms of your visa. It will only be a matter of time before you are picked up by the immigration service and removed from the United States, perhaps forcibly.'

Again, the phone went quiet, for quite a while. Then he said, 'So, there's nothing the consulate can do for us?'

'I'm sorry. I really am. There's nothing.'

'OK. Thanks, anyway,' he said, and then he was gone.

I never spoke to him again, so I don't know how he resolved his situation, but about three months later I found myself in Fort Lauderdale after a meeting with a lawyer. I had a mouth like Gandhi's flip-flop and I needed some refreshment. I remembered the name and address of Steve and Lucy's diner, so I decided to go over there and give them some business. I was on the Triumph, which I parked just down the street from where I could see the name of the place. As I approached, hoping to find it busy, I saw that it was closed. In fact, it had been abandoned. I peered through the glass, shading my line of sight from the sun with my helmet, and it was empty. No people, no menus, no tables or chairs – just dust.

I felt very sad for the couple and their children. I got back on my motorcycle and headed over to the other diner Steve had told me about, just a few blocks away. It was quite busy; there were people outside on the pavement eating and drinking, and waiters frantically running in and out. As he'd said, this one had a name remarkably similar to the old one. I took my business elsewhere. Sometimes the greed and sheer underhandedness of some people in this world depresses me.

Strangely, only a month or two later I took a call from another British guy who was complaining about a hair dressing salon he'd bought to get his 'E' visa.

'I bought the place on the basis of the figures and accounts they showed me,' he said. 'When I got there, I found that the previous owner had most of the staff off the books, cash-in-hand.' This had helped her avoid medical costs and other liabilities, but it was completely illegal. 'If I now put all those payments through the books, which I'm supposed to do, the salon isn't profitable. It's bound to go under. What do you think?'

'I think you have a problem,' I said. Sometimes understatement can be very effective. If he followed the same route as the previous owner and got caught, he'd be arrested and he'd lose the business. If he didn't, he'd lose it anyway. Either way, he'd be deported pretty soon afterwards.

'What should I do?' he asked.

'The only advice I can give you is to obey the law. You're going to have to put it all through the books, and suffer the consequences. Having said that, I think you have very good grounds for a legal action against the vendor. You could probably recover some or all of your investment from her, and frankly, she could go to jail.'

I heard him sigh. 'Yeah, but I can't do that.'

'Why not?'

'She still works here for me, and she's a really, really nice old lady.'

I had to stifle my laughter. 'Well,' I said, 'it's probably not really for me to say this, but you'll need to decide whether to watch your business and probably your life in America go down the pan, or whether to pull the plug on the charlatan that sold you the business, and save your own backside. It really is your call. I can't tell you what to do.'

'I know,' he said. 'Honestly, though, what would you do?'

'Me? I'd shop the old witch. Let her spend a couple of months in jail – that'll fix her.'

At least we were able to share a laugh about that.

Before we hung up, he told me to drop by for a free haircut one day. About a year later, I was in his neighbourhood and I decided on the spur of the moment to get a mullet. All I can say is they were in fashion in the States at the time. The shop was still there, with a Union Jack outside and plastic bulldog on the steps. I went in and introduced myself to the owner, who was delighted to see me. Clearly, he'd decided to go with the off-the-books option.

'I shall cut your hair personally,' he shrieked.

'But what if you get nicked halfway through?' I asked him. 'I'll end-up with a half-mullet.'

He didn't get nicked, and I got my haircut – though looking back, it wasn't one of my finest. On the way home, I thought about him. He was probably having a lot of sleepless nights, just waiting for the knock on the door at dawn, and the trip to the deportation centre. I wouldn't fancy it myself.

* * * * *

Whilst I had become competent at advising people on managing their professional lives, I was not so expert at managing my own personal life.

I was out for dinner with Cheryl one evening. It was a fine restaurant, high above the city with the lights of Orlando all around us. The food was excellent. We ate like this fairly often. Our circumstances allowed it as we both worked, and we had few financial obligations. It was a lovely way to live, and that evening I remember thinking that I did not have a care in the world. We had been together for a few years by this point, with no tangible change in our domestic arrangements: we still lived separately and had never had a conversation about moving in together, which suited me. We didn't even have keys for each other's apartments.

I suppose I should have known it couldn't last.

'What is it exactly that you want?' she asked, as we were finishing the main course.

'I was thinking of the soufflé.'

'Don't be a smart ass.'

I sipped some wine, a lovely Chablis, but I was drinking it to buy myself a few extra seconds. I put the glass down slowly, aware that she was watching me closely. With the same gut-wrenching feeling you get the instant you realise you've braked too late to avoid hitting the car in front of you, I braced myself for a crash with reality.

'I don't know. I like things how they are,' I said. 'I'm not ready for a change right now.'

'And how long am I supposed to wait before you are ready for a change?'

'I don't know,' I said.

She shook her head at me for a moment and I felt like an infant. It seemed as if an eternity passed before she asked her next question.

'Would this situation be any different if I wasn't black?' she asked.

That question was like a knife plunged into my chest. No such thing was in my heart or in my consciousness, and I couldn't believe she would even think it was possible. The question was even more shocking to me for being so unexpected, so unanticipated. Was this what she'd really been thinking? Had I really given her cause to believe that? For me, in truth, dealing with the cultural differences of her race was much less of an issue than dealing with the cultural difference of her being American.

'Of course it wouldn't,' I said. 'How could you say or think that?'

'If you don't want to marry me and have a family with me, you're leaving it a long time to let me know.'

'I think I've been honest with you, haven't I? I'm just not ready for that.'

Then the waiter walked by, and Cheryl asked for the bill.

She drove me back to my place, but she wouldn't come in. She said she wanted to go home and she sped off before I could talk her out of it. I couldn't sleep, and at about three in the morning I jumped on the Triumph and drove over to her place. I knocked several times. She eventually opened the door in her silk nightgown. Her eyes were all sleepy. She walked back to her bedroom, leaving the front door open. I went inside, closed the door, undressed and got into bed with her. We made love, and fell asleep in each other's arms. We hadn't spoken a word.

16

AN HORRIFIC SCENE greeted police as they pushed open the door to suite 1215 at the plush DuPont Plaza Hotel in downtown Miami.

One man lay riddled with bullets on the ground floor of the expensive suite; upstairs, another had been executed in cold blood, shot through the head as he knelt by a wall. The rooms were spattered with blood – as was the corridor outside. One of the victims had tried to crawl away, only to be dragged back inside by his killer – or killers – and finished off.

The two dead men were a father and son, Derrick and Duane Moo Young.

Their murderer – so police believed – was a colourful British entrepreneur called Krishna Maharaj.

Maharaj had made a multi-million pound fortune in the fruit and veg trade in London, bought a holiday home in Florida, then set up a newspaper in the state in slightly bizarre circumstances.

He would end up on Death Row – and he is in jail in the States to this day, despite the fact that many people think he is an innocent man.

Maharaj was born in Trinidad to a good family of Indian descent. His brother was to become Trinidad and Tobago's Attorney General, but Krishna's ambitions lay in London, to where he emigrated as a teenager in the 1960s. He started a business importing fruit and vegetables from the Caribbean and was soon making serious amounts of money trading to the capital's growing West Indian community. So successful was it, in fact, that Maharaj at one time owned a fleet of Rolls-Royces and a stable of racehorses.

During the early 1980s, he flew to Florida to search for a vacation home. His stay in the USA became protracted and while he was there he had a falling out with Derrick Moo Young, a Jamaican national of Chinese descent and an old family friend.

The dispute was bitter and angry, each claiming the other owed him hundreds of thousands of dollars for various business deals. As far as I know, no-one has ever established who owed what to whom, but what was later discovered was that, at the time of his death, Moo Young had $2 million stashed away in secret bank accounts hidden from the US taxman. He was, at the very least, a sharp operator.

To his many supporters and friends, Krishna Maharaj was the polar opposite.

I remember very well the first time I went to visit him on Florida's Death Row, a prison within a prison at Union Correctional Institution, near the aptly-named Starke.

Once inside the secure perimeter of Union, you walk a short way across the compound before you come to a gate leading into a tunnel of chain-link fencing. You walk along this for about 200 metres before you arrive at the entrance to the Death Row building itself. It's an eerie feeling arriving there, knowing the fate of those held within.

After going through some formalities, I was led to an extremely small cell – maybe four feet by five feet – in which there was a table, and two fixed chairs. Maharaj was waiting there for me – his feet shackled and his hands manacled behind his back, as if he would be likely to leap forward and kill me at any moment. It seemed draconian, but those are the rules.

We talked for half an hour. The duration of the visits on Death Row are strictly limited and enforced, and the time passes very quickly, for visitors at any rate.

I wanted to talk to him about his health. He was, by this time, almost 60 and he had already been on Death Row for over 10 years, and that takes a toll.

'I'm fine, thank you very much,' he said. 'My health is a matter of little consequence to me, though I wonder if you would mind writing to the prison's warden on my behalf to ask if he would allow me to have my hands bound in front of me when I am out of my cell? This is very uncomfortable.'

I agreed to do that.

He had a certain charm, even humility. I don't know what people on Death Row should be like, but, whatever it is, he didn't seem to be it. He seemed meek, submissive, victimised. He was polite and respectful, and I warmed to him in a strange way. Over the following seven years, we became friendly with each other. He always called me Hugh; I always called him Kris. He always asked after my family; I always asked after his.

He was undoubtedly an intelligent man, and also tenacious. During that first meeting, he wanted to discuss only one thing, and it was a conversation that repeated itself on every occasion we met thereafter. He was like a dog with a bone, and the bone was his innocence.

Before leaving my office to make this visit, I had carefully read the case file, which included full transcripts of the court hearings. The evidence against him appeared strong and clear, and his lawyer during the original trial had done little to rebut the facts presented to the court.

But now, sitting across from me in this tiny cell, he challenged most of the evidence with the creation of doubt based in possibility. Most of it; but not, I felt, all of it. As he was talking me through his version of the events on the day in question, I wanted to believe him – as I have always wanted to – but something nagged away at me.

The dispute with Derrick Moo Young had rumbled on through the 1980s, fuelled by a series of damaging articles that appeared in a West Indian expatriate newspaper, the *Caribbean Echo*. In an attempt to put his side of the story more forcefully, Maharaj went so far as to start his own newspaper, the *Caribbean Times*.

During August and September of 1986, Maharaj had attempted on a number of occasions to meet Derrick Moo Young so the men could settle their differences. But he was unsuccessful, and felt that the 53-year-old Moo Young was avoiding him.

In September 1986, a man called Neville Butler, a journalist with the *Echo* and an acquaintance of Moo Young, contacted Maharaj and told him that he was unhappy working there. He sought a position with the *Times*.

Butler is a central figure in this story: he was in the room when the horrific double killing happened, and it was primarily his evidence that nailed Krishna Maharaj.

Bulter's story was as follows.

Maharaj told him to arrange a meeting with Derrick Moo Young at the DuPont Plaza hotel. Butler claims he told Moo Young that this was so that he (Moo Young) could meet two Bahamians to discuss an import/export opportunity. In fact, as Butler knew, Maharaj would be there and the plan was – once again, according to Butler – that Maharaj would confront Moo Young about the money owed.

At the appointed time, Derrick Moo Young appeared at the hotel suite, but, unexpectedly, he had with him his 23-year-old son, Duane.

Butler invited the two guests in, and from that moment the whole thing started to go badly wrong. Maharaj appeared from behind a door with a pistol in one hand, and a small pillow in the other, although Butler said he did not know Maharaj was armed. Immediately, according to Butler, an argument broke out between the two older men, and Maharaj shot Derrick Moo Young in the leg. He then ordered Butler to tie up both the Moo Youngs with electric cord. As Butler was tying up Duane, Derrick advanced on Maharaj who fired several more shots at him.

Presumably believing Derrick to be completely incapacitated and mortally wounded, Maharaj then turned his attention to Duane, shouting at him about the money his father owed. Duane lunged at Maharaj, but Butler intercepted him. Meanwhile, Derrick Moo Young had recovered consciousness and dragged himself to the door of the suite. He opened it, and had made it into the corridor of the hotel before Maharaj realised what was happening. He rushed into the corridor, shot the crawling man once more, this time fatally, and then dragged him back inside.

Butler told the later murder trial that Maharaj then forced Duane Moo Young at gunpoint to the upstairs room of the suite. Duane had known Maharaj all his life, and for most of that time, Maharaj had been a friend of the family. Butler testified that the young man pleaded for his life as he was being forced upstairs; the last words Butler heard, probably the last Duane spoke, were, 'Please, Uncle Kris, why are you doing this?'

A moment or two later, said Butler, he heard a single gunshot from the room above. The two men then left the hotel together, and split.

Not long afterwards, a hotel cleaner found a 'Do Not Disturb' sign on the outside of the suite door. On that sign was a bloody handprint. The blood was Derrick Moo Young's and the handprint belonged to Krishna Maharaj.

Inside, she found the furniture in disarray and two dead bodies.

Later that same day, Neville Butler called the Miami Police Department and spoke to a Detective Burmeister, telling him everything. That evening, Maharaj called Butler and, Butler said, arranged to meet him at a diner close to Miami airport to plan their alibis. When Maharaj arrived at the diner, detective Burmeister and another officer were there to arrest him.

Maharaj denied killing the Moo Youngs. He pleaded not guilty, hired an expensive lawyer – he was then still a wealthy man – and prepared for a fight.

The trial lasted for two weeks, and a few days in something extraordinary happened: the presiding judge, Howard Gross, was arrested in his chambers by federal marshals and charged with accepting a bribe in an unrelated case. [He was subsequently cleared and returned to the bench.] A new judge, Harold Solomon, was immediately assigned to the case; Solomon offered Maharaj the opportunity to start the trial again from the beginning, or to allow him to review the court transcripts from the preceding few days and continue from that point – not unusual in Florida courts. Maharaj and his attorney discussed the situation, and elected to continue.

As well as Butler's evidence, a motive was provided by the acrimony between Maharaj and Derrick Moo Young. Additionally, Maharaj had rented the room in question the night before the killings, although there was no sign that he'd spent that night there. But there *was* evidence that he had been in the hotel room on the day of the murders – it was covered in his fingerprints. A firearms expert also proved that the lethal shots had been fired from a pre-1976 Smith & Wesson 9mm semi-automatic pistol with a serial number under 270000. Maharaj owned such a weapon – it had the serial number A235464 – but it was missing. Other points were raised, too: like the fact that Maharaj had been carrying various weapons in the boot of his car, and had attempted to force another driver off the road with the intention of killing him.

The main defence was an alibi. Maharaj admitted being in suite 1215 on the day in question, but said he had arrived at around 8am, waited for about an hour to meet the Bahamians so he could discuss the import/export deal, and had then left for meetings in Fort Lauderdale when they failed to show. Strangely, Maharaj's lawyer did not call a single alibi witness to back this up: in fact, he didn't call any witnesses. Nor did he attempt to refute much of the prosecution's evidence.

Who did carry out the murders? Maharaj could suggest no-one plausible.

It wasn't a great strategy, and it failed utterly. Maharaj was found guilty of both murders.

The prosecution had sought the death penalty. Under Florida law, the jury has a major say in sentencing; it advises the judge, and judges almost always go along with that advice. For murdering Derrick Moo Young, the jury recommended that Maharaj receive a life sentence. For killing Duane Moo Young, by seven to five, they recommended that he be executed.

On 1 December 1987, Judge Solomon formally imposed the death penalty on Krishna Maharaj, and he was transported to Death Row at Union Correctional Institution.

A few days after the trial ended, an academic from the University of Florida in Gainesville who had a professional interest in the death penalty contacted the British Consulate General in Atlanta to ask about the British Government's views on the situation. This was the first anyone knew about any of it; once again, notwithstanding their obligations and the high seriousness of the matter, the Miami Police Department had failed in its obligation to inform the consulate. The vice-consul in Atlanta at the time, Maureen Howley, immediately wrote to Maharaj asking him to establish his claim to British nationality. Howley went to visit Maharaj at Union CI in January of 1988: that was his first consular visit.

* * * * *

There were 287 death sentences passed across America that year; as in any year, few of those sentenced – if any – accepted their fate and went quickly to the gas chamber, electric chair or needle. Most go through an exhaustive series of appeals, both against conviction and sentence. Maharaj was no different.

Over the next few years, he appeared before the Supreme Court of Florida on several occasions, exploiting various avenues of appeal. Mostly he was unsuccessful, but in 1995 the court decided he should be allowed to challenge his conviction on the basis that the evidence against him was flawed. At the same time, having run out of money to pay attorneys, he asked the British Consulate to approach the well-known, US-based anti-capital punishment lawyer and British citizen Clive Stafford Smith to work on his case.

Quite coincidentally, a vice-consul at the British Consulate General in Atlanta was due to have lunch with Stafford Smith as the latter had been representing Nicholas Ingram, another British national on Death Row – this time in Georgia – and the meeting was to review the developments in that case. (Ingram was finally executed in 1995.) During the lunch, Maharaj's appeal was discussed. Although Stafford

Smith said it was unlikely he could help because of a heavy caseload, he did eventually start working on it.

I know and like Clive – he has dedicated his professional life to assisting indigent people in dire straights. Often he and his staff have worked without payment, and he has been critical of the British Government's failure to do more to help Britons facing the death penalty.

He became completely convinced of Maharaj's innocence, and he told me that if he could get a retrial, he was certain that he could establish that his client did not murder the Moo Youngs. His optimism seemed unfounded when the evidentiary hearing was finally held in Miami in October 1997. It lasted for a week, and Stafford Smith finally did what the original trial lawyer should have done – he produced witnesses to support the alibi. In fact, six people now came forward to say that they had been with the appellant in Fort Lauderdale – 45 minutes away – at the time of the killings.

Despite this, the judge threw out Maharaj's appeal for a retrial, on the grounds that none of the evidence he was offering was new. These witnesses were available and should have been produced at the original trial, and it was now too late. The guilty verdict stood, and Maharaj remained on Death Row.

But Stafford Smith was persistent and the appeals process ground on, reaching the Florida Supreme Court in November 2001. Again, Maharaj's appeal for a new trial was rejected, but there was a glimmer of hope – they ordered the penalty to be re-determined. At a re-sentencing hearing back at the Dade County Courthouse in Miami in March 2002, a new jury made a new recommendation: this time, by a majority of eleven-to-one, they requested that the death penalty be commuted to life with no possibility of parole. The judge concurred.

Within a few days, Maharaj was taken back to Union Correctional Institution, but this time he was held in the general population, rather than on Death Row.

A further attempt to get a retrial failed in 2004.

Undaunted, Stafford Smith pursued an avenue of appeal through the federal system. Although Maharaj had been tried and convicted of a state crime, and sentenced to time in a Florida prison, Stafford Smith argued in a federal court that because the Miami Police had failed to inform the British consulate of his arrest, his constitutionally guaranteed rights had been breached. The US federal 11th circuit court in Atlanta denied this petition, which eventually found its way to Washington. But finally, in 2006, the US Federal Supreme Court refused to hear the case, effectively ending any prospect of the case being resolved by the federal authorities.

Maharaj can now only hope for clemency from the Governor of Florida. Such clemency is extremely rare, and it is now almost certain that he will die in prison, far from home.

Derrick Moo Young was no angel. During the three years before his death, he reported earnings to the US tax authorities of less than $25,000 per annum, yet he had assets totalling over $2 million in secret bank accounts, shielded from the IRS. There is no explanation for this that I am aware of.

But is Kris Maharaj innocent of those two murders?

The BBC has run numerous stories suggesting he may have been the victim of a terrible miscarriage of justice. Thousands of supporters have bombarded the US authorities asking for his pardon. And Clive Stafford Smith – extremely experienced in such cases – firmly believes in his innocence. During the re-sentencing hearing in Miami in 2002, I found myself sitting next to Clive during a recess.

We were discussing the case in general manner, when there was a pause.

'Can I ask you,' I said, 'how it is that, when the evidence against Kris seems overwhelming, you are so confident you could get him acquitted if he gets a retrial?'

He seemed genuinely surprised that I had any doubt about it, and went on to dismiss the evidence against Maharaj in very short order.

'Firstly, there's no dispute that he was in that hotel room on the day in question, so the fingerprint evidence is irrelevant. We have good alibi evidence that he was elsewhere at the time of the murders. The fact that he owned a Smith & Wesson firearm with a serial number of under A270000 is speculative – so do a quarter of a million other people, and the murder weapon itself has never been found. I think we could show that Butler was a liar, and his counsel was incompetent. The Moo Youngs were either dealing in drugs or laundering money – their accounts show as much. I think they were probably killed by Colombians, and I think I can even name the killer.'

I think I raised my eyebrow at this suggestion.

Stafford Smith returned my look of surprise. 'You're still unconvinced?' he said.

'There's just one thing that's nagging away at me,' I said.

'What's that?' he asked.

'The handprint. How did Kris's handprint, in Derrick Moo Young's blood, come to be found on the outside of the door if he was 30 miles away?'

Stafford Smith dismissed this with a wave of his hand. He said he could prove forensically that if a fingerprint was already on something, which subsequently became contaminated with blood, the fingerprint could appear, ostensibly, to have been on top of the blood. It proved nothing. With that he stood and walked away to attend to his business in court.

Clive Stafford Smith is tall, elegant and handsome; he is articulate, urbane and sophisticated. He cuts a dash. If I were ever in serious trouble – and, frankly, it's only a matter of time – he is someone I would want on my side. His dedication to humanitarian causes is admirable. He has defended many dozens of inmates on Death Row throughout the United States, almost always *pro bono*, and in this he raises himself head-and-shoulders above most of his colleagues in the legal profession.

It troubles me that I view the evidence so differently to him, but I do, and there it is.

17

AS CONSULAR WORK started to gain a higher profile in the media, Consular Directorate in London formulated plans to deal with incidents such as natural disasters and major terrorist attacks. One of the first things they did was to create a Consular Emergency Response Team (CERT) in London – a group of experienced consular officials who participated in a rota-of-availability to travel anywhere in the world at a moment's notice and provide support to local consular teams.

Additionally, each post was required to formulate a consular emergency plan (CEP). The plan was supposed to help us cope with a major incident, whether it was a terrorist attack or a natural disaster. Each plan was localised, but based on a template prepared in London. There were important lessons to be learned from our responses in New York on 9/11 and on Bali in 2002, and they were to be learned at every level in every post.

In February of 2004, two senior consular staff flew out from London to spend a day with us in Orlando explaining the important principles to bear in mind. We worked through a tabletop exercise, learned a lot about London's resources and expectations, and ended with a debriefing during which the message was hammered home: the Treasury had made a fund of money available (over £5 million) to finance our response to significant consular emergencies, and we needed to react quickly and pro-actively.

'Don't worry about overreacting,' said one of the instructors. 'It's better to overreact, and then scale back later if necessary. Be bold.'

To my thinking, this was good stuff. For the first time, in my experience, the FCO was recognising that it had obligations to the ordinary British public, and that the public had expectations as to the consular assistance they should receive in a major emergency, and we were being trained and financed accordingly. Not before time, really.

Within a few months, we had occasion in Florida to see these new consular arrangements in action.

In late August 2004, Hurricane Frances formed in the Atlantic and began its journey towards Florida. It was the second hurricane to hit the state that year – Hurricane Charley had come ashore in Punta Gorda on 13th August – but Frances was a much bigger weather system. The North Atlantic hurricanes, the ones that hit Florida, begin in the doldrums of the Atlantic Ocean, about 10 degrees north of the equator, and they occur between June 1 and November 31 every year. The surface temperature of the ocean is warm, so the water evaporates in vast quantities. Once the vapour reaches a certain altitude it condenses with a terrific release of energy, and this is the primary power source of a hurricane (in some parts of the world, the same weather system is called a cyclone). Additional factors contributing to the mechanics of a hurricane are the earth's rotation and gravity.

Hurricanes are usually measured in terms of the wind speed found at their heart, and categorised from force one to force five (the most ferocious). Frances was building into a force four, but the wind speed was not the most interesting or dangerous thing about this hurricane. What was unusual about it was its size: it was *huge*, the size of the state of Texas. Put another way – to give British readers more perspective – it was three times as big as the entire United Kingdom. Also significantly, it was moving slowly. The predictions were that the storm would hit the shore around Cocoa Beach, a small surfing and retirement community about 40 miles east of Orlando, and then drift slowly over the state, perhaps even coming to a complete standstill for a while.

The biggest component of danger in a hurricane is the flooding that follows (as Katrina showed in New Orleans). This occurs because the sheer quantity of rainwater that falls saturates the ground, overwhelming natural and man-made drainage systems. It goes on to disable power systems, knocks out highways and train tracks, submerges airport runways and leaves people isolated, without much chance of rescue. Then it turns stagnant, and becomes a fetid breeding ground for every species of vile, infectious insect known to mankind. Raw sewage seeps into the lakes of trapped water, turning them poisonous. In short, it's not nice.

I watched the media reports as Hurricane Frances made its way towards us, and Governor Bush regularly updated the state's residents. It looked as though the storm might well flood central Florida, leaving airports inundated, the emergency services overstretched and sanitation unavailable for days or weeks. People who could leave the area were advised to go, but few of the tourists from the UK would be in a position to evacuate very far.

Two days before Frances was expected to make land – the earliest point at which its trajectory and power could be predicted with any degree of accuracy – I contacted the consul general in Atlanta.

'I think we should invoke our consular emergency plan,' I said. 'There's only the five of us here. If things get difficult we're going to need extra staff, so let's get them into Orlando now before the storm hits. It's going to be difficult, if not impossible, to do that after the storm.'

'I agree,' he said. 'I'll leave you to move ahead with it, but please keep me posted.'

I contacted Consular Directorate in London to ask for the funds we would need. I wanted at least four additional staff, with consular experience, to come and help us for up to a week. I had spoken to other posts around the USA, and colleagues were prepared to come from New York, Houston, Chicago and San Francisco, provided I cover their airfares, accommodation and any other incidental expenses. I was hoping we might even get CERT from London. I needed these extra people because if things got bad we'd need the office open 24 hours a day and we might need to send officers out into the field, visiting hospitals, hotels, emergency accommodation sites and so on.

In view of what we had been told in countless circulars, and by the senior brass who had visited six months before, I thought my request would be a formality, so I was surprised when I was told that I would have to wait for several hours for my answer. When it came I was shocked. They refused us the money, and the CERT.

I was incredulous.

'What possible explanation can there be for this?' I demanded to know from a colleague in London.

'It's complicated,' said my desk officer. 'It seems the Treasury intended the fund to be reactive, so because the hurricane has not yet struck Florida you don't qualify for the assistance.'

I protested, as usual – as a matter of principle I protest about almost everything – but I was wasting my time.

This was going to be a problem. We would almost certainly need extra people, but how would we pay for them? I couldn't afford it from my tiny Orlando budget – I had about $10,000 per year for office travel, on which I had to visit, on average, over two hundred prisoners, in addition to all my other outside commitments – and I knew that budgets were also tight around the other consulates. I called around to the other posts, but the response was much the same at each: we can't afford to spend a significant chunk of our budget to come and help you for a week. The feeling was simply that if it wasn't all that important to London, why should it be so important to anyone else? Although it left me in a difficult situation, I couldn't really blame them.

The storm came ashore in Florida on 4th September at Vero Beach, a small retirement community around 50 miles south-east of Orlando. All hurricanes lose power over land, and Frances had dropped to a category two by the time it got to Orlando. The wind speeds were down, but there was still a massive amount of rain. We all hunkered down at our homes for the storm itself and it poured on us for 36 hours. As soon as it passed I headed into the office to launch our response.

There was extensive flooding, although not as much as some had anticipated. The airports would be shut for several days, partly because of water on the airfields, but primarily because oil tankers had been unable to dock anywhere in Florida for a week, and the reserves of jet fuel were down to zero. We started to get many calls from British nationals stranded in Florida, and from family members in the UK.

I wanted to open temporary emergency consulates at both of Orlando's international airports (OIA and Sanford), but to do that I'd need two staff at each airport, plus I would need at least three people in the office, and two others (including myself) to travel around visiting people and co-ordinating the effort.

Predictably, the media coverage of the hurricane back in the UK was sensationalised, with stories and photos of British tourists stranded in school gymnasia sleeping on the floor. Also predictably, the FCO brass in London wanted to be able to report that we were responding proactively. There was now a panic, which was also predictable.

'Hugh,' said my desk officer in London when I picked up the phone, 'what are you doing about all these people trapped in schools? The minister wants to know.'

'I'm trying to arrange visits to them where possible, but I also have to open temporary consulates at two airports and keep staff at the office to field phone calls and liaise with you. The problem is, I don't have enough staff.'

'Why not?' he asked, without a hint of irony.

'I was going to ask you the same question.'

I called my consul general in Atlanta to give him an update.

'Suddenly this has become a priority in London,' I told him. 'The press are lapping up the stories of stranded tourists, and the senior management want to know what we're doing.'

'How are you managing?'

'I'm doing my best,' I said, 'but without more people, we're limited.'

'I'll send you four people from here,' he said.

'It's 400 miles, how will they get here?'

'Drive, I suppose. There's no other way.'

'That hurricane has diminished into a tropical storm,' I said, 'but it's still a powerful system with a lot of wind and rain, and it's now heading right up the interstate towards Atlanta. Do you think the roads will be passable?'

'I'll get a team together and talk to them. I'll let you know when we've made a decision.'

He called me back a couple of hours later and told me that he had four volunteers prepared to attempt the journey down to help us; they would be departing that afternoon in a Land Rover, but he had told them to turn back if it was dangerous.

In the end all four of them arrived safely in Orlando, but it was a dangerous journey and a couple of them were quite shaken up by the time they got there. One, an ex-soldier, told me it was the most dangerous thing he'd ever done. Another one, a London-based woman who was in Atlanta on temporary duty after having done a year in Kinshasa, said it was the closest to death she'd ever been.

We spent the next week responding to public and FCO inquiries about the developing situation. As soon as flights into and out of Orlando recommenced, there were long lines of Britons at both airports, all clamouring to get on the first planes home. There were not enough airline staff to deal with this situation, so, once again, we set up temporary consulates. We staffed them from about 10am until after the last flights left each evening, helping to keep the waiting passengers informed of flight information, arranging priority boarding for those who needed it and finding beds for those who couldn't get on a flight.

It was a hectic week, but we did our work quietly and unsung, which is as it should be. The whole thing left a bad taste in my mouth, though. Once again, after lots of policy chatter in London and a public declaration of how much we'd learned from past mistakes, it was business as usual: poor planning, unrelated to the realities on the ground; critical failure to act decisively at the right moment; lots of groping around in the dark and miscommunication during the event; all followed by a frenetic campaign in London to persuade the media that the FCO was on top of things. Tragedy, or comedy?

* * * * *

Frances wasn't the only major hurricane we had to deal with that year. Hurricane Ivan looked pretty innocuous at first: a category two storm, it arrived ashore in the United States on 16th September near Pensacola in the Florida panhandle, close to Alabama, and missed all our major population centres.

But it was the damage that it had done 500 miles away during the previous day which was to catch us on the hop. The first I heard of it was when a colleague from our consulate in Miami, Nina Robinson, called me to alert me to a growing nightmare at Miami airport. Before reaching the States, Ivan had smashed its way across the Caribbean and along the way it had devastated the Cayman Islands. People were fleeing by the thousands, many leaving their possessions, passports and money behind in the rush. Some of these people were holidaymakers and business people from the United Kingdom, but, and this was the sting in the tail, the Cayman Islands are a British territory, so everyone from the Cayman Islands has a British passport with the right to live in Britain. (British citizens from the UK, sadly, do not have a reciprocal right of abode in the Caymans.) Hundreds of people had begun arriving in Miami that day, many with no passports or means of identification, and the US immigration officials at the airport did not know how to process them. The chief immigration official in Miami had called Nina and she'd called me.

'I'll get a rental car, get some emergency supplies together, and I'll meet you at Miami airport in three hours,' I told her.

'See you there,' she said, full of enthusiasm.

You might ask why – given that the Caymans are a British territory, controlled, essentially, by the Overseas Territories Department (OTD), which is part of the FCO – our officials in London seemed to know nothing about what was happening there. Or, if they did, why none of them had informed us, and let us know what emergency plans the OTD were making for the British citizens of that island?

But I didn't have time to address those questions. I grabbed a large pile of emergency passport documents, along with some other pre-prepared emergency supplies, and headed straight to Miami. I met up with Nina at the airport and we immediately went to speak to the chief US immigration official (CIO).

Embarrassingly, while we might not have known what was happening on our own island the Americans did. The CIO gave me a briefing. The Caymans had been battered by the hurricane: there was no power, no water, no sanitation, and, from the accounts the Americans were getting from their people there, not much in the way of law and order, either. Anyone who could get out was doing so. They were leaving in large numbers and as quickly as possible.

The problem at Miami was that crucial lack of ID; the US immigration service did not know how to deal with these people, and all the usual procedures were out the window.

'I'm in a difficult position,' the CIO said. 'I recognise that this is humanitarian crisis of sorts, and I want to do the right thing, but I can't just let thousands of people into the country with no form of control. Do you have any suggestions?'

'If you can get us airside, we can meet each plane as it arrives,' I said. 'As the passengers disembark, we can sort the Brits into those who have passports and those who don't. We'll issue emergency documents to those who need them so they can get through immigration. Then we can deal with them from there. Would that work for you?'

'Yes, I can do that. I'll get you both airside, and as long as we don't have people turning up at the immigration desks without documents, I'll be happy.'

After Nina and I went airside, we met with a representative from Cayman Airlines and I asked him for an update.

'We only have four planes, and because there's no power on the island they can only take off and land during hours of daylight. The last flights will leave Grand Cayman just before sundown, arriving here in the evening. All four aircraft will stay here overnight, depart virtually empty first thing in the morning and aim to arrive in the Caymans as the sun comes up. Each plane can make four round trips before the sun goes down. That's the best we can do.'

'That's a good start,' I said. 'We can be here at the gate to meet all 16 flights every day until further notice. Anyone on board without a travel document should speak to us as they disembark, and we'll get them fixed up.'

'What about non-British nationals?' he said. 'What do we do about them?'

I hadn't thought about that, so I called the CIO on his cell phone. He told me he'd already spoken to the Italian and South African consulates, but he didn't want consuls from any other countries to go airside, or the whole thing was going to get out of hand. I asked him to give all the other consuls my cell phone number and have them call me. I'd have to improvise as best I could.

I wasn't sure what to expect when the first flight landed, but I was amazed at the terrible physical condition of the passengers, many of whom literally fell off the plane. Many were mothers with babies and young children, and quite a few lacked travel documents and had only the clothes they were wearing. Nina and I took them into a separate room to interview them and issue emergency passports.

We soon heard from them about the situation in the Caymans. Without lighting – the main grid was completely down, but a few places, such as the radio station, had generators – the streets had become dangerous at nights, with widespread looting. In the general chaos, there were stories of assaults and rapes. Hospitals were turning people away, and patients already inside were receiving little treatment. Within 24 hours, food was running out as some people panic-bought and ships couldn't yet dock to offload new supplies.

To help mitigate the panic on the island, Cayman Airways had announced over the radio that it would carry to Miami, free of charge, anyone wishing to leave the island. Of course, thousands then flocked to the airport to try and escape, and the police and soldiers trying to guard it were using a heavy hand to protect the perimeter. The airline had suggested that those with babies and small children, or those in urgent need of medical treatment would be given priority to leave the island. The problem was that the soldiers weren't letting anyone near the terminal, and the vulnerable ones couldn't fight their way through the cordon. Several people told me they'd heard shooting. It sounded like hell.

As each flight arrived. Nina and I issued dozens of emergency passports, advised the bewildered passengers to clear US immigration and wait for us opposite the BA desk. Once we'd finished processing emergency passports, we'd rush through to the terminal to help people with travel to another destination, or finding somewhere to stay, or getting medication, or any of a thousand other issues. I also spent hours dealing with non-British nationals and making frantic phone calls to the consulates of Italy, Germany, Israel, Holland and South Africa, among others.

After two days, it was clear that this wasn't going to end quickly. I sent a message to Graeme Wise, the consul at our embassy in Washington, asking for assistance. He immediately made arrangements to travel down the next day along with his deputy, Adam Radcliffe.

I also sent a message to OTD in London describing what we were hearing from the arriving passengers and asking them for assistance. I said that the Cayman Islands were being evacuated and that many people were arriving in Miami with no money and no papers. They were asking, quite reasonably I thought, for financial help, which I didn't have the resources to arrange.

I dropped in to the Miami consulate the next morning before going to the airport, and picked up the emailed response from OTD. The department had taken a firm line on my request. They said words to the effect that the Cayman Islands were not being evacuated, as they had not ordered that they be so. Furthermore, they were pleased the police were taking a strong line with the public, as this would prevent widespread panic. As far as the money was concerned, there were relatively few British nationals arriving in Miami, and we should be able to deal with them using normal consular arrangements.

This reply dripped with the kind of pomposity, arrogance and sheer out-of-touchness that only a senior FCO official can conjure. If the infrastructure of an island has failed, there is widespread disorder and everyone is trying to leave, that's an evacuation, whether you define it as such or not. Secondly, how could they know 4,000 miles away what the law and order situation was? Who were they talking to? Certainly not the bedraggled passengers I was confronted with. Thirdly, they seemed to be under the assumption that we were only offering consular assistance to British citizens *from the UK*. I wished we had that choice.

Nina, who hadn't seen the message, was sitting across the desk from me when I read it. 'What does it say?' she asked.

'Just some cant from London,' I said.

I was tired and frustrated by the end of the third day. I chose that time to draft a vitriolic response to OTD, but before I had a chance to send it Graeme and Adam arrived from Washington. I showed it to Graeme, and he wouldn't let me send it. If he had, I have no doubt I would have been summarily dismissed. It would almost have been worth it.

The next day, I found myself dealing with an interesting problem. A man approached me at our temporary consulate on the airport concourse.

'Excuse me, are you the British consul?' he asked.

'Yes, I'm Hugh Hunter. How can I help you?'

'I've been refused permission to fly to Grand Cayman, and I was wondering whether you could assist?'

'Why would you want to go?'

'I'm a journalist, and I want to know the situation is on the island. The Cayman Airways station manager here is refusing me passage.'

'I'll speak to him and see what I can do,' I told him, and he came with me to listen in to the conversation.

'This man says you won't let him fly to Grand Cayman. Is that correct?'

'Yes, that's right,' he told me. 'I'm under instructions from London to prevent him from flying.'

'Why?'

'You'll have to ask them that.'

I called London on my cell phone, and eventually found my way through to OTD.

'I have (I named the journalist) here, and I've been told by Cayman Airways that he is not to be permitted to fly to the island. Is that true?'

'Yes, he's not allowed in,' I was told.

'Why not?'

'He may write something detrimental.'

Funny: I'd thought there was nothing going on to be detrimental about.

'I'm sure he might,' I said, 'but surely this is a free country? We don't do things like that, do we? Where are we, North Korea?'

'He might get in the way of the recovery operation.'

'First of all, what recovery operation? Secondly, are we banning him in case he's critical, or in case he gets in the way?'

'Sorry, I can't help you further. He's not allowed in, and that's the end of it.'

I was dumbfounded, and more than slightly embarrassed to have to report it to the gentleman concerned.

'I'm sorry,' I said, 'and I'm shocked. I don't know what to tell you. I'm ashamed to represent a country that would behave in that way.'

'Don't worry,' he said. 'I appreciate that you tried for me.'

The four of us worked at Miami airport for another four days before the situation calmed down enough for us to deal with it from the consulate. Graeme and Adam flew back to Washington, Nina stayed in Miami and I drove back to Orlando. On the way back I was tired, disillusioned and angry. That was some of the most difficult and intense consular work I'd done, yet, if it hadn't been for Graeme's intervention, I could have got myself fired for it. That just seemed wrong.

* * * * *

At the beginning of 2005, the deputy consul-general (DCG) in Atlanta came to visit the office to address the whole staff.

'I have some wonderful news,' she said. 'You all did so well during the hurricane season last year that we have arranged for you to get a bonus of 500 dollars each.'

She seemed overjoyed to be giving us this information. The others smiled at each other and I am sure they were enjoying both the recognition for their efforts and the prospect of some extra cash.

'You can keep mine,' I said.

'Keep it?' she responded, obviously not expecting my reply.

'Yeah, keep it. I don't want it.'

'You don't need the 500 dollars?'

'Of course I need 500 dollars,' I said, 'but I want no part in this nonsense.'

'Well, I find that a bit odd,' she said.

'I don't think it's odd at all. The whole thing's a sham and it's about time a few people stood up and said so.'

'The consul-general had to write to London and make a case for this,' she said. 'I hope you understand that that was quite an involved process and took a lot of effort.'

'I'm sorry to disappoint you, but in my case it was a waste of time. He needn't have bothered.'

Within a few minutes the mood of the room had changed completely. The DCG became terse, and started to pack her things to leave. The rest of my team seemed embarrassed at my reaction, and were probably concerned they might lose the cash.

'I'll remember that the next time anyone suggests rewarding you for a job well done,' she said.

'Please do,' I answered.

She stood up and said a quick thank you to the others before leaving for the airport. I don't think she was angry with me, but she was astonished by my attitude and seemed to have taken it personally. It seemed clear to me that she had completely accepted the concept of monetary reward for good performance and had not anticipated that others felt differently. This bonus culture had cascaded down from Whitehall, and it appeared that everyone in the Diplomatic Service who wanted a career had bought into it without question.

At the end of the month, $500 appeared in my bank account with the rest of my salary. I wrote a cheque for the full amount and sent it to Atlanta, but they never cashed it so I still have their 500 bucks.

It wasn't just that I objected to the insinuation that we wouldn't do our job properly without bonuses, it was also that I remembered clearly how poorly London had responded to our requests for assistance, despite their promises less than a year ago. I also remembered how close I'd come to losing my job.

By this time, my job was not the only thing I ran the risk of losing.

Cheryl's determination to move our relationship to the next stage was growing in direct proportion to my increasing inertia. I liked things how they were: I worked hard, I liked to go flying on the weekends and I loved to sit around reading alone. I always had a great time with her, knowing that I had my own place to go back to at the end of the day. She was always direct and honest about how she felt. I thought I was also direct and honest, but, in retrospect, that probably wasn't true.

She played her cards well. Months would go by, during which the subject of commitment would never be broached. I felt I was being given latitude to introduce the matter of my own volition. I never did. After a suitable period of time, Cheryl would give me a little push to help me along. I began to feel ever-so-slightly trapped in a corner, and I was running out of ideas to escape.

One Sunday lunchtime, she came to collect me for an afternoon drive. It was a perfect day; we had the top of her convertible car down, and the wind was in my hair.

'Do you mind if we go to see a couple of houses while we're out?' she asked.

'No, I don't mind,' I said. 'Is it for work?'

'No, I thought we might go and see some places we could buy together.'

We had never seriously discussed even living together, so the casual suggestion of buying a place as a couple was so unexpected that I thought it was a joke. But I didn't laugh. I sat there quietly panicking whilst she drove us to a modest, unremarkable family home in a pleasant, undistinguished area of Orlando. She was forcing the issue. Either I went along with this, which would imply that I was up for it, or I needed to say something soon to clarify the situation. There was no question of my being ready for this step. I was becoming unsure about my future at the consulate, and as my immigration status was tied to my diplomatic visa I was uncertain that I would even stay in the United States. Nor did I want to take out a giant mortgage to buy a house that I couldn't afford, didn't like and wouldn't enjoy. Buying a house was also the first step towards marriage and then children, and I was increasingly feeling like a stranger in a foreign land. Cheryl was so American, and, having lived abroad for almost 20 years, I was becoming paradoxically more and more British. As an American, she believed that love would conquer all, but as an Englishman, I knew it wouldn't. This was going too far. I needed to be clear and decisive with her, and I needed to do it now.

Naturally, I bottled it. I spent the next two hours walking around nondescript houses making vacuous, insincere comments about 'space' and 'atmosphere', feeling guilty about the obvious pleasure on Cheryl's face and wishing I were safely back in my apartment.

18

PRISON VISITING WAS not popular with many of my colleagues. It meant hours, if not days, away from the office when there were other priorities to deal with. It also meant spending time in depressing jails, dealing with the difficult prison system bureaucracy and to talking to sometimes hostile and unappreciative prisoners. Many also felt that the visits themselves were unproductive.

This was music to the ears of the purse-holders back in London. If I flew to Pensacola, spent two days visiting four prisoners, with a night in a hotel and expenses, it could easily cost the best part of a thousand dollars. Budgets in every civil service department had been under pressure for years, so it was decided that maybe we shouldn't visit prisoners as assiduously. After all, who's going to stand up and defend spending money on convicts in foreign jails?

It all came to a head at a consular conference I hosted in Orlando for various British consuls from around the USA and Canada and colleagues and managers from London. Our prisoner visiting policy was at the top of the agenda, and it was quickly clear that many people felt we could sidestep a lot of the work by asking whether some convicts were really British or not, or simply changing the requirements to visit people.

Many of our prisoners had left the UK as children and had grown up in the USA as, essentially, Americans. They often had family and friends in the States but not in the UK. Despite their British citizenship, they often regarded themselves as being American and didn't really understand why we were visiting them. Many of my consular colleagues had unofficially all but stopped providing assistance to such people; the question was, could we make this official?

I was in a minority on this, and if you removed the neutrals from the equation I think it was a minority of one.

'Why would we give them consular assistance if they don't want it, or can't see the point of it?' one chap argued.

'There are several reasons,' I said. 'As felons they will all be deported from the USA on completion of their sentence. They will then be living in Britain, whether we like it or not. We get the opportunity to help prepare them for the life they have ahead of them, and we also get an opportunity to forewarn the appropriate services in the UK that they're coming. Some of these people are violent murderers, paedophiles and rapists.'

'That's not our job, that's a police job or a social services job,' was the response from one colleague.

'We're here to assist prisoners,' I said, 'but we should also ensure our government is properly notified of pertinent information. If we don't engage with these people whilst they're in prison, we lose our opportunity to do that.'

My opinion wasn't popular with my America-based colleagues, and when the top man from London spoke I realised it wasn't that popular there either.

'I think we're going to have to accept that we should target our limited resources on those with a really strong connection to the United Kingdom or our territories. I think the newspapers would have a field day if we spend too much of our time and effort with a convicted rapist who left the UK when he was six months old, has no family there and has never even visited the place.' This was greeted with approval around the table.

'Hang on a second,' I said. 'I think you're getting into dangerous territory if you're going to start saying some Brits are more British than others. There can only be one determination for this – if you qualify for British citizenship, you're British. If you don't, you're not. If you're saying there are degrees of "Britishness", the next thing you'll be asking people is which cricket team they support. Then you'll be on a sticky wicket.'

Nobody laughed; I realised they felt as strongly about this as I did.

'Look, Hugh,' said the top man from London, 'I understand you, but there are certain realities we have to face. We don't know exactly how many people outside of the UK have an entitlement to British citizenship. The real number is probably unknowable, but every reasonable estimate is between five and ten million. We cannot afford to be responsible for that kind of financial commitment.'

'But consular work is self-funding,' I countered. 'Every time a British person buys a passport, ten pounds of that fee goes directly to fund consular work. How can the finances not work out?'

(According to the rules, all those tenners are supposed to be ring-fenced for the FCO's Consular Directorate; later I tried to discover whether it was actually being held discretely, but could not find any clear accounting trail showing that it was.)

'I think we could talk this into the ground,' said the London brass. 'Let's leave it there for now. There will be ongoing discussion about this in London and we'll let you know what we decide in due course.'

To everybody else's relief the conference moved on, but I knew it wasn't going to end there for me.

* * * * *

Alec McDougal is the kind of guy who was going to be affected by this change of emphasis. As far as I can tell, he has the longest prison sentence of any British citizen anywhere in the world.

In 1983, a Florida judge sentenced him to 1,285 years in jail. Even when he dies he will still have well over 1,000 years to serve, and he didn't even kill anyone.

McDougal was born in Britain, and grew up in south-west London. When he was in his teens, his mother married a US airman, and a few years later the family moved to Florida.

For McDougal, it was downhill from there on in.

He started getting into trouble pretty regularly, and by the time he was 20 he was a habitual offender and a convicted felon.

One hot summer's night in August 1983, high on drugs and carrying guns, he and two friends burst into a large house in Okaloosa County in northern Florida, where a dinner party was in progress. They forced the 12 guests into a downstairs toilet at gunpoint, and held them there whilst they ransacked the house for valuables. Unbeknownst to the perpetrators, a silent alarm had been activated and, as McDougal and his accomplices made their escape, they were intercepted by the police and quickly arrested.

It was a pathetic folly from the start, exacerbated by their choice of victim: the host was a senior member of the Florida establishment, a judge and prominent Republican politician.

McDougal was charged with 12 counts of kidnapping; it's worth knowing that, in Florida, if you force someone to go *anywhere* against their will, even if it's only from one room of a house to another, that qualifies as a kidnapping. In addition there were charges of possession of a firearm by a convicted felon, and armed burglary.

He was offered a plea bargain of 60 years imprisonment if he pleaded guilty; he thought this was a bit steep, so he decided to take his chances at trial.

That was a mistake.

He was convicted by a jury and sentenced to 100 years imprisonment for each charge of kidnapping, 70 years for armed burglary and 15 years for possession of a firearm by a felon. All of these sentences were to run consecutively.

'Perhaps,' declared the judge at his sentencing, 'this will teach you a lesson, Mr McDougal.'

That must be one of the all-time great understatements.

He was pleased to see me the first time I turned up at Union Correctional Institution to visit him. I was the only visitor he had received in 16 years. His surviving family members had long since broken off all contact with him. Sadly, this was something that I saw quite often: when someone you love goes to prison for the rest of his life, it is sometimes best for everyone to consider him dead. However, McDougal's initial excitement at meeting me was soon overtaken by melancholy. I can't fault him for that: I think I would have felt much the same in his situation.

During that first meeting, we talked for over an hour about one thing and another. He told me his life story, and regaled me with accusations of corrupt Florida judges, and a deeply prejudiced and flawed legal system: something, unsurprisingly, you frequently hear from prisoners. While he was talking I watched him carefully, and tried to imagine the aggressive, violent and irrational man that he once must have been. It was difficult. His shoulders slumped, his head hung down and his hands shook as he smoked a cigarette. After all those years in prison, and with no prospect of release, his spirit had been castrated by the Great State of Florida. He desperately wanted to be free again, but he had made a Faustian pact and exchanged a few youthful years of high-octane excitement for this purgatory. He had completely wasted his life at a time when he was lacking the wisdom to understand what he was throwing away.

As I started to wrap up what was already an overly long conversation, he held up a hand. 'Hang on,' he said. 'I want to tell you something.' He slunk out of his seat, quickly checked outside the door of our meeting room to make sure nobody was listening and then leaned in close to me.

'Listen,' he whispered. 'I want to confess to something. I've never told anyone about it, and it's been eating me up.'

My interest was aroused. 'OK,' I said, and leaned in closer.

'When I was a young kid growing up in Battersea, I was mates with some other boys from my council estate, including one who was about three years older than the rest of us. He was kind of our gang leader. He was a lot bigger than the rest of us, and this guy was a psychopath. He used to lie down between the railway tracks and let the trains go over the top of him. He was an ugly kid. One of his eyes was a lot bigger than the other one, his nose was crooked and most of his mouth was on one side of his face. It looked like someone had welded two halves of separate skulls together to make his head. We used to joke that his mum didn't have a bed for him, so she hung him by his mouth on a coat peg every night to sleep. But he was a bully and a really scary guy. We were all terrified of him.'

I nodded. 'Sounds like a real charmer,' I said.

'One evening,' said McDougal, 'we was playing down by the river, down by the Thames there, and it was starting to get dark. Most of the other lads had gone off home for their tea, and in the end it was only me and this other kid left. We decided to get north of the river on a railway bridge. So we get about halfway over, and he stops and challenges me to hang off the edge of the bridge by my fingertips.'

McDougal held up his fingers to me, miming clinging on to something for dear life.

'I was terrified,' he continued. 'The tide was going out, the river was running fast and it was a long way down. I couldn't even swim! It was madness. I wanted to say no, but I could just tell that if I did that this guy – he was a maniac, to be honest, completely unpredictable – was just going to beat me up, and probably throw me off the bridge.'

He paused, and I sensed that he was reliving the moment in his mind. I said nothing, and waited for him to continue.

'So what I did was, I said I'd do it as long as he went first, thinking he'd back out of it. But he said okay, he would, and he climbed over the edge. I think as he started lowering himself down he must have realised how stupid it was, and seen that there was no way he could hang on by his hands or pull himself back onto the bridge afterwards. I saw him look down at the water, with his legs flying around everywhere, and then he started to freak out. I could see it in his face – really scared, he was. He was sort of propped up on his elbows, just hanging there with his feet waving around. He started trying to haul himself back up, but he couldn't do it. Then he started shouting at me, "You do it! You do it!" I was so scared. I think I started to cry. I didn't want to do it, but I knew he'd kill me if I didn't. I didn't know how to get out of this, so I panicked. I kicked him in the face and started stamping on his hands and arms. Just stomping, stomping, stomping. He let go and fell straight into the river, screaming. It was a long way down. I saw him go under the water, but I never saw him come up again.'

'Bloody hell!' I said. 'Are you serious?'

'Yes.'

'Did he drown?' I asked.

'Well, they never found a body,' said McDougal. 'The police got involved after his mother reported him missing, but they never found nothing out. In the end they said he'd just disappeared. They didn't even know that I was the last person to see him. About a year later, we moved to Florida and that was that.'

'Who knows about this?' I asked.

'Me and you.'

We sat in silence for a while, and I studied his face carefully. I wondered if he was lying, but how can you know? He was obviously waiting for me to say something, but I didn't even know where to start, so I began doodling on my writing pad whilst I thought about it.

'Mr Hunter,' he said, after a couple of minutes of quiet, 'if you can get me extradited back to England to pay for my crime, I am prepared to confess and make a full statement to the police. Do you think you can do that? What would I get for murder in England? I was a juvenile offender, don't forget, so there should be some leniency. Ten years? Surely not more than 15?'

To my shame, my reaction was to laugh; but he didn't laugh with me and I realised that I was going to have to take this seriously.

'Can you remember what the victim was called?' I said.

He thought about it for a moment. 'Nah, I can't. We all called him "Fuckface", but I don't think that was his real name.'

'Did you call him that even if he was there?'

'No, if he was there we called him Popeye.'

'When did this happen, exactly?'

'I guess I was about 12 or 13, so around 1965.'

I asked a few more questions, but he was unable to provide any more information.

'So, do you think you can get me to England?' he asked, as I was putting my notes away.

'I doubt it, but I'll see what I can do.'

I suspected this desperate story was nothing more than an ingenious escape plan; but sometimes I wonder. Either way, even if it had contained any truth, it would have not been remotely likely to result in his release from a Florida prison.

Nevertheless, out of a sense of duty, when I got back to the office I contacted the Metropolitan Police in London and put the case to a detective. As I had expected, he told me that with nothing more than the inadequate information McDougal had given me, there was little if anything to be done. He didn't even offer to check that far back in the missing persons file.

* * * * *

Despite my best efforts, the rules were changed after that conference, and British consuls in Europe and North America are now only required to visit prisoners soon after their arrest and once again after their conviction. Thereafter, a visit is only made if the prisoner has strong ties to the UK – after all, such a prisoner's family could complain to their local MP – or in the event of a humanitarian need.

I ignored this, and continued to visit all my long-term prisoners every year – we had over 150 of them – citing a humanitarian need on each occasion: after all, the factors contributing to a humanitarian need are quite subjective. But it wasn't popular in London and my boss, the consul general in Atlanta, was asked to curtail my activities. I flew to Georgia for a dressing down.

'London tells me you keep visiting long-term prisoners even though the policy has changed,' he said.

'Yes, that's correct.'

'Why is that?'

'There are humanitarian reasons,' I said, 'and I think it's important.'

'Well, officially it's not. Please try to do it less, or, even better, not at all.'

He obviously didn't like getting reports from London that his subordinate vice-consul was insubordinate.

I decided to ignore that, too: I would continue to visit prisoners in much the same way that I had been doing for the last five years. It would only be a matter of time before this came to the attention of London, and they probably wouldn't like it; I knew that the next time I was ordered up to Atlanta to discuss the matter, I wouldn't be getting a warning. But it was a point of principle. To take Alex McDougal, he was a British citizen, born in Britain to a British mother – and I was supposed to consider him, and others like him, as somehow less British? I came to learn that the British government could be slightly hypocritical on the subject of nationality. The concept of who is or isn't British, or how British you are, is a moveable feast, as the case of Felix Johnson shows.

The phone rang one morning. It was the US immigration service reporting the arrest of a British national, the aforementioned Felix, who had attempted to enter the USA at Miami Airport the day before. During his immigration check, it had been discovered that he had been previously convicted of murder in Florida and had been deported after serving his time.

I went to see him in jail the next day to find out the background to his arrest. It caused me some consternation.

Felix Johnson was born in Jamaica and lived there until he was 16, when he travelled to Florida. It was supposed to be a three-week holiday with his cousin, but he decided to stick around; being unable to work legitimately, he started up in business dealing drugs to get by. As so often seems to happen in the unregulated world of narcotics trading, problems soon arose.

'Basically, two friends of mine wanted to meet another guy I knew, a drug dealer,' he said. 'They said they wanted to buy some weed off of him. They said they needed an introduction, that they couldn't get to meet him otherwise. So I agreed to help them out.'

Johnson and the two others drove to the house where the other man lived.

'I knocked on the door, and he was like, "Who is it?" Like, he didn't open the door to no-one unless he knew them real well. I told him it was me, I got some guys with me want to buy some weed. He know me, we never had no falling out or nothing, so he open the door and we start the talking.'

The man trusted Johnson and agreed to walk over to the car to meet the occupants. As he drew close, a tainted window lowered and a fusillade of shots was fired at close range. The man fell dead.

All three fled, but they were arrested shortly afterwards and prosecuted. Under Florida law, all were equally culpable of the murder if they were in a common enterprise, and each knew what was going to happen. Johnson argued in court that he didn't, that he thought he was just arranging a meeting between mutual friends; but the jury decided he was lying and convicted him. The judge sentenced him to 10 years in the big house. He was released from prison about seven years later, and immediately deported back to Jamaica. As with all people who are deported from America, there follows a period of exclusion. In Johnson's case that period was life.

He only stayed in Jamaica for a few months before deciding that his prospects were better in the United Kingdom. After his arrival in England, he met a British woman and married her. He then applied to the Home Office for 'leave to remain' in the UK – another way of saying he applied to become a permanent resident of Britain – on the basis of his marriage. On the form he completed as part of this process, he was required to declare whether he had any criminal convictions: he stated that he did not. After living in Britain for the qualifying period of three years, he applied for British nationality, which was granted.

A few years later, Johnson's father was taken seriously ill in Florida and was expected to die (ironically, he subsequently made a full recovery). In his desperation to see his father, Johnson took a chance and made the trip to Miami. Although he knew he was excluded from the United States, he believed that by travelling on his new passport he might evade detection from the US immigration authorities. He was wrong, and that's how we met.

Although I was committed to providing him with proper consular assistance, I was troubled by how he had managed to get his British nationality. When I discovered that he had lied on his application form to get his citizenship, it seemed wrong. Interestingly, some new legislation designed to combat international terrorism had just passed through Parliament. This legislation permitted the Home Secretary to remove acquired British nationality if it could be shown that the person had lied or misrepresented his circumstances when he had applied for it. This seemed to me to be exactly what Johnson had done, notwithstanding that there was no suggestion that he was involved in terrorism.

I wrote a report about the case and sent it to the then head of the nationality section of Consular Directorate in London, the late Paul Ronchetti, whom I knew well, liked and respected. In my report, I suggested that the Home Office (HO) should pursue this case with the intention of revoking Johnson's British citizenship. Paul sent the report to an official at the HO, who replied a few weeks later to the effect that this was not the sort of case the Government had in mind when it passed the legislation, and that the HO had no intention of acting upon it. Paul sent me a copy of the report the next day, saying that that was the end of the matter. I wrote back to Paul explaining that the HO official who had written the report had no idea what he was talking about: first of all the HO should not be applying its own rules selectively, and at the very least it should be tested in court; secondly, if there was to be no sanction against someone who had lied upon an official application form, what possible incentive could there be for an applicant to tell the truth in future? That kind of information quickly travels around the type of communities where it is useful. Paul's reply was quick and to the point: I was told that it was not our position to instruct the HO how to process its own business, and that I had to drop it.

Within a few months, the US immigration service decided that because Johnson had not attempted to change his name or date of birth in order to deceive them, and had readily admitted his previous conviction and deportation, he should be dealt with leniently. He was deported back to Britain after four months in detention.

The last I heard he was living comfortably in the London area with his wife and children. In all probability he has turned his life around and is now a productive and law-abiding member of the community, but that's hardly the point. Many other countries revoke citizenship in circumstances such as these, the Americans among them – but unlike us, they have the political will and courage to enforce their rules.

McDougal, born in England to a British mother, is officially ignored, considered for practical purposes to be an American. Johnson, a convicted murderer from Jamaica who lied to gain British nationality, is to be permitted to retain the full rights of citizenship with the blessing of the Home Office.

It's farcical.

I went to visit McDougal every year whilst I was in Florida. I was the only visitor he ever had and the last time I saw him was when I came to leave Orlando. I told him this would be our last meeting. I also told him that he was unlikely to get any more consular visits, as the policy had been changed in London. He nodded, and seemed sad – I was probably the only person in his recent life who came even close to being a friend, the concept of friendship in a prison being significantly different to that on the outside – but I looked into his eyes and saw nothing there. This was a man with no hope and no reason to go on. I wished him luck, but we both knew there would be none. We shook hands and I said goodbye forever.

19

A LOT OF the people you deal with in consular offices are not who they claim to be.

People use false ID when travelling for a number of reasons. They might be wanted by the police; they might have been deported previously, or owe money to someone, or be hiding from other criminals, or trying to avoid getting a criminal record in their real name.

I spent many hours trying to establish the true identities of Brits who had found themselves in the Florida justice system, or working on people who were *claiming* they were British, but weren't.

The British passport is highly prized by foreign nationals who want to travel on a false identity. This is because there are relatively few visa requirements for British nationals travelling internationally and there are also many ethnically non-Anglo Saxon British nationals. It's not at all unusual for people whose antecedents are in Africa, the Caribbean or Asia to be authentically British, whereas a Nigerian might attract more attention if he presented a Russian or Cambodian passport.

Additionally, there is an extensive criminal network that can help you obtain a British passport. I'm afraid we've not made it particularly difficult for them. I reported many dozens of cases of passport fraud to the United Kingdom Passport Authority (UKPA) over the years, though to the best of my knowledge only one of them resulted in a prosecution. I'm talking about cases where there was clear evidence, including documents and incriminating statements, all of which were offered on a plate to the UK authorities, and almost none of which were ever utilised.

All that would happen – in the worst cases – was that the names of the fraudulent individual and of the person whose identity might have been stolen would be added to a warning list, usually causing more difficulties for the innocent person than the criminal.

I was called by a US immigration service officer attached to the Broward County Jail Women's Facility in Fort Lauderdale. They had a woman who had been arrested a few days ago for attempting to bring cocaine into America. She had arrived at Fort Lauderdale Airport on a flight from Jamaica, and had presented her British passport to immigration officials before being arrested by customs officers. She gave me the woman's name: Penelope Agnes Chalmondley. Place of birth: Cheltenham, Glos.

Later that day, I requested a copy of Chalmondley's passport application form from the UK Passport Service. The form was duly faxed through to me, and I had a look through it. Everything seemed to be in order, except for a few nagging details.

The first was that the given name and place of birth suggested – I put it no higher than that, of course – that the applicant would probably be a white woman, whereas in fact she was Afro-Caribbean.

The second was that there were some odd spelling mistakes in the application; for example, her hometown was written as 'Cheltenam'.

The third was a spelling mistake made by the counter-signatory: this supposedly professional person had written the name of his employer as 'Brown & Asosiates'.

The final point of interest was that this woman was 34 and yet was apparently applying for her first passport; this is not terribly rare, and is obviously not an offence, but it is slightly unusual.

Anyway, I went to visit 'Penelope' a few days later.

The person in front of me was unmistakably the person whose photograph was on the passport, and, by cross-referencing it to the passport application form, the person to whom the passport had been issued. During the interview, however, she was quite evasive with me. She didn't look at me much whilst I was talking to her, and kept glancing through the window into the room next door: I very much got the impression that she wished she were there rather than with me.

Furthermore, she simply didn't know the answers to some basic questions about things she should have known.

'Can I ask, how do you say your surname?' I said.

'Chall-mond-lee,' she replied. Normally, it is pronounced 'Chumley', of course.

'You have a very strong Jamaican accent,' I said.

'I live on de island when I was little,' she said. 'For a laang time.'

'You say you live in London now, Ms Chalmondley?' I asked.

She nodded. 'In Kensington.'

'Can you tell me the name of the nearest tube station to your house?' I said.

There was a long silence, and then she shook her head.

'I know Kensington quite well,' I said. 'Which supermarket do you shop in?'

Again, she was silent.

'Can you name *any* British supermarket chains?'

'Why you ask me all this?'

Afterwards, I spoke with the immigration official.

'I'd like to retain this passport,' I said. It had only been issued a few weeks before in London, but, tellingly, it bore no entry stamp for Jamaica, from whence the woman had just arrived.

When I got back to the office, I contacted the UKPA and requested that they examine the application for this woman and let me know whether they were happy with it. They got back to me a few days later and told me that they could see nothing wrong with it, and that as far as they were concerned it was a legitimate issue. I still wasn't satisfied, so I contacted the passport office at the British Embassy in Washington, and told the Chief Passport Examiner (CPE) there about my reservations. The CPE was Sean Ferguson – a slightly abrasive character who wouldn't win many popularity contests, but a helpful and extremely competent passport examiner with whom I'd developed a good relationship over the years.

'I'll look into it, Hugh,' he said. 'Leave it with me.'

He called me back about ten days later.

'We found out a few interesting things about this case,' he said. 'Your suspicions were bang on. There is a Penelope Chalmondley from Cheltenham, but your woman isn't she. The real Penelope is white, and she's never left the town in her life – she was born severely mentally and physically disabled, and she lives in a care home. I got this from the Benefits Agency.'

As strange as it may sound, this was a real break. It's rare for information to be exchanged by normal channels between government departments. Partly, this is because of ethical objections: some people think it is simply wrong to share or request information about a particular individual from other departments. It is also partly because of a lack of mechanism: short of picking up a phone and calling someone on spec, there are no established channels of communication.

A few days later I headed back down to Fort Lauderdale to confront the inmate.

We met in the same room, and she was just as evasive. I have a feeling she knew what was coming.

'I know you're not Penelope Chalmondley,' I said. 'If you're honest with me I'll do what I can to advise you. But if she continue to lie to me, I'm going to walk out of here and tell the whole story to the US immigration service and you're on your own.'

She thought for a moment or two, and then sighed. 'OK, I am really Jamaican,' she said. 'My name is Janelle Douglas. I was ask' to smuggle some coke into the United States, for a laat of money, but I have a conviction back home for drug smuggling so I cannot get a visa. The man, he say to me, get another passport. My aunt, she work in England at a hospital or someting. She look after this lady, Penelope Chalmondley, and knew that she would never leave the hospital. So someone get a copy of her birth certificate and apply for a passport usin' my picture.'

'Who applied for you?' I said.

'I can't tell you that,' she replied.

The passport had been mailed out to Jamaica – hence, no entry stamp to that country – and Douglas had used it as her own.

I thanked her for her honesty – after all, I'd benefited from learning how she'd managed to undertake this fraud – and asked if she needed any advice from me. She seemed relieved to have got this off her chest, and for the first time in either of my meetings with her she smiled. She said she would appreciate some help, so I sat with her for a while and gave her the best advice I could.

I'm sure my initial suspicions about this case, were, in themselves, probably outside the bounds of some people's definition of political correctness. But the fact remains that if I had not reported them to the Chief Passport Examiner in Washington, the deception would probably never have come to light. It certainly would not have been detected by the UKPA using their usual methods of examination. Think of that laxity applied across thousands of applications – some of them made for highly sinister purposes.

When I had first arrived in Orlando, deportation officers often kicked out British nationals without telling the consulate; provided they had the detainee's current passport, they would simply arrange the removal without contacting us.

This caused me some anxiety, as I felt that the people concerned might not be getting the advice and support they needed. I was also concerned that, in some cases, people potentially using false identities might be deported to Britain without being checked out properly.

I asked the US immigration officials to refrain from deporting British people until we could arrange consular access; at the same time I undertook to do these visits as quickly as possible, and usually this was done within a few days.

The immigration officials at each of the three deportation centres in Florida – Bradenton, Krome (in Miami) and Orlando – were very co-operative with us, and were a great credit to their service. As a result of this relationship, we managed to prevent a significant number of unlawful entries to the UK, including a certain Mr Hussain.

I got a call from an officer at Bradenton who had picked up a man named Mohammed Hussain, a British national who had entered the USA several years before as a tourist and had overstayed.

It appeared to be, for all intents and purposes, a straightforward case.

They had his unexpired British passport, and they were anxious to deport him as quickly as possible – as usual, their cells were full.

I obtained the passport application form from the UKPA, and everything looked to be in order. The next day I went to visit him in the jail. As with 'Penelope Chalmondley', the man I was talking to looked to be the same man whose photograph was on the application form, but during our conversation it again quickly became apparent that something wasn't right.

He claimed he had lived in Bradford all his life until he had come to the USA five years ago, and the immigration stamps in his passport did support this version of events. Yet he had a very strong Asian accent, without the slightest trace of Yorkshire in it – no sign of an 'oop' or a 'bar t'at'.

'Can you tell me the name of your local football team?' I asked.

'No, sorry. I don't like football.'

'Can you tell me the name of the nearest motorway to Bradford?'

'No, I don't drive, you see.'

He was unable to answer a number of similar questions, so after the meeting I asked deportation officer to give me a little more time to investigate.

The next day I contacted, *inter alia*, Interpol in London to see what information they might have on this individual, and it so happened that they had quite a bit: the most interesting part of which was that he was currently detained at Her Majesty's pleasure in HMP Strangeways.

This presented me with a dilemma. The British police were quite certain that they had the right man. Their person had been in trouble with the police frequently over a long period of time, going back to his youth, and they had matching fingerprints on him throughout. I decided to go back and challenge the man in detention in Bradenton.

'I don't know who you are,' I said, 'but I know you are not Mohammed Hussain.'

He shrugged and admitted it. 'I am from Pakistan,' he said.

'How did you get the passport?'

'See, my parents get it for me at a grocery store in Khyber Pass.'

I didn't believe a word of that, of course, but it became clear he wasn't going to change his story. But it didn't really matter at this point. He then gave me what he claimed was his real name, place and date of birth, and I told him he would have to sort it out with the Americans. This would involve US Immigration officers taking this character, under armed guard, on a plane to Washington DC and presenting him to the consular section of the Pakistani Embassy for an interview. Assuming he was then given a Pakistani passport, he would then need to be brought all the way back to Florida to be dealt with for the original offence of overstaying.

It's worth pointing out here that – in the United States at least – the officials from many embassies and consulates, including Pakistan, often don't bother to send consular officers to visit their nationals in US immigration service deportation jails. We *always* went, in person, within a few days, and we always resolved nationality and identity questions as quickly as we could. No wonder we had such a good relationship with the deportation officers in Florida! But it didn't just work for them. If I had not interviewed 'Hussain', he would almost certainly have been successfully deported to the UK – and the only remaining line of defence would have been an interception by a British immigration officer on arrival. Chances are he would have waltzed back into Britain and would still be travelling the world on his British passport with impunity.

* * * * *

In the above two cases, foreigners used a false British identity and passport to travel and commit offences. In the next two cases, British nationals used false British identities.

A woman called Fiona McTulloch was caught smuggling drugs into Miami Airport on a flight from Jamaica. I flew down to visit her a few days later. Before going to the jail, I dropped by to talk to the US Customs officer who was dealing with the case and during our discussion he gave me the passport the woman had been using. It had been issued only a month before, for a woman aged 19, and while the woman I interviewed was clearly the person in the passport photo, she looked to be at least 30. Well, maybe she'd had a hard life; although Afro-Caribbean in origin, she certainly had a British accent, and she knew enough about Britain to convince me that she was from England. Still, there are routine questions to be asked, so I asked one.

'Can you tell me the address you were living at when you applied for the passport?'

'Er... well... it's... '

For the first time in our discussion she became a little agitated.

'It was only issued a month or so ago,' I said. 'You must know where you were living then?'

It turned out she didn't. I delved deeper, and she became increasingly evasive. Eventually, getting nowhere, I said, 'Is there anything untoward you want to tell me?'

She said there wasn't.

When I returned to the office a few days later, I called Sean Ferguson up in Washington and he agreed to look into it further.

I also telephoned an Interpol contact about the woman.

'Let me see what we have,' he said. I listened to the tapping on his computer keyboard for a minute or two. 'Well, we have nothing on any "Fiona McTulloch", but the address she used to obtain the passport is one we know about. A number of people arrested in the UK for drugs offences have given that as their home address.'

Interesting.

Sean got back to me a few days later with more from his own investigations. He had spoken again to the Benefits Agency to see whether there was any live claim against this identity. There was: a single mother was in receipt of child's allowance and housing benefit being issued from an office in Bristol. Sean called the Bristol benefits office to speak with whomever was dealing with that case.

The conversation went something like this: 'Hello, my name's Sean Ferguson. I'm calling you from the passport office of the British Embassy in Washington. I wanted to speak to you concerning a claim being made by a certain Fiona McTulloch. Do you happen to know who's running that case?'

'Yes, that's one of my cases, actually. I know her well. In fact we were at school together.'

'So, you could definitely give me a good description of her then?'

'Yes, of course I could. In fact, I could let you speak to her if you want. She's in the waiting room right now. We're going to lunch together.'

'She's there now?'

'Yes.'

'Can you just give me a quick description of her please?'

'About 5ft 6in, blonde hair, blue eyes, fair complexion.'

'OK, that's great. Thanks very much.'

'Is everything OK?'

'Yes, thanks, that's all I need to know. It's just a routine enquiry.'

They must have had quite an interesting lunch.

Armed with this knowledge, I went back to visit the woman in detention. She admitted the deception immediately.

'They offered me some money to bring some drugs from Jamaica to England, but I got arrested in Jamaica a few years ago for trying to smuggle drugs. I was in prison there for quite a long time, and when they let me out they deported me and told me I couldn't come back to Jamaica. They even made me pay my own airfare, but I didn't have no money so I borrowed it from the British High Commission in Kingston. I had to give them my passport as security but then I never paid them back.'

'So you got yourself a new passport as Fiona McTulloch?'

'Yes.'

'How?'

'I paid her £500. She gave me her birth certificate and said she wouldn't apply for a passport herself. Not for a year, anyway. It was easy.'

Five hundred pounds is quite serious money to a single mum living in a council flat; once again, without a personal interview with the perpetrator, and a subsequent investigation, this fraud would have gone undetected until such time as the real McTulloch applied for a passport.

These cases are getting more common and harder to spot, not least because of the huge numbers of children now born out of wedlock or raised by men other than their fathers. Imagine a boy born John Smith, to Mrs and Mrs Smith. His parents break up a year later, and Mrs Smith hooks up with a Mr Brown. She has another child with Brown and, in the interests of family unity, 'John Smith' becomes 'John Brown', assuming the surname of his *de facto* stepfather. It's perfectly legal, and there is no requirement for anyone to do anything, other than start using the new surname, for it to become John's legitimate and legal surname. (The supposed requirement for a deed poll is an urban myth.)

If we travel forward in time, John is now 20 years old. He applies for a passport in his assumed name, supplying his birth certificate along with testimony that his surname is now different. The passport is then issued in the name of John Brown.

Two years later, he decides to apply for *another* passport – this time using his name as it appears on his birth certificate. If no mention is made on this application of the other identity, there is no mechanism for the passport authority to cross-reference it.

The person will then have two passports in two different names, and nobody is any the wiser.

Here's a case in point.

Two men, Gary and Terry, came into the consulate one morning. They said that they had been working in Massachusetts for a few weeks, but that their boss had failed to pay them; there had been an argument, and the two men left without money. For some reason that they were unable to explain, they then drove their rental car over a thousand miles to Florida. They had come to the Orlando consulate in the hope that we could help them financially, and buy them an air ticket home. They both had their British passports, which they gave to me to establish their identities.

A quick check on the computer revealed that a few days previously they had been into the British consulate in Boston and given a similar story there. My colleague in Boston had taken sympathy with them and had a whip round in the office to give them enough money to get air tickets home. That was a very generous and trusting gesture. When I spoke to the vice-consul in Boston and told her the situation, she was surprised and disappointed that these gentlemen had then driven to Florida using that money.

I went back out into the waiting room to speak with the itinerant rascals.

'So you need this money to get home?'

'Yes.'

'You're just planning to spend it on flights, right?'

'Sure.'

'Anything else you think I ought to know?'

'Er... nope.'

'How about letting me know that you pulled the same stunt in the Boston consulate a few days ago?'

There was an embarrassed silence, and they even had the good grace to blush. Then Terry, the older of the two, slapped his forehead. 'Gah! You know what, yes, of course we were there, that's just...

how stupid is that? To have forgotten like that? It was only last week but…'

Listening to rubbish like this is, unfortunately, the lot of many public servants these days.

'Listen guys,' I said. 'I'm not buying this at all. We'll do whatever we can to get in touch with your folks back home, get them to wire the money out here by Western Union, but we're not handing you another 500 dollars or whatever, forget it.'

'Trouble is,' said Gary, 'there's no-one in the UK who could help us with the cash.'

'No friends?' I said. 'No family? No-one you worked with or for?'

'No.'

It's an all-too-familiar process, and they were clearly practised in it.

'Look,' I said. 'You'd better think of someone, because otherwise you're up the creek without a paddle.'

I left them in the waiting room for a while.

Several hours passed before they came to realise that this wasn't going to be as easy as Boston; Terry finally suggested an ex-girlfriend who might be able to help. We called her and, remarkably, she immediately agreed to send him enough money to pay for his air ticket home that evening, and some subsistence. Half the problem was thus solved.

Gary's situation was proving more difficult. He resolutely refused to give me any information that would enable me to contact someone back in the UK on his behalf.

He claimed that his parents were both dead, that he had no aunts or uncles, that he had no brothers or sisters, no friends, no colleagues, nobody – possible, but extremely unusual.

We continued on for some time in this manner – me proposing an avenue of assistance back in England, him closing it down – before I adopted a different tactic. I'd had his passport application form faxed over to see what contact details it might contain. There were none other than his own, so – in a genuine effort to establish his *bona fides* and find a way of helping him – I contacted Interpol in London. They said they had nothing on anyone with that name. I was surprised at this: he seemed like the type of geezer who might have had the occasional misunderstanding with law enforcement personnel.

'What home address do you have for him?' asked my Interpol contact. 'I'll run that through the system.'

It was on Moss Side, Manchester, and I read it out to him. There was a moment's pause while he keyed it in, and then he said, 'Well, we certainly know the address. If you can hold the line, I'll give the intelligence people at Greater Manchester Police a bell to see what else I can find out?'

'Sure.'

He came back on the phone a few minutes later.

'Is the guy was still at the consulate?'

'Yep, he's in the waiting room now.'

'Is he around 5ft 10in tall, 20 years old, stocky, with short black hair?'

'Yes, yes, yes and yes.'

'Do me a favour, go back in there and get a quick look at his right hand, could you? Let me know if he has part of his little finger missing.'

I went back to the waiting room and asked the man to sign his name on a form. As he did so, I saw that he was missing a chunk of his pinky finger.

I gave the information to the Interpol officer.

'He's well known to the police in Manchester,' he said. 'In fact, he's wanted at the moment for a serious assault. The only thing is, he's known here as Gary Sharpe and you've got him as Gary Read. It would be interesting to know how he got an apparently genuine passport in a different name?'

I didn't know the answer to this question, but I was determined to find out.

I went back to Gary and Terry. 'OK guys,' I said. 'I think we're going to be able to sort something out but you'll have to come back tomorrow.'

They grumbled a little – one of them complained that it would mean sleeping in the car they'd rented (and failed to take back over a month ago) – but they ambled off.

I got straight onto the passport office in Peterborough and asked them to send me information regarding any passports issued to a 20-year-old Gary Sharpe from Manchester. After reviewing those papers and making further inquiries with Sean, I discovered that Gary had grown up with his mother and his mother's partner, who was not his real father. He had lived almost all of his life using his stepfather's surname, Sharpe, and was well known to the police under that identity. He had applied for, and been given, a passport in that name some years before: all you need to do in these increasingly common circumstances is supply your birth certificate along with testimony that your surname is now different.

Then, a few months ago, and in an effort to create a covert identity, he had simply applied for and been issued a second British passport in his birth name, Read. This time, he'd simply sent in his birth certificate and made no mention of the fact that he already had a previous passport under a different name. Since there was no mechanism or practice by which the passport authority could cross-check and detect his lie, he was free to carry out the fraud. Once again, without the interview and the investigation he would have remained undiscovered.

The two guys returned the following morning.

'Right Gary,' I said. 'We can pay for your flight but I need to retain your passport as collateral for the money. You'll get the passport back when you repay the money, and in the meantime you can travel back to the UK on a temporary passport.'

'Oh, that's sound, man,' he said. 'That's great, cheers. Thanks Hugh.'

It was as if we were old friends and, as they left the office that afternoon, laughing and slapping each other on the back, I think they felt they had scored a victory over stupid officialdom. My irritation at this was mitigated by the fact that I knew what was coming; I hope they enjoyed their flight back, because there was an official reception party waiting for one of them at Manchester airport the next morning.

* * * * *

The next day I found myself down at Palm Beach County Jail visiting Paul Carr from Burnley – the guy who'd 'accidentally' taken the cocaine after visiting Martin Luther King Boulevard at 2.30am – and on the way back, I called Linda Nassar up in Atlanta. They'd had a meeting that morning with two diplomats based in Washington who were visiting all the consulates to explain new conditions of service that were being imposed on all locally-employed staff. Needless to say, these new contracts were less favourable in every sense to the old ones. Some staff members with long service records were being offered early retirement, or redundancy, and Linda was among them. The next day, when I was back in the office, I asked her how it had gone.

'Well, I have never been spoken to so disrespectfully in my life,' she said.

'How so?'

'There was no acknowledgement of the work and service the people in this office had given over the years. The way this one guy spoke, it was like we were an inconvenience. I'm only glad they've offered me a way out. I would hate to have to stay and work for people with that kind of attitude.'

'It was that bad?'

'Well,' she said, 'you'll find out the day after tomorrow when they get to Orlando.'

But by this time, work wasn't my only concern. During the previous few months, things with Cheryl had started to cool down. Whereas we once spent four or five nights a week together, now it was more like one or two. The conversation between us, once so easy and alive, had now become routine and sometimes even banal. Why it had changed, and when, I couldn't really say: I just knew that it was different now. I still loved her, and I believe she still loved me, but there was little of the intensity we'd once had. Like a wilting flower, it could probably have been saved with a little warmth, water and sunshine, but I've never been much of a gardener and Cheryl couldn't do it on her own. So, one day, we had to talk.

We met for dinner. I was nervous, and hoped we could simply ignore the facts and continue as if nothing had changed. Don't get me wrong, I believe it's essential in life to confront the hard truth at any cost, but I just don't want to be part of the equation. We met at a restaurant we'd been to dozens of times. At first, she didn't seem talkative, so I took the reins and spent some time telling her about the guy with the missing pinkie finger and how we'd worked out who he really was. I quickly began to realise that she wasn't that interested.

'What's wrong?' I asked.

If she was upset, or she had something important to say, she had a habit of pausing before she spoke. So I knew before she said a word she wasn't best pleased with me.

'You spend all this time telling me you don't know who this guy is, but you know something, I don't even know who *you* are. I've been with you for years, and we have fun, and we hang out and we sleep together, but I have no idea what you want in life. There's a whole side to you I know nothing about. Whenever we start to talk about the future, and where we're going, you change the subject. You know what, I'm damn well fed up with it. So, what's it gonna be?'

'What's what going to be?'

'You don't know?' she said.

'What is it you want to talk about?'

'What do you think I might want to talk about?'

'I don't know,' I said, although it was a lie, and I knew perfectly well what she wanted to discuss.

'Honey, take a guess.'

'I really don't know.'

There was another long pause before she spoke again.

'Okay, I think I'm done here,' she said. 'I have nothing left to say to you, I really don't. I'm going home. Call me if you have something important to say to me, but if not please don't bother. I mean that. Don't come around in the middle of the night like some ol' creeping tomcat, or call me because you need someone to go to dinner with. I'm done with it.'

She stood up from the table and walked out of the restaurant without even looking around. I hated to see her leave like that, but I had to respect her decisiveness: we hadn't even finished the starters.

It wasn't the first time we'd danced around this subject, but this time I could tell she was serious. I needed to think this through and make a decision, but I knew I didn't have much time to do it.

20

THE DAY AFTER Cheryl had left the restaurant in such glorious style, we had our visit from the Washington-based team. During the previous two years, we'd received a number of circulars from Head Office telling us the FCO was short of money, and savings were necessary: I'd been expecting a swift kick in the gonads for some time. Even though the diplomats themselves were receiving their annual pay increments in London, the LE staff in the United States had long been on a pay freeze. We were now moving on to a performance-related pay scheme, and these two diplomats were here to tell us how it would work.

'The FCO wants to offer terms and conditions that will enable it to recruit and retain the best LE staff,' said the main man, consulting his notes to ensure he didn't go off-message. 'As it stands, staff are rewarded with annual increments for time served regardless of effort or ability. We have a number of personnel who are being paid well but have long since stopped making any real effort and this is patently unfair. We shall be moving to a system of incentive and bonus payments, so that staff are properly recruited and rewarded for their abilities and efforts.'

This was disingenuous: the annual increments he was referring to were already performance-related, and they hadn't been paid out for the last two years, anyway. And the truth was, systematic mismanagement by senior UK-based DS staff meant any policy of this type was susceptible to incompetence. I say 'systematic' because it wasn't really their fault. Every three years, DS personnel change job, country and culture. They get a new boss, new colleagues and new staff. Not unreasonably, it takes them a year to learn their new job and adapt to their new boss. It takes them another year to work out which of their staff are good and who are the lazy, troublesome ones.

Getting rid of staff, even bad ones, is a difficult process so when DS officers only have a year left to serve in post most of them prefer to leave it to the next person.

The guy from Washington then went on to describe how staff would be expected to perform well, and would be rewarded for high achievement. This sounds good in theory, but already I sensed a real problem. In some areas of FCO work, such as trade promotion, inward investment or even political reporting, where most of the work is proactive, I could see that there was scope for incentive. But consular work is, essentially, a reactive operation, much like firefighting, disaster relief or any other humanitarian job.

I've spent almost all of my working life in public service. It is rarely well paid, but it has its own rewards. I have always done the best I could, and most of the people I've worked with have done the same. Sure, at times I could have been more highly motivated, but by monetary reward for performance? I doubt it. How would that work? As a humanitarian, whether you're trying to save somebody's life, arrest a violent criminal or comfort relatives after a death, it can only come from your soul. If that love doesn't live in your heart you need to find another vocation, because no amount of money is likely to remedy the situation.

When the diplomat finished addressing us, he looked rather pleased with himself. Perhaps he was on a bonus scheme.

'Any questions?' he asked us.

'Yes,' I said, 'what are the criteria for achievement in consular work?'

'We haven't decided yet,' he said. 'We have criteria set for every area of FCO work other than consular and visa operations. We're still working on those.'

That didn't surprise me.

'Can you give us any idea at all?' I asked him.

'Not at the moment, but we'll be there soon. Any business can be made more effective with incentives.'

'But consular work isn't a business, it's a service, surely?'

'In today's world we need to justify all our operations and account for our expenditure. In this respect we need to reflect best business practice, and bonuses work.'

'None of the firemen and policemen who went into the World Trade Center on 9/11 did it for a bonus,' I said.

'I don't know what that has to do with us,' he said. 'I only know it is now well-established business practice that performance-related pay works effectively in all areas of employment.'

I shrugged. I had never done it for the money; I was only ever interested in the experience.

Some of my colleagues began asking questions about early retirement and the pension scheme, but I was done.

I've heard it said that any large company, organisation or government department eventually becomes more focused on itself than its purpose. To me, this certainly seemed true of the FCO. I was reminded of a conversation I'd had with Linda not long after I'd first started in Orlando all those years ago. I'd just returned from a few days at the Embassy in Washington, and I was telling her how uninterested in public service most of the senior diplomats seemed to be.

'The ones in the political section seem to think they're actually politicians,' I told her. 'The ones in the commercial section think they're business executives, and the ones in the press section think they're journalists. Few of them seem to behave like public servants.'

'That's because FCO has the same basic problem as the airlines,' she said.

'The airlines? How's that?'

'Well, working as cabin crew is a hard slog and it's not at all glamorous. It's like being a cross between being a geriatric nurse and a waiter. But many of the people who apply for the job really are only interested in being paid to fly all over the world, stay in top hotels, meet pilots and business people and get cut-price travel. They think the routine work is beneath them, and they resent it; they're only interested in the image. It's the same thing for a lot of the diplomats. For them public service is something the lower orders do.'

My experience as the vice-consul had given me little reason to challenge Linda's view. By its very nature, the FCO attracts some of the brightest and best-educated people, many of them seeking, in the words of Carne Ross, founder of the not-for-profit organisation Independent Diplomat, 'status, esteem and recognition'. For the lucky few, the rewards are significant: to be an ambassador is a grand thing indeed. Yet, it seems to me that, despite the intellectual abilities of many senior FCO diplomats – or, arguably, because of them – an unhealthy, self-reinforcing culture seems to have developed within the policy ranks. Most of them have the same background, the same outlook and the same ambitions. Provided they don't screw up, they're destined for high office and honours and the best way to avoid making a mistake is to avoid actually doing anything in the first place. I've frequently heard senior diplomats speak in meetings, but it usually seemed their objective was to make themselves appear erudite, impressive, a force to be reckoned with, not with actually doing or changing anything.

I find it a strange culture, to be sure, but it's not without parallel.

I once did a prison visit to Santa Rosa Correctional Institution in the Florida panhandle. I was there to see a British man with the unlikely name of Angel Rodriguez, who was serving 25 years for a double manslaughter. He was truly an enormous man, with an impressive physique. After I had introduced myself, I asked him whether he was having any problems at the prison. I had meant this in the general sense: was the food acceptable, and was he getting enough exercise and so on. Unfortunately he seemed to think I was asking him whether he had been subjected to any sexual abuse. He fixed me with a long cold stare, before he responded.

'Problems? Me? Are you crazy? Who's gonna fuck with me?' he said.

I thought this was a rhetorical question, but, just in case it wasn't, I answered 'I don't know.'

He stood up. He was around 6ft 4in and I would guess he weighed about 18 stone. There wasn't an ounce of fat on him. He flexed his arms to demonstrate the size of his biceps. His forearms were the size of my thighs.

'Who's gonna fuck with me?' he demanded, shouting this time. Before I could reply, he kissed his biceps and began ululating loudly.

A correctional officer, who had been detailed to oversee the meeting and was reading a newspaper at the other end of the large room, looked up casually and then carried on reading, as if nothing were out of the ordinary. Rodriguez sat back down again, almost breaking the seat.

He leaned forward and asked me, quietly this time, 'Who's gonna fuck with me? Are *you* gonna fuck with me?'

'No, I'm afraid that won't be possible today,' I said, hastily. 'I have two more people to see after you, and then I have to be over at Century Correctional Institution by two this afternoon.'

Rodriguez used the *lingua franca* of the cellblock. His behaviour was designed to convince people that it would be a mistake to challenge him, and it was probably quite effective. Of course, if he successfully avoids the challenge, he is certain to avoid an embarrassing defeat with all its consequences. It is not so much that I doubted his ability to take care of himself in that world – far from it – it's just that it isn't a productive way to promote good relationships with the other inmates, the guards, or anyone else for that matter. And that, in my opinion, is a big problem in the FCO: intellectual ululation and a metaphorical kissing of the biceps. The prisoners aren't the only ones to become institutionalised.

Another problem I had recognised, as the FCO struggled to find a role in a changing world and decided to try to be all things to all men, was well stated by a diplomat speaking at an FCO seminar I attended. 'I am increasingly being required to know less and less about more and more,' he said. 'In the end I shall know nothing about everything.'

There were nods of understanding around the room.

In the job marketplace there is a word for people who fit that description: unskilled. When I was young, many of my friends' dads made their living by doing a bit of this, and a bit of that. These days, all of this and most of that is done either by computers or people on a minimum wage. We are in an age where the key advantage is to be extremely good and highly experienced in a particular discipline, and in this respect the FCO is out-of-step with the zeitgeist. For example, a diplomat might be sent to Japan for two years on full pay to learn the language, prior to a posting there. But, after a three-year posting in Tokyo, he might never go near the place again in his career. His language skill will quickly fade, and his knowledge of the country will soon become largely redundant. This pattern is likely to repeat itself throughout his career, giving him skills that are never fully developed and only temporarily useful. Does that make any sense to you?

I think the FCO missed a trick in the early part of the 21st century, when the old Consular D_ivision became the Consular Directorate. Whilst the new directorate ostensibly gained a higher profile within the FCO, in truth it remained the disenfranchised and neglected rump of the Foreign Office. What I think should have happened was that all consular operations should have been hived off into a separate, self-funding, self-managing consular service, as already happens in some other countries. Such an organisation would attract, cultivate and be managed by practical, service-minded people, not technocrats or policy boffins, and I think British citizens living and travelling all over the world would be better off for it.

I worked for the FCO for over a decade. During that time, as with most public services and government departments, it became increasingly corporate; it wasn't enough just to do your job well, you needed to prove it somehow. You needed statistics to measure your effectiveness, you needed to tick boxes and constantly improve. Major corporations such as Enron and WorldCom were able to demonstrate their effectiveness by virtue of their rising share prices. Investment bankers, such as those working at Lehman Brothers or Madoff Securities, could demonstrate their value by virtue of the concrete returns they were giving their investors. In such a successful global commercial environment it was only right that those of us in the public sector follow their example.

So, in homage to the revered private sector and mindful of a government obsessed with private finance initiatives and business consultants, the FCO management board set measurable objectives and targets that were cascaded down through the ranks. But that's the easy bit. The difficult bit is to be the officer on the ground dealing with the problem – the unexpected, unquantifiable, dynamic problem. The strategy targets landed on our heads like gravel tipped off a dumper truck, and we were blinded by the dust. For consular officers, the focus was no longer compassionate, intelligent, personalised service delivery, but statistical analysis, call-filtering and the avoidance of legal vulnerability.

The work was beginning to become a stranger to my ideals and I knew that if I stayed I would have to fight the changes at every opportunity. That wouldn't be much fun for anyone, especially me; anyway, ten years is enough time to spend doing anything in this short life. It was time to quit.

I called my friend and colleague, Graeme Wise, the consul in Washington. I told him that I'd given my notice in and would be leaving.

'That's too bad,' he said. 'You'll be missed. You're held in high esteem here.'

High esteem! The last I heard you could get ten years for that shit. It was definitely time to get out.

* * * * *

During the last few weeks I said my goodbyes and packed my things. I sold the Triumph to a friend for a song, and he let me keep it until my last day. I had put 40,000 miles on it, and it was starting to need some real attention. My friend was a mechanic, so I knew it was going to a good home, but I would miss it.

I called Linda one evening.

'I hope you're not calling me to say goodbye,' she said.

'I was, actually.'

'Well, honey, you'd better think again!'

We still talk regularly.

I'd had a great time working for the FCO and I shall treasure the memories. What I learned will stay with me for the rest of my life, and I wouldn't have missed a minute of it. I could have done something else, and maybe made more money, but on those days when I'm trying to put everything into perspective I often think of a man I once talked to in prison. He was a Londoner who'd already done half of a 30-year stretch for an armed robbery. I had just told him that his mother had died back in the East End – he hadn't seen her since before his arrest – and it took a while for it to sink in that he'd never set eyes on her again.

'Are you okay?' I asked, after he recovered his composure.

'I feel like the money weren't worth the time,' was his reply.

'It never is,' I said.

A few nights before I left, I rode the Triumph over to the street where Cheryl lived. I had not seen her, or spoken to her, since the meal at the restaurant weeks before. I didn't know what I was going to say, but it seemed like the right thing to do. I sat on my bike at the entrance to her apartment complex, and I could see her car parked outside her flat. She would be inside, probably making dinner or watching television. I wondered what I could say to make things right, but, deep down, I knew that the only thing she wanted to hear was that I loved her, and that I wanted to marry her and spend the rest of my life with her. I also knew that I couldn't say those words, and that nothing else would do.

I wondered whether I should just knock and say goodbye, but in truth I'd been saying goodbye for years. I turned the bike around and went home.

She was everything you could want in a partner – intelligent, beautiful, funny, caring and accomplished. It didn't get any better than that, yet I still couldn't take that final step and I didn't know why. It was becoming the story of my life: tragedy, or farce?

The day finally came for me to leave Orlando, and I put my federal consular identification card into envelope to send back to the US State Department – during all the years that had passed since I'd got hold of the damned thing, not a single Florida law enforcement officer I'd shown it to had known what it was.

I dropped by the office to say a final goodbye to everyone, and I noticed on the top shelf in the storage room the automated telephone system that I'd purchased years before, in its box, unopened, and gathering dust. On top of it was a door sign that said 'Open 9am – 2pm'.

They were small victories, but no less sweet for that.

That night, as the plane took off into the night sky, I looked down on the city of Orlando and I followed the lights of the interstate out to where Cheryl's apartment was. I wondered what the future held for her, who she might meet, who she might spend her life with and whether she would have children. I wondered why things work out the way they do. Do we make the choices, or do the choices make us? The plane banked hard to the right, and we continued to climb to the east. From my window on the left, I could now see the small airfield where, as a pilot, I'd landed so many times. I could see the green, flashing beacon above the control tower that had so often guided me safely home in the dark. It looked like an old friend. Then it disappeared from view under the wing and after a few more seconds the plane broke into cloud, and I could see nothing more of Florida.

Also from Monday Books

Sick Notes / Dr Tony Copperfield
(ppbk, £8.99)

Welcome to the bizarre world of Tony Copperfield, family doctor. He spends his days fending off anxious mums, elderly sex maniacs and hopeless hypochondriacs (with his eyes peeled for the odd serious symptom). The rest of his time is taken up sparring with colleagues, battling bureaucrats and banging his head against the brick walls of the NHS.

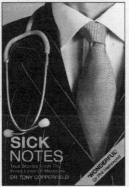

If you've ever wondered what your GP is really thinking - and what's actually going on behind the scenes at your surgery - *SICK NOTES* is for you.

'A wonderful book, funny and insightful in equal measure'
– Dr Phil Hammond (Private Eye's 'MD')

'Copperfield is simply fantastic, unbelievably funny and improbably wise... everything he writes is truer than fact'
– British Medical Journal

'Original, funny and an incredible read' *– The Sun*

Tony Copperfield is a Medical Journalist of the Year, has been shortlisted for UK Columnist of the Year many times and writes regularly for *The Times* and other media.

**From all good bookshops, online from
www.mondaybooks.com or via 01455 221752.**

Second Opinion: A Doctor's Dispatches from the Inner City
Theodore Dalrymple (hdbk, £14.99)

No-one has travelled further into the dark and secret heart of Britain's underclass than the brilliant Theodore Dalrymple. A hospital consultant and prison doctor in the grim inner city, every day he confronts a brutal, tragic netherworld which most of us never see. It's the world of 'Baby P' and Shannon Matthews, where life is cheap and ugly, jealous men beat and strangle their women and 'anyone will do anything for ten bags of brown'. In a series of short and gripping pieces, full of feeling and bleak humour, he exposes the fascinating, hidden horror of our modern slums as never before.

'Dalrymple's dispatches from the frontline have a tone and a quality entirely their own... their rarity makes you sit up and take notice'
– *Marcus Berkmann, The Spectator*

'Dalrymple is a modern master'
– *Stephen Poole, The Guardian*

'The George Orwell of our time... a writer of genius'
– *Denis Dutton*

**From all good bookshops, online from
www.mondaybooks.com or via 01455 221752.**

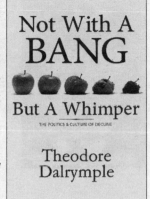

***Wasting Police Time* / PC David Copperfield** (ppbk, £7.99)

The fascinating, hilarious and best-selling inside story of the madness of modern policing. A serving officer - writing deep under cover - reveals everything the government wants hushed up about life on the beat.

'**Very revealing**' – *The Daily Telegraph*
'**Passionate, important, interesting and genuinely revealing**' – *The Sunday Times*
'**Graphic, entertaining and sobering**' – *The Observer*
'**A huge hit... will make you laugh out loud**'
– *The Daily Mail*
'**Hilarious... should be compulsory reading for our political masters**' – *The Mail on Sunday*
'**More of a fiction than Dickens**'
– *Tony McNulty MP, former Police Minister*
(On a BBC *Panorama* programme about PC Copperfield, McNulty was later forced to admit that this statement, made in the House of Commons, was itself inaccurate)

**From all good bookshops, online from
www.mondaybooks.com or via 01455 221752.**

Perverting The Course Of Justice / Inspector Gadget
(ppbk, £7.99)

A senior serving policeman picks up where PC Copperfield left off and reveals how far the insanity extends – children arrested for stealing sweets from each other while serious criminals go about their business unmolested.

'**Exposes the reality of life at the sharp end**'
– *The Daily Telegraph*

'**No wonder they call us Plods... A frustrated inspector speaks out on the madness of modern policing**'
– *The Daily Mail*

'**Staggering... exposes the bloated bureaucracy that is crushing Britain**' – *The Daily Express*

'**You must buy this book... it is a fascinating insight**'
– *Kelvin MacKenzie, The Sun*

In April 2010, Inspector Gadget was named one of the country's 'best 40 bloggers' by *The Times*.

From all good bookshops, online from www.mondaybooks.com or via 01455 221752.

When Science Goes Wrong / Simon LeVay
(ppbk, £7.99)

We live in times of astonishing scientific progress. But for every stunning triumph there are hundreds of cock-ups, damp squibs and disasters. Escaped anthrax spores and nuclear explosions, tiny data errors which send a spacecraft hurtling to oblivion, innocent men jailed on 'infallible' DNA evidence…just some of the fascinating and disturbing tales from the dark side of discovery.

'Spine-tingling, occasionally gruesome accounts of well-meant but disastrous scientific bungling'
– *The Los Angeles Times*

'Entertaining and thought-provoking'
– *Publisher's Weekly*

'The dark – but fascinating – side of science… an absorbing read' – *GeoTimes*

**From all good bookshops, online from
www.mondaybooks.com or via 01455 221752.**

A Paramedic's Diary / Stuart Gray
(ppbk, £7.99)

STUART GRAY is a paramedic dealing with the worst life can throw at him. *A Paramedic's Diary* is his gripping, blow-by-blow account of a year on the streets – 12 rollercoaster months of enormous highs and tragic lows. One day he'll save a young mother's life as she gives birth, the next he might watch a young girl die on the tarmac in front of him after a hit-and-run. A gripping, entertaining and often amusing read by a talented new writer.

As heard on BBC Radio 4's Saturday Live and BBC Radio 5 Live's Donal McIntyre Show and Simon Mayo

In April 2010, Stuart Gray was named one of the country's 'best 40 bloggers' by *The Times*

From all good bookshops, online from www.mondaybooks.com or via 01455 221752.

So That's Why They Call It Great Britain / Steve Pope
(ppbk, £7.99)

From the steam engine to the jet engine to the engine of the world wide web, to vaccination and penicillin, to Viagra, chocolate bars, the flushing loo, the G&T, ibruprofen and the telephone... this is the truly astonishing story of one tiny country and its gifts to the world.

**From all good bookshops, online from
www.mondaybooks.com or via 01455 221752.**